Profiles of Pioneer

Women Scientists

Profiles of Pioneer

Women Scientists

Elizabeth Moot O'Hern, Ph.D.

Introduction by Morris Schaeffer, M.D. Ph.D.

1/99

O.P.

ACROPOLIS BOOKS LTD.

WASHINGTON, D.C.

ACROPOLIS BOOKS, LTD.
Colortone Building, 2400 17th St., N.W.,
Washington, D.C. 20009

Art Director, Robert Hickey   Designer, Chris Borges   Artist, Pamela Moore

Printed in the United States of America by
COLORTONE PRESS
Creative Graphics, Inc.
Washington, D.C. 20009

Attention: Schools and Corporations
ACROPOLIS books are available at quantity discounts with bulk purchase
for educational, business, or sales promotional use. For information, please
write to: SPECIAL SALES DEPARTMENT, ACROPOLIS BOOKS LTD.,
2400 17th ST., N.W., WASHINGTON, D.C. 20009

**Are there Acropolis Books you want
but cannot find in your local stores?**
You can get any Acropolis book title in print. Simply send title
and retail price, plus 50 cents per copy to cover mailing and
handling costs for each book desired. District of Columbia
residents add applicable sales tax. Enclose check or money order
only, no cash please, to: ACROPOLIS BOOKS LTD., 2400 17th
ST., N.W., WASHINGTON, D.C. 20009.

Library of Congress Cataloging-in-Publication Data

O'Hern, Elizabeth Moot.
    Profiles of pioneer women scientists.

    Bibliography: p.
    Includes index.
    1. Women medical scientists—United States—
Biography.   I. Title.
R153.036   1986   509.2′2   [B]   86-3515
ISBN 0-87491-811-1

CONTENTS

Introduction 7

Foreword 11

NEW YORK CITY AND VICINITY

Chapter I   SARA JOSEPHINE BAKER (1873–1945) 21
Socialite turned reformer, she made New York City a healthier
place for babies and children. Encountering unrelenting sex
discrimination, she nullified the effects by her forceful personality.

Chapter II   ANNA WESSELS WILLIAMS (1863–1954) 32
Shortened the diagnosis of rabies from weeks to hours at the New
York City Department of Health Laboratory where she researched
all ongoing infectious diseases from the turn of the century until her
forced retirement at age 70.

Chapter III   FLORENCE RENA SABIN (1871–1953) 47
First to graduate from the Johns Hopkins Medical School, first on
the medical school faculty there, first full member of Rockefeller
Institute, first elected to the National Academy of Science, and in
retirement an intrepid lady prodding the Colorado legislature for
better health measures.

Chapter IV   FLORENCE BARBARA SEIBERT (1897–) 57
Discovered cause of "protein fevers" in contaminated water and
perfected tuberculosis diagnostic skin test through research at
Phipps Institute, Philadelphia, and University of Uppsala, Sweden,
all under handicap of polio suffered as a child.

Chapter V   REBECCA CRAIGHILL LANCEFIELD (1895–1981) .. 69
First woman president of American Association of Immunologists,
she sought cause and cure of rheumatic fever and brought order to
disorderly field of streptococcal infections.

Chapter VI   GLADYS LOUNSBURY HOBBY (1910–) 81
Pioneer in field of antibiotics (penicillin, streptomycin, viomycin,
Terramycin[R]) and in chemotherapy of tuberculosis; founded
journal on antibiotics and chemotherapy.

Chapter VII   RHODA WILLIAMS BENHAM (1894–1957) 87
Inspired research on mycotic disease, first medical school course on
the subject, reduced confusion among the fungi, differentiating the
pathogenic from the harmless.

Chapter VIII   ELIZABETH LEE HAZEN (1885–1975) 95
Co-discoverer of Nystatin[R], antibiotic used against fungous
infections in turkeys, in trees, in bananas, and even against some
mycotic diseases of humans. Income from her patent supported
mycological research for many years.

Chapter IX   LEONA BAUMGARTNER (1902–) 103
First woman commissioner of health of New York City, she
promoted preventive health measures through speeches, books, and
broadcasts. Serving in State Department under President Kennedy,
she extended her influence worldwide.

THE NATIONAL INSTITUTES OF HEALTH

Chapter X   IDA ALBERTINA BENGSTON (1881–1952) 119
Won Typhus Medal for research on Rocky Mountain spotted fever
and other tick borne infections, spent fruitless years hunting cause
of trachoma eye infections, but developed early diagnostic tests for
botulism and related diseases.

Chapter XI   ALICE CATHERINE EVANS (1881–1975) 127
First woman president of Society of American Bacteriologists,
renowned for research on undulant fever, urged pasteurization of
milk against opposition of dairymen, through personal misfortune
demonstrated chronic nature of the illness.

Chapter XII   SARA ELIZABETH BRANHAM (1888–1962) 141
Battled meningitis bacteria for years in laboratory tests, resolved
vaccine and antiserum production against the meningococcus, and
was first to show efficacy of sulfa drugs against the disease.

Chapter XIII   BERNICE ELAINE EDDY (1903–) 151
Virologist at Biologics Control Division of NIH, subjected to usual
fate of whistle blower for timely report on infectivity of test polio
vaccine in monkeys; warnings led to safe vaccine. Won Superior
Service Award for work on influenza.

Chapter XIV   SARAH ELIZABETH STEWART (1906–1976) 161
Investigated viruses as cause of cancer, co-discoverer of polyoma
virus, agent of malignant tumors in rodents. Received Federal
Woman's Award and was first woman to obtain M.D. from
Georgetown University.

Chapter XV   MARGARET PITTMAN (1901–)................ 171
Crusader in pertussis vaccine production, world traveller for
vaccine standardization, and phenomenal research investigator at
age 85. Received Distinguished Service Award and Federal
Woman's Award for achievements.

WESTCOAST, MIDLANDS AND ELSEWHERE

Chapter XVI   BERNICE ULAH EDDIE (1903–1969) HOOPER FOUN-
DATION FOR MEDICAL RESEARCH 183
Spending a lifetime of research at Hooper Laboratory, she securely
established her expertise in arthropod-borne diseases.

Chapter XVII   ELIZABETH MCCOY (1903–1978)................ 195
One of foremost women in the history of bacteriology, she engaged
enormous energy in research on lake eutrophication, plant root
bacteria, and bacterial fermentations for which she held a patent.

Chapter XVIII CORNELIA MITCHELL DOWNS (1892–) 205
Engaged in secret "biological warfare" research during World War
II, became expert on tularemia, highly infectious disease of rabbits,
ground squirrels, and of human beings. Developed fluorescent
antibody staining technique.

Chapter XIX   PEARL LOUELLA KENDRICK (1890–1980) 213
Showed great innovation in early development with Grace Eldering
of pertussis vaccine in cramped quarters with minimal supplies and
support. Became world-renowned consultant and recipient of
foreign medals.

Chapter XX   MARY INGRAHAM BUNTING (1910–) 225
President of Radcliffe College, member of Atomic Energy
Commission, she opened a rich vein of research in bacterial
genetics at a time when bacteria were thought to have no sex life at
all.

Footnotes 235
Glossary 251
Index 257

INTRODUCTION

Recent times have afforded considerable relief from the severe restrictions of the past. Many new avenues have been opened for women's progress and further accommodations are in sight, albeit some barriers still persist. Despite the difficulties, many women reached their goals with creditable professional achievements. Their emergence from intellectual obscurity has been documented in books and articles appearing in ever increasing numbers to depict the careers and struggles of accomplished women in the sciences.

In this book Elizabeth O'Hern presents, biographically, twenty women engaged in scientific activity in the United States during the past one hundred years. Incidentally, she also provides us with a view of the role of women in the development of microbiology (and public health) during one of the most productive periods in its history. The careers of these women developed more or less contemporaneously to form an important segment of the scientific community. Seven of these remarkable ladies are still alive, and just as concerned about the progress of science as ever, although they are now fully or partially retired.

It has been my good fortune, during the course of fifty years in my own career, to have met nearly all of the twenty women on one occasion or another. Besides becoming acquainted with at least half of them, I have had the exciting experience of working closely with three (Hobby, Williams, and Baumgartner) during different periods of my two stints at the New York City Department of Health. In addition, Eddy and Pittman were among my most highly regarded colleagues at the Bureau of Biologics in Bethesda. This firsthand knowledge leaves me quite convinced that O'Hern has selected some truly extraordinary individuals as well as outstanding scientists who deserve to be honored and remembered for their notable contributions.

The preponderance of microbiologists among the group of women scientists profiled here may be due partly to an understandable bias on the part of the author, who also qualifies as one of this category; but there may be another compelling reason. For that we must examine the contemporary scene and surrounding circumstances.

At the turn of the century women found it easier to gain entrance into higher education. This paved the way for careers in science and an expansion of the acceptance of women began. However, persisting patterns of discrimination and the professionalization of science fostered the retention of restrictions on women's employment. Women were infrequently considered eminent by their fellow scientists. They had fewer job opportunities and the jobs available were of lower status and at lower pay. Few women were permitted to enter medicine and almost none were admitted into such highly "masculine" fields as engineering, mathematics, agronomy, or pharmacy.

Thus, in comparison with other scientific fields, inordinate numbers of women were welcomed into microbiology. There they kept hard at work and happy for the opportunity while the men preferred instead to lecture and travel and write and administer or chair departments and officiate in professional societies. Sometimes they would share credit with the women who provided the vital laboratory support; often they would hog it all. Examples of such occurrences run through the individual biographies in the pages to follow.

Virginia Woolf's book, *A Room of One's Own,* was based on a brilliant series of lectures delivered in 1928. She expounded on why there had been so few women writers up to that time. The message was that the formal right to think for oneself was not enough. Women lacked the resources, the time, and suitable conditions for developing their thoughts and talents. What was required was an income and a room of one's own.

Woolf's analysis can readily be extended beyond women of literature to women in science. Those who gained access to the laboratories obtained exactly what they required for the development of their talents—an income, resources, and a room of their own. They were left usually pretty much on their own in their workrooms and there they flourished.

These women won their laurels because they possessed important attributes, generally ascribed to successful men, such as courage, ambition, drive, integrity, pursuit of purpose, and a tough but pliable hide. Leona Baumgartner was, in my opinion, the best commissioner the New York City Health Department ever had. Previously all had been men. She was adept as a public health leader because she could combine her technical knowledge with her innate ability to deal with people. She could be a gracious lady or a tough hombre, using each role appropriately and advantageously as befitted the occasion.

Margaret Pittman is by nature a very polite, unobtrusive, and considerate lady. Indeed, she could be considered quite shy. Let the occasion demand it, even now in her eighties, and she is sharp, peppery, articulate, convincing, and unswerving in defense of her ideology. Although each is a quite different individual, all of the women described here appear similarly stalwart in character. How else could they have overcome the prejudice and restrictions to attain their eminent positions in our society?

Now that women are attaining equal status, in which directions will the future take them? Lewis Thomas, in his most recent book, *The Youngest Science: Notes of a Medicine-Watcher* (Viking Press, 1983), believes that they will supersede men in helping to solve the important problems of our aching civilization. He says:

> There is a deep center of immaturity built into the male brain, always
> needing steadying and redirection, designed to be reconstructed and
> instructed, perhaps analogous to the left-brain center for male birdsong,
> which goes to pieces seasonally and requires the reassembling of

neurons to function properly each spring. Women keep changing the upper, outer parts of their minds all the time, like shifting furniture or changing purses, but the center tends to hold as a steadier, more solid place.

Also, another matter, the world has become crowded with knowledge, and there is more to come. The fair redistribution of knowledge will be a more important problem in the century ahead than at any time past. Women have not had much hand in this up to now. The full education of children, up through adolescence into early adult life, will soon become the great challenge for humanity, once we have become free of the threat of bombs. All the more reason, I think, to put the women, born teachers all, in charge. Send the men, for the time being anyway (the time being a hundred years), off to the showers, for the long, long bath they have earned.

It is not likely that Thomas' suggestion will come to pass. But what if it should? The men then would have a lot of catching up to do and it might take them more than a hundred years.

Morris Schaeffer
Bethesda, Maryland

FOREWORD

Little did I realize when I received Alice Evans' *Memoirs* that I was embarking on an undertaking of this magnitude and that I would be seriously involved in such rewarding experiences while interviewing and researching the lives and published works of these women scientists. My interest developed from the research I did on Alice Evans for the American Society for Microbiology's journal *ASM NEWS*.

Alice Evans, long a member of the American Association of University Women (AAUW), made a donation to the new Federal City College in Washington, D.C., through the AAUW at the time when I was president of the Washington Branch in 1968. Thus it was that I received a copy of her *Memoirs*. Some time later I visited her at Goodwin House, a retirement home in Alexandria, Virginia, where she was then living. At lunch there was great excitement among the women seated at a large table with one of the new residents, a widower who had just arrived. Alice Evans professed no interest in all the flurry. On reading the draft of the article I had written about her she insisted that her research on the streptococci be included. In this she was quite right as a recent publication has shown.[1]

Rebecca Lancefield was the second woman president of the Society of American Bacteriologists (now American Society for Microbiology, ASM); Alice Evans had been the first. Dr. Lancefield was interviewed in 1975 in her laboratory at the Rockefeller University where she accomplished most of her research with the streptococci which had been her life for so many years. After a long and leisurely discussion we topped off the day at the campus bar. Following publication of this profile in the *ASM NEWS*[2], *MEDIA CIRCLE*, a Japanese journal, requested permission to publish it in Japanese. After receiving the reprint, Dr. Lancefield wrote me, "I never expected to see myself in Japanese."

A special luncheon had been arranged to honor Cora Downs at the 1974 ASM meeting in Chicago but Dr. Downs was not well enough to attend. So I flew to Kansas to interview her at her home in Lawrence. It was spring and the flowers round her spacious home were in full bloom. Dr. David Paretsky, then chairman of the Department of Microbiology at the University of Kansas, came with his wife for lunch, adding to the conviviality. Dr. Downs discussed her early efforts to carry on research at the university on a very limited budget and her interesting experiences at Fort Detrick engaged in secret research.

In February 1976, I interviewed Elizabeth McCoy in her laboratory at the University of Wisconsin where she was an emeritus professor but still actively engaged in research. She was particularly interested in discussing her graduate students and identified specific research projects with specific students. In talking with her I had the impression that research absorbed all her interest. I was later to discover that this was not entirely the case for, devoted as she was to research, she also had a great interest in her farm, in the university, and in the Wisconsin Academy of Science. This information emerged from an interview with Dr. E. B. Fred, emeritus professor and former president of the University of Wisconsin, who spoke with great admiration for his former student and colleague, and from correspondence with Miss Ruth Dickie, professor of nutrition at the university and an Academy associate of Dr. McCoy.

When I interviewed Gladys Hobby in the fall of 1977, she had only recently moved from her Fifth Avenue apartment in New York City to a retirement community in New Jersey. Her apartment was not completely furnished but her own paintings were there, along with many of the porcelains acquired by her father in his travels. Dr. Hobby was very cooperative during the interview and seemed to enjoy discussing her career, particularly the years with industry during the first wave of antibiotic discovery and production when antibiotics were discovered, tested, and used on patients in remarkably short time and often with dramatic results, cures of formerly hopeless infections. But when it came to reviewing her profile she was quite insistent about cutting out all but the essentials, leaving little but the framework of her professional career.

I flew out to Grand Rapids in June 1977 to interview Pearl Kendrick and Grace Eldering who met me at the airport and drove me out to their lovely home overlooking the Grand River. Once in the suburbs, the house was by then nearly surrounded by the city and the trees had grown so tall that the river was no longer visible. However, they did have a large yard enclosed by trees and shrubs where Dr. Eldering could study the birds she so loved. Dr. Kendrick had prepared for the visit by bringing out photograph albums and reprints. She spoke about the early days at the Grand Rapids laboratory when she worked there alone and about her trip to Russia. At lunch we discussed her childhood days. She emphasized how much her father had done for her and readily remembered his name. But when asked her mother's name, she couldn't remember.

The interview with Leona Baumgartner came late in October of 1977 on an afternoon when the weather was pleasant in Boston yet my ticket to Martha's Vineyard was stamped "Landing Doubtful." Although I had my doubts about getting aboard, the two other passengers showed no concern. However, as predicted, the plane was unable to land on the island in the fog and returned to New Bedford. From there we three stranded passengers took a taxi to Woods Hole and then a ferry to Martha's Vineyard. Five hours late, I nevertheless phoned to let Dr. Baumgartner know I had arrived. Her husband, Dr. Langmuir, answered the phone, told me she had retired for the night, and invited me to stay with them. In the morning Dr. Baumgartner appeared for breakfast in red and white checked slacks and a scoop-neck sweater, a trim figure at age 75. We spent so much time discussing her extensive career that I nearly missed the noon plane. Additional information was provided by the dissertation manuscript about Dr. Baumgartner prepared by Dr. Julia Bess Frank and made available by the Countway Library of Harvard University.

When I interviewed Bernice Eddy in 1978, she was still living in her charming home on Selkirk Boulevard, a wooded section of Bethesda, Maryland. She described her research in considerable detail and spoke of the happy years of her marriage and of her children. She described the troubled years when she was under much tension and under repression very carefully and without too much bitterness. On reviewing the draft of her profile she made more corrections than any of the others, returning to the library to be exact about references and dates.

Margaret Pittman was very helpful in many ways, not alone with respect to her own career. She provided information about the Bureau of Biologics and the other organizational units of the NIH in the earlier days. Since she had known all of the other profiled NIH scientists and had worked with many of them, she rounded out the picture of their lives and the environment in which they worked. She made available all of Sara Branham's reprints and provided insight on Ida Bengston. Dr. Pittman's own career, still in development at age 85, shows a remarkable enthusiasm for research and a thorough appreciation of the foreign lands she visited.

Mary Ingraham Bunting was visiting her son in Washington, D.C., at the time I interviewed her in 1977. One of her grandsons was playing nearby. She was particularly thoughtful in including personal incidents and anecdotes about her family and her students. She discussed her early unconventional education, the intellectual atmosphere in which she grew up, and the logical progression of her career.

Florence Seibert I had once met at a conference sponsored by the George Washington University School of Medicine when I was teaching there. I did not interview her because her autobiography, *Pebbles on the Hill of a Scientist,* is so well detailed recounting her struggles with poliomyelitis, her remarkable trips to Sweden, and her rewarding research career.

After Sarah Stewart's death her sister, Dr. Laura Stewart, came to Bethesda to dispose of Sarah's home. Her mother, who had lived in the home with Sarah for many years, was also present at the interview. Laura Stewart had also been a research investigator at the NIH so she was familiar with the environment and with all of Sarah's research. She and her sister, Mrs. Helen Brown, were most generous in making available reprints, photographs, and news clippings of which there were many since Sarah acquired many honors during her lifetime.

I had known Bernice Eddie of San Francisco as a professor when I was a student at the University of California at Berkeley and graduate student at the UC San Francisco. Her headquarters were at the George Williams Hooper Laboratory which, in my student days, was housed in an old ivy-covered building nestled against Sutro Forest. By the time I returned to interview her associates in 1977, the Hooper Laboratory had become a nondescript section of the basic science building on a campus almost completely redeveloped. Dr. Eddie's assistant, Minnie Sung, was helpful in so many ways, providing photographs, referring me to good sources of information, and putting me in contact with Dr. Hulda Thelander, Bernice Eddie's close friend and travelling companion whom I visited at her home in Tiburon. Built at the water's edge, the home sits in a children's playground. Dr. Thelander is a pediatrician. She had requested to see me for she felt she could give me some insight into Dr. Eddie's personality which might not have been obvious to her associates at the laboratory, the warm and friendly person whom she had known for so many years. On another visit to San Francisco I talked with Bernice Eddie's sister, Mrs. Marcelline Cannon, who lived in a large home descending through several floors to a garden overlooking the city and the Golden Gate Bridge. She had unfortunately given away or destroyed all of Bernice's travel photos but she added so much about their early days, especially about their mother who had been so influential in their lives. She also described the beautiful apartment where Bernice had lived with her mother for many years, nearby her sister and not far from the Hooper Laboratory.

Dr. Margarita Silva-Hutner at Columbia University College of Physicians and Surgeons was very helpful in providing data about Dr. Rhoda Benham. Photographs were very few for the Dermatology Laboratory collection had been lost or destroyed. Dr. Benham's niece, Rhoda Benham Johnson, was also very obliging in providing information and a photograph of a painting of Dr. Benham which she herself had painted. Being by training a mycologist myself, I had known of Dr. Benham for many years and had seen her reputation grow as a pioneer in the field and I had attended the first presentation of the Rhoda Benham Award by the Medical Mycology Society of the Americas in 1967.

Dr. Silva was also a great help in providing background about Dr. Elizabeth Hazen. It was Dr. Silva who put me in contact with Stevenson Bacon who was researching Dr. Hazen's background for a biography. I had known Elizabeth Hazen in New York City when I was teaching at the Downstate Medical Center and serving as an officer of the Medical Mycology Society of New York. Dr. Hazen often participated in the society meetings. By nature rather reserved, she was however very definite about her research.

Anna Williams left a collection of papers for some time in the possession of Dr. Annis Thomson, a colleague at the New York City Department of Health Laboratory. While in New York City to participate in the 1979 New York Academy of Science conference on "Expanding the Role of Women in the Sciences"[3], I had a visit from Dr. Thomson at my hotel. She brought with her some tantalizing tidbits from the Williams collection, newspaper clippings about her retirement and a letter from Anna Williams' mother written when Dr. Williams was studying in Europe before the turn of the century. A few years later I was able to explore and review several boxes of the Williams collection after it had been reposited with the Schlessinger Library of Radcliffe College. The collection contains some fiction that Dr. Williams seems never to have finished as well as descriptions of actual events. One event she described is a trip she and some others from the New York City Department of Health Laboratory took with Dr. Park to Canada in a 1916 Buick touring car. For the trip Dr. Williams had bought a complete outfit for the great adventure: khaki pants and jacket and a khaki hat. On the first day they made 67 miles, from New York City to Kingston.

Dr. Marian Wilson, assistant director at the New York City Department of Health Laboratory, was most gracious in providing bibliography, histories, and photographs (glass negatives) from Dr. Williams' days at the laboratory.

Each of these scientists knew and worked with at least one other of the profiled assemblage: Leona Baumgartner worked briefly with Alice Evans; Gladys Hobby with Anna Williams. Cora Downs and Elizabeth McCoy had connections with the Hooper Laboratory, thus with Bernice Eddie; Florence Seibert and Florence Sabin served on a National Tuberculosis Association committee for several years. The Eddy-Stewart research collaboration is well known. Margaret Pittman and Pearl Kendrick cooperated on many problems dealing with the whooping cough (pertussis) vaccine. Several attended the same college: Gladys Hobby and Mary Bunting graduated from Vassar; it was Josephine Baker's inability to attend Vassar after her father's early death that pressed her into medicine. Rhoda Benham, Elizabeth Hazen, Rebecca Lancefield, and Gladys Hobby obtained degrees from Columbia University; Leona Baumgartner and Florence Seibert received doctoral degrees from Yale; Elizabeth McCoy and Mary Bunting from the University of Wisconsin and Pearl Kendrick and Florence Sabin from the Johns Hopkins University. Sara Branham, Sarah Stewart, and Margaret Pittman all received doctoral degrees from the University of Chicago.

Many of the problems encountered in public health and control of infectious diseases were dealt with by the nine individuals in the group working in New York and vicinity: as physicians, as research scientists, and as administrators of public health policy. Their period of influence extends from the late nineteenth century (Dr. Anna Williams and Dr. Sara Josephine Baker) through the discovery and development period in the history of infectious diseases (Drs. Anna Williams, Rebecca Lancefield, Florence Sabin, and Rhoda Benham) to the present period of specific therapy (Drs. Elizabeth Hazen and Gladys Hobby). Dr. Baumgartner's sphere of action in prevention and control of disease extended to the promotion of good health.

The National Institutes of Health grew out of the Laboratory of Hygiene, a bacteriology laboratory, established in 1887 for research on cholera and other infectious diseases. In 1891 the Laboratory was moved from Staten Island, New York, to Washington, D.C. It is there that we pick up the story with Alice Evans, Drs. Ida Bengston, Sara Branham, Bernice Eddy, Sarah Stewart, and Margaret Pittman. Their research concerned infectious diseases and their control, which was the original emphasis of the Laboratory of Hygiene and little reflects the expansion of interest, direction, and significance of the present-day National Institutes of Health.

Public health practice and laws in New York and vicinity were stimulated by the threat of cholera. On the West Coast, it was plague that served as the impetus to public health laws and to laboratory research. Dr. Bernice Eddie and the other research scientists at the Hooper Laboratory (Beatrice Howitt and Janet Gunnison and Hilda Heller) exemplify by the practical research problems they dealt with some of the major concerns of the period. In this group Cora Downs is unique in her association with Fort Detrick as Elizabeth McCoy was unique in her involvement with soil, water, and agricultural bacteriology. Yet all of these researchers were in some measure in the mainstream of discovery and development. Dr. Mary Bunting's geographical sphere, as well as her fields of action, are more diverse and lead into the present period.

The reasons for the career decisions of these women scientists are not obvious but surely resulted from wise choices at critical points in their lives. That few of the women were married is probably not surprising, marriage being the full-time commitment that it was in those days of large families. The few who were married, Leona Baumgartner, Sara Branham, Mary Bunting, Rebecca Lancefield, and Bernice Eddy, seem to have found marriage no obstacle to the development of their careers, certainly a credit to the character of each one of them. Most of them had very supportive families. Some were closer to their mothers: Bernice Eddie and Sarah Stewart; others had strong, protective fathers who promoted their careers: Pearl Kendrick, Margaret Pittman, and Florence Seibert; while a few appear to have been quite independent: Sara Josephine Baker, Florence Sabin, Alice Evans, and Anna Williams.

Sexual discrimination was part of their lives as it was part of the times. Some of these women scientists were particularly sensitive to it as was Alice Evans. Others were quite aware of it and effectively evaded it as did Leona Baumgartner and some were forced to openly combat it as did Sara Josephine Baker. Pearl Kendrick mentioned her awareness that her salary was less than that of men of similar rank and position but accepted it as normal for the times. Elizabeth McCoy and Gladys Hobby denied ever experiencing any discrimination.

I am grateful for the immeasureable contributions of all those mentioned above and extend my thanks to Mr. Wyndham Miles and to Mrs. Lucinda Keister of the National Library of Medicine for access to the oral history files and to photographs; to the Schlessinger Library of Radcliffe College for use of the Anna Williams files; to the National Academy of Sciences and to Mr. Noley Mumey of Denver, Colorado, for information about Florence Sabin; to the Rockefeller University and Dr. Merrill Chase for photographs and other materials concerning Dr. Lancefield. I am particularly appreciative of the assistance of Dr. Marian Wilson and Dr. Morris

Schaeffer, formerly of the New York City Laboratory and the Public Health Research Institute of New York City respectively, who read the manuscript in draft and provided such helpful suggestions and encouragement.

Permission is gratefully acknowledged for use of material and photographs from the following books: Macmillan Publishing Company for use of *Fighting for Life* by Josephine Baker; E. P. Dutton for material in *The Man Who Lived for Tomorrow* by Wade Oliver; to the Countway Library of Harvard University and to Julia Bess Frank for her manuscript, *A Personal History of Leona Baumgartner;* to Florence Seibert for use of her autobiography, *Pebbles on the Hill of a Scientist.* To the Colorado Associated University Press for photographs from *Florence Sabin* by Elinor Bluemel; to Mr. Noley Mumey of Denver, Colorado, for news clippings about Dr. Sabin; and to the Ferdinand Hamburger Archives of Johns Hopkins University for photographs of Florence Sabin. I am also indebted to the American Society for Microbiology for permission to publish chapters on Alice Evans, Rebecca Lancefield, Cora Downs, and Elizabeth McCoy which appeared in the *ASM NEWS.*

E.M.O.

New York City
and
Vicinity

CHAPTER I

Sara Josephine Baker

*". . . A true crusader for children's health
and welfare; a socialite turned reformer."*

Women physicians were a rarity at the end of the last century constituting less that one percent of all of them. Few medical schools were open to women and their opportunities for medical practice were severely limited. The few women who chose medicine as a profession did so from extraordinary conviction. One of them was Sara Josephine Baker who, upon the death of her father, took it upon herself to support the family by becoming a physician. Ill-prepared for such a venture by her finishing school education, she took some serious subjects for admission to medical school and in 1908 became director of the Bureau of Child Health in New York City where her determination served her well. In the city and beyond her policies made an enormous difference for her time and long after, even to the present day.

An Idyllic Early Life

In her autobiography, Josephine Baker describes her wonderfully happy childhood in Poughkeepsie, New York, where she was born on November 15, 1873, to Orlando Daniel Mosher Baker and Jennie Harwood Brown (Baker). Her father was a well-to-do lawyer of Quaker stock; her mother, a descendent of Samuel Danforth, one of the founders of Harvard College, had been a member of the first class to enter Vassar College. Known at home as Josephine, she added her first name, or initial, only later in life to distinguish herself from the famous singer. She was one of four children; she had two sisters and a brother, none of whom lived to become adults. When she was 16 her father died of typhoid fever. This change in the family structure caused her to abandon her plans to enter Vassar College and to take up the study of medicine.

As a consequence, skating, ice yachting on the Hudson, and the boat trips down the river to New York City for shopping and the theater fell into the leisured past as Josephine earnestly undertook to prepare herself for studying medicine. Advised against such a course by her family physician, by all her friends, and even by her mother at first, she nevertheless persevered in her intentions. Her preparation for Vassar at the Misses Thomas' School for young ladies, in Poughkeepsie, left her ill-prepared for medical school—and she recognized it. She found that she would need a certificate from the New York State Board of Regents to enter medical school so she studied privately for a year, took the necessary examinations, including biology and chemistry, and obtained the requisite credentials.

A Medical Education Begins

Josephine Baker selected the Women's Medical College of the New York Infirmary for Women and Children because she knew of no other school that accepted women. The college was at that time, 1894, headed by Dr. Emily Blackwell, sister of the more famous Dr. Elizabeth Blackwell. It was one of the few medical colleges that offered women the opportunity for clinical work, denied them elsewhere. It had been founded by the two Blackwell physicians and Dr. Marie E. Zackrzewska in 1856. By the time Baker arrived, Elizabeth Blackwell had departed for England to open opportunities for women there and Dr. Zackrzewska had gone to Boston, where she was instrumental in opening a hospital where women physicians could obtain graduate training. Baker was later to intern there.

Not quite 18 when she entered medical school in a class of 35, Baker found life at the medical college rather terrifying. However, after her first few months when classes had become routine and even boring, she acquired a more casual attitude and sometimes rode the horse-drawn trolley to the carbarn at 84th Street where the horses were changed, then back to the city, all for ten cents. At other times she went to the theater, and like all medical students, always carried her bag of bones. She lived in a boarding house on 17th Street between Fifth and Sixth Avenues and was at first quite alone. Gradually, as she became more and more absorbed with medicine, she made friends among her classmates. Many of them remained her friends for life, among them Dr. Florence M. Laighton, with whom she practiced medicine and shared a home for many years.

Ironically, the only subject she failed in medical school was "The Normal Child," a subject which had interested her very little. However, on repeating the course she read everything assigned and was therefore well prepared when later the opportunity came to work with child welfare. She received her M.D. degree in 1898, second in a class that had dwindled to 18. The following year Dr. Blackwell closed the college believing that it was no longer needed since Cornell University had that year opened a coeducational medical college where for the first time women could work on equal terms with men.

Josephine Baker interned at the New England Hospital for Women and Children in Boston, which was staffed entirely by women of high caliber, by her reckoning. She became quite interested in surgery, felt that it was "clean, definite with visible results." Nevertheless her intention was to go into general practice. During the internship she spent three months in an out-clinic on Fayette Street which served Boston's worst slums, receiving $4 per week for her services. Here she faced the medical realities—"fever, pain, delirium and mutilation"—and her medical texts were of little help to her. Dealing with the slum population, she found medicine "a calamitous thing," but she was by then thoroughly committed to it. Once attacked by the drunken husband of a patient she was attending in the home, she knocked him down the stairs.

At the end of the year in Boston she and Florence Laighton, who had also interned at the New England Hospital, returned to New York City and set up practice. Contrary to all advice against practicing in New York City, they opened an office on 91st Street near Central Park. The advice proved only too sound for their income for the first year was only $185. The next year they managed to become medical examiners for an insurance company which brought them a steady income and some interesting visitors, Lillian Russell for one.

A Rude Awakening

Baker's next venture was to take the Civil Service Examination for medical inspector for the City of New York Department of Health. This served to launch her career in public service. Her first assignment was to examine children in the public schools—at $1 per day. To her dismay and disgust the job proved to be a farce: she was allowed one hour per day to visit three schools. She was authorized to send home any child who was sick. The procedure called for a follow-up visit at home but no time was allotted for the follow-up. In practice, many inspectors never left their offices, never set foot inside a school. This sad state of affairs changed in 1902 when Ernest J. Lederle was appointed commissioner of health. Walter Bensel, sanitary superintendent, became Baker's chief and remained so for several years. He assigned her to the Hell's Kitchen district for which her Boston experience had well prepared her, for there too people lived in squalor and abject poverty. Baker's public service hours were from 7:00 to 11:00 A.M. and 4:00 to 6:00 P.M.; her private practice was fitted in between and after hours. As she relates, she "climbed stair after stair, knocked on door after door, met drunk after drunk, filthy mother after filthy mother and dying baby after dying baby." Infant deaths during the summer months were appalling, at times 1,500 deaths per week, mostly carried off by dysentery. The mothers did not follow the doctor's instructions, did not bring babies to the clinic. It was truly discouraging.

Sanitation in New York City was at a low level. Dead horses could be found in the street, milk was unpasteurized, sold from rusty, open cans. For two years Dr. Baker worked as an assistant in the office of Herman Biggs, medical officer of the City of New York, where she and Dr. William Studdiford were able to work on public health planning and where she learned a great deal about infectious diseases. It was during this time that she decided on a career in public health. Later she was assigned to the office of Dr. Thomas Darlington, commissioner of health (1904–1910). From him she learned to think of a mass attack on health problems rather than in terms of individual cases, and she learned to deal with the problems of a community. She was sent to the Bowery flophouses, with a policeman, to vaccinate the inhabitants against smallpox between midnight and 6:00 A.M., after which the inhabitants dispersed. During the meningitis epidemic of 1905–6, she "dashed around New York taking cultures, making spinal punctures, diagnosing cases and supervising treatment." She was, in fact, a trouble-shooter.

The Discovery of Typhoid Mary

In 1907 she was dispatched to visit Mary Mallon, the famous cook who became known as "Typhoid Mary." George Soper at the Department of Health Laboratories had investigated seven family epidemics of typhoid going back to 1900. He found that they were all linked to the cook in each family. Baker was sent to collect specimens for culture. On her first visit, Baker had the door slammed in her face. The next day, when she returned with several policemen, Mary answered the door and again tried to slam it shut, but a policeman's foot was in the door. Mary ran into the house and could not be found in a search of the house. But looking out the rear window, Dr. Baker noticed a chair against the fence and footprints in the snow. Mary was found next door hiding in a closet. She was most uncooperative and fought against having blood taken so she was forcibly transported in an ambulance to a hospital where specimens were obtained. The blood and urine cultures were negative but the stool culture was teaming with typhoid bacilli. Captured on March 20, 1907, Mary Mallon was confined to Willard Parker Hospital for two years and 11 months during which time every available remedy was tried to rid her of the typhoid organisms. All efforts failed. On the promise that she would return every three months to the laboratory and take up some occupation other than cooking, Mary was released. She promptly disappeared and it was more than five years later when her trail was picked up, once more through epidemiology. She made no struggle against the second capture. This time she was sent to North Brother Island where she remained for 23 years, to the end of her life in 1938, a special guest of New York City.

Discussions of the ethics of her case, the morality of depriving her of liberty, had commenced at the annual meeting of the American Medical Association in Chicago in 1910. Concurrently there was consternation over the probability that many more typhoid carriers must be at liberty in many communities.

One of Baker's major school problems was caused by truant officers. Children with infectious diseases were sent home and often the truant officer would send them back. The teachers could do little about it. Ernest Lederle, then commissioner of health, sought help from Lillian D. Wald, head of the famous Henry Street Settlement. Her suggestion was that she lend one of her best nurses, Miss Lina Rogers, to work with Dr. Baker. After Miss Rogers, probably the first public health nurse in the country, carried out a few months of experimental work in a particularly bad school, a scheme evolved for checking the spread of minor infections. It involved home missionary work and skillful conditioning. Pediculosis (head lice), for example, which had been accepted as a matter of course, came to be seen as a disgrace. This arrangement proved so successful that a school nurse program was eventually set up in all the city schools by the Department of Health. Some years later while teaching at Columbia University Medical School, Dr. Baker commented on the great success of the nursing program in the schools. When she wished to present cases of the skin disease impetigo, the eye infection trachoma or of pediculosis to the medical students, the cases were hard to find.

Battling Disease and Death

Another of Baker's assignments was to work with the Bureau of Municipal Research, a privately financed organization which checked on the affairs of the city wherever political administrations failed to seek out the facts. When the bureau started investigating New York City's scandalous death rate, Josephine Baker was assigned to work with them. This was not just another assignment for the facts uncovered by the bureau proved the final determinant in her career direction. The specific facts were that one-third of all who died in New York City every year were under five years of age, and one-fifth were babies less than a year old. With all her experience in the tenement district, Baker recognized that many of these infant deaths could be prevented. Preventive medicine was scarcely a formulated concept at that time. Health departments worked on the principle that if nothing had happened there was no point in doing much. Through fortuitous cooperation with Dr. Baker, the bureau recognized that health care could be improved. They recommended to the Health Department that a separate bureau be established to deal with preventive medicine and public health education. The recommendation was approved and Baker was given the opportunity to test the idea.

To start with an impressive sample, Baker selected in the summer of 1908 a district with a very high baby death rate. She chose, as she describes it, "a complicated, filthy, sunless and stifling nest of tenements on the Lower

East Side of the city."[1] She dispatched some thirty school nurses to the homes of newborns to instruct the mothers in proper care of babies. Seeing their babies flourish despite the hot summer, the mothers cooperated and the result was impressive; there were 1,200 fewer deaths that summer in that district than there had been in the previous year. "And there," to quote Baker, "if we have to be dramatic about it, was the actual beginning of my life work."[2] The success of this test led to the creation of the Division of Child Hygiene, later Bureau of Child Health, with Josephine Baker as its chief.

During the 15 years (1908–1923) in which she served as director of the Bureau of Child Health, Baker made many changes in established practices, some against great opposition. Midwives, for example, were finally approved and licensed after a long battle with the physicians represented by the New York Academy of Medicine. Baker had stated publicly that if she had a daughter she would rather she be delivered by a Scandinavian midwife than by the average practitioner and that American midwives could be equally good. Finally, she published figures showing that the maternal death rate for women delivered by physicians in hospitals was far greater than the rate for those delivered at home by midwives. The Academy of Medicine investigated and came up with figures even more favorable to the New York City midwives.

At the time the midwives were brought under City Health Department regulation there were "hundreds and hundreds of children in the New York Blind Asylum." Josephine changed this situation both by regulation and by the fairly foolproof dispenser she helped design for administering silver nitrate to the eyes of all newborns to prevent infection and subsequent blindness from gonococcal ophthalmia neonatorum.

Another item that she gave her attention to was the design of sensible clothing for babies. The undergarments and outerclothes could all be laid open piled one on top of the other so that the child's arms could be pulled through all layers at one time, a simple operation and comfortable clothing. The McCall's Pattern Company produced patterns for these clothes.

With a well-trained staff of physicians and nurses organized for inspecting, treating, monitoring, and teaching and with enforcement authority, Baker brought under control the once haphazard health care of babies in the New York tenement district. She gradually gained the confidence of the mothers who became willing to bring their babies to the clinics where they themselves could be educated in proper child care. The morbidity and mortality rates for infant diseases were reduced through improved home care and with preventive medicine as vaccines became available. Many child care clinics, called "Baby Health Stations," were set up. They dispensed clean milk at lower than market prices and offered general advice to mothers.

The Battle Against Discrimination

The extent to which her efforts and her successes were recognized became evident during a period of political harassment when efforts were made to displace Josephine Baker from her position with the city. The *New York Globe* stated that "the main reason that 900 out of 1000 babies survive their first year is that a woman of rare intelligence looks after them." At the New York Academy of Medicine resolutions of unqualified endorsement of Baker were passed. At one point a group of mothers marched to Mayor Hylan's office to protest the proposed dismissal of Dr. Baker. She herself fought the dismissal through the Civil Service. However, for many months of 1919 much of her time was wasted with hostile inspectors going through her files. Appropriations for the Bureau of Child Hygiene were cut. It was a demoralizing period of persecution. But the bureau was well organized, her staff was loyal, and they weathered the storm. A bonus of a sort was the enormous publicity the bureau received day after day.

Josephine Baker organized Little Mothers Leagues as a consequence of a book that appeared about 1910. These "little mothers" were girls, some eight or nine years old, who were forced to take care of the younger children because the mother was struggling to hold down a job in order to feed her family. When Baker read the book, which was critical of the "little mothers," calling them a menace because they were dirty and neglectful of the smaller children, she strongly objected to the criticism. It was a challenge to her for she readily recognized that these little mothers needed training in hygiene and proper child care—and motivation. She approached the schools to teach hygiene but they scorned the idea, except for one, where Ms. Margaret Knox of P.S. 15 agreed to sponsor the first Little Mothers League in her school. Thereafter, school after school fell into line disregarding the Board of Education. The girls received a gold-washed badge of honor as recognition of their attendance at meetings. The girls were eager to obtain the badge. They learned baby feeding, dressing, bathing, and they in turn became missionaries in the tenements.

Some protested the Little Mothers Leagues as "enslaving the young girls so their mothers could be irresponsible, go to the movies or get drunk."[3] Even some physicians were opposed, "If we're going to save the lives of all the women and children at public expense, what incentive will there be for a young man to go into medicine?" one is quoted as saying in testimony before a Congressional committee.[4] At the same hearing Dr. Baker testified in favor of the leagues and in support of the budget for the Federal Children's Bureau of the U.S. Department of Labor.

Another, and perhaps worse, example of opposition that Dr. Baker received from her fellow professionals, the physicians, came in the form of a letter of protest forwarded from the mayor's office. A petition signed by thirty or more Brooklyn physicians had been sent to the Mayor protesting the Bureau of Child Hygiene because "it was ruining medical practice by its results in keeping babies well." They demanded that the bureau be abolished in the interests of the medical profession.[5] Dr. Baker wrote to the mayor, "This is the first compliment I've received since the Bureau of Child Hygiene was established. I am profoundly grateful for having seen it," and sent the letter right back to the mayor's office. Nothing more was heard of it.

In 1915 Dr. William H. Park, dean of New York University medical school, as well as laboratory director in the New York City Department of Health, invited Josephine Baker to lecture on child hygiene in a course to be offered in a new program leading to the Doctor of Public Health degree (DPH). Being very committed to public health, Baker offered to bargain with Park. She would agree to lecture if she were allowed to enroll in the program herself. At first he refused absolutely; no women were allowed in the DPH program. However, after some time and considerable argument, the school agreed to accept her as a student and she received the DPH degree in 1917 with a thesis on the relation between classroom ventilation and respiratory diseases among school children.

Her first encounter with the class as a teacher was a rude shock. As she relates, "I stood down in a well with tiers of seats rising all around me, surgical-theater fashion, and the seats were filled with unruly, impatient, hardboiled young men. I looked them over and opened my mouth to begin the lecture. Instantly, before a syllable could be heard, they began to clap— thunderously, deafeningly, grinning and pounding their palms together." To save face she roared with laughter, and they stopped. She began to lecture like mad. At the end of the hour the "horrible" clapping began again. For fifteen years, from 1915 to 1930, every lecture she gave at NYU-Bellevue was clapped in and out in this contemptuous rhythmic whacking.[6]

This was not her first encounter with bias. When she was appointed director of the Division of Child Hygiene the six physicians with whom she had been working amicably as a health inspector for several years all resigned because of the disgrace of working for a woman. She persuaded them to try it for a month; they did and stayed on.

Her awareness of the bias influenced her dress. The shirtwaist had come into fashion and Dr. Baker wore a severely masculine-looking outfit in public life. She wore a long skirt, but when seated she almost appeared to be one of the men. For similar reasons she used her initials rather than her name for quite some time. Many who were not in personal contact with her did in fact think of her as a man. One grateful client sent her a fine mustache cup with "Dr. S. J. Baker" lettered in gold along the side.

In 1914 she was invited to present a paper at the Philadelphia College of Physicians. She accepted and on arrival found a note at her hotel inviting her to dine with the physicians at the Union Club. Many of the members of the club were astonished to discover that Dr. S. J. Baker was a woman, but they were polite. After a formal, stately dinner they proceeded to the college where the president of the College of Physicians introduced her, noting that it was the first time a woman had been allowed to enter the premises since the founding of the college in 1787. He admitted that it was only after months of debate that the directors of the college had decided to invite her there.

Josephine Baker became involved early in the women's suffrage movement. Drawn to it by the conviction that, "women are as much human beings as men are," she was one of five to six original members of the College Equal

Suffrage League, an organization of college women working for the right to vote. She was one of the 500 marchers in the first suffrage parade on Fifth Avenue braving the public scorn; fifty courageous men marched with them. She noted that every year the parade was larger and the public more friendly. She did some street corner stumping at noontime in Wall Street and also lectured in a vacant hall on Nassau Street where a small crowd of hecklers would drop in, all scornful of women. Josephine Baker was among the group of suffragettes who met with President Wilson at the White House. The president's statement of support was considered a great help to the cause. But after the Nineteenth Amendment was ratified, the great women's army of suffragettes disbanded, and by 1939, when Josephine Baker wrote her autobiography, she noted that young women of that day didn't "care how, when or why."[7] She also expressed her distress at seeing so few women in public office, at seeing boom times put women into jobs and the depression sweep them out again.

During her earlier years as a health inspector, while the Bureau of Child Hygiene was developing, Dr. Baker pursued a steady toil, taking only two weeks vacation leave during the whole period. She was completely absorbed by her work. When she had too many things to remember she wrote them down on a penny postcard and mailed them to herself. And such were the mails in those times, the very next morning she would receive the card to read with her coffee.

Doctor as Activist

Dr. Baker became active outside her immediate domain out of necessity: the need for outside funds for starting new projects, such as the Baby Health Stations. She persuaded the wealthy, socially prominent Mrs. J. Borden Harriman to chair a fund-raising committee. With the $165,000 they raised, 30 health stations were set up. When the funds were nearing exhaustion, Dr. Baker went to the city fathers with a successful project underway which the authorities agreed to continue with city funds. It was during this period that she devised a formula for cow's milk adding water, lime (calcium carbonate), and lactose to make it suitable for newborns. The quantity of the formula was based on the child's weight. The use of this formula became standard practice.

Josephine Baker was a director of the board to several children's foundations and public health organizations. When in 1923 she retired from the Bureau of Child Hygiene she also retired from 16 board of director positions. Dr. Baker was also a prolific writer. She published five books, *Healthy Babies* (1920)[8], *Healthy Mothers* (1920)[9], *Healthy Children* (1920)[10], *The Growing Child* (1923)[11], and *Child Hygiene* (1925).[12] She contributed 150 or more articles in the popular periodicals and nearly 50 articles in professional journals, such as the *American Journal of Public Health*. In 1939 an autobiography, *Fighting for Life* appeared.

In 1918–19 Dr. Baker served as president of the American Child Hygiene Association and in 1935–36 as president of the American Medical

Women's Association. She was a consultant on child hygiene with the United States Public Health Service and with the New York State and New Jersey Departments of Health. In 1923 she became consulting director in maternity and child health in the United States Children's Bureau, Department of Labor. She also represented the United States on the Health Committee of the League of Nations. She was a member of the board of trustees of a number of associations: Medical Board of the Maternity Center Association of New York; New York Academy of Medicine; the New Jersey Infirmary for Women and Children; the American Public Health Association; and she was a member of the board and consulting pediatrician to the Clinton, New Jersey, Reformatory for Women. She was an associate member of the American Academy of Pediatrics and an honorary member of the Medical Society of the State of New Jersey and the Somerset County Medical Society. She was also made honorary president of the Children's Welfare Federation of New York City, an organization which she had created in 1911 as the Babies Welfare Association. In addition to her membership in the Women's Equal Suffrage League, she belonged to some social clubs such as the Women's City Club, Cosmopolitan, and Present Day clubs and a discussion group known as the Heterodoxy Club. The Heterodoxy Club earned her the reputation of being a radical because so many unconventional women were members.

Dr. Baker lectured widely throughout the United States. Some of the speeches to the League of Women Voters were reported by *The New York Times* and other New York newspapers. The *Times* published a feature article on her child welfare work (September 9, 1929) and in the November third issue of 1932 reported on Josephine Baker's appeal by radio to parents to vote for Franklin Delano Roosevelt. Her election as president of the Medical Women's National Association was reported in 1935. At the time of her death *The New York Times* noted that through her pioneering efforts, New York City had been made one of the safest cities for babies to be born in.

A True Crusader

Josephine Baker served as the first director to the world's first tax-supported agency which was devoted to improving the health of children. Unimpeded by precedents, she developed her own standards of preventive medicine. She pioneered in public health education, devising effective and influential means of bringing existing medical knowledge and techniques to the people who needed them.[13] She was an exceedingly determined woman who handled prejudice against her with good grace. A true crusader for children's hygiene and welfare, she attained well-deserved honors and acclaim for her success in changing the conditions of life for babies and the concepts of care and of public responsibility for such care.

Josephine Baker was an extraordinary woman with a great zest for life. Her last four years were spent at Trevenna Farm in Bellemead, New Jersey, where she died in 1945.

CHAPTER II

Anna Wessels Williams

*". . . A lifetime spent fighting the
spread of infectious diseases."*

While she was young, Anna Williams suffered from the experience of seeing
her sister lose a baby, born dead, from eclampsia, a toxemia of pregnancy.
This made a lasting impression on Anna and she determined to become a
doctor, to learn how to prevent such a tragic outcome. After she graduated
from medical school—the same medical school attended by Sara Josephine
Baker—she tried general practice of medicine. It was a brief stint as she
quickly recognized that too little was known about effective treatment of
disease to make this practice of medicine a satisfactory pursuit for her. Thus
it was that in 1894 she accepted an appointment in the New York City
Department of Health Laboratory where she studied the cause and cure of the
diverse infectious diseases known to afflict humankind. Her contributions
extend beyond her specific research investigations for she lectured widely and
authored textbooks[1] which became the standard of their day.

Anna Wessels Williams was born in Hackensack, New Jersey, on March
17, 1863, to William and Amelia Van Saun Williams. She entered the Women's
Medical College in New York City in the fall of 1887 and almost gave it up two
years later when her father died. But her mother persuaded her to continue
although there was little money. To save, Anna sometimes walked the two

miles from her home to the Hackensack ferry. She also taught chemistry in the evening. Graduating in 1891 from the college where Elizabeth Blackwell, the college founder, had been her professor of obstetrics and gynecology, she stayed on at the college as an instructor in pathology for a year before venturing on a brief trial of medical practice. Soon discouraged with life as a general practitioner, she borrowed money from her grandmother to join her friend and classmate, Dr. Sara Belcher, who was studying in Germany. While there she studied in Vienna, Heidelberg, and Leipzig. In Berlin she visited the great Robert Koch, the discoverer of the tubercle bacillus. On her return from Europe she continued teaching pathology and hygiene at the Women's Medical College until she learned of an opportunity at the New York City Department of Health Laboratory. Wade W. Oliver, writing of her entry into the laboratory in *The Man Who Lived for Tomorrow,* says, "The outstanding acquisition of 1894 was Anna W. Williams as Assistant Bacteriologist, an untried volunteer who became more indispensable to [the Director, Dr. W. H.] Park with each year of service."[2] Her debut in the laboratory came via a box of cheese weighing 60 pounds, sent by a chemist for bacteriological examination. There was at first some excitement about the cheese because organisms resembling diphtheria were found, but they proved harmless.

The Threat of Diphtheria

Diphtheria was a problem of increasing concern to physicians and public health officials of New York at that time. There had been a sharp rise in the death rate from 1893 (1,970 deaths in the city) to 1894, when there were 2,359 deaths.[3] Anna Williams immediately became immersed in the diagnostic work and in the production of antitoxin.

Dr. Herman Biggs, Chief Inspector for Pathology, Bacteriology and Disinfection of New York, was in Paris in 1894 and had heard the papers on antitoxin at the International Congress of Hygiene and Demography. They were presented by the renowned scientists Emil von Behring, from Koch's laboratory, and Emile Roux from the Pasteur Institute. The audience burst into cheers at the news that diphtheria could be controlled by antitoxin. Dr. Biggs then visited Koch's laboratory to learn the technique of antitoxin production. On learning the procedure, he wired home to Park to start making antitoxin. On his return he tested sample antitoxin brought with him from Koch's laboratory on children in Mt. Vernon, New York, where the mortality rate had been 40 to 50 percent in untreated cases.[4] The mortality rate fell to 25 percent in those who received antitoxin. Spread of the disease was stopped in Mt. Vernon by administration of antitoxin to cases, but 12 days later new cases appeared. Again he treated all the children and the disease stopped.[5] This was the first evidence of the short duration of antitoxin protection.

One strain of *Corynebacterium diphtheriae* isolated by Williams in 1894 was found to be a uniquely constant toxin producer. Williams believed that this strain should be named for her since Park was on vacation at the time she discovered it. Park, however, insisted that the strain be named for him since he was the director of the laboratory and Williams was only an assistant. And so it was. The strain first known as the Williams strain, later became "Park 8" strain, and was the standard strain of C. diphtheriae used for toxin production for many years.[6]

Anna Williams' first responsibility at the City Laboratory was with diagnostic bacteriology. When not engaged in routine examinations she indulged in research. By 1894 when she arrived, Park's laboratory had become known as the Research Laboratory. He emphasized that research work was the basis of practical invention. The laboratory went into production of antitoxin in 1895 making it available to physicians for ten cents per 100 units of antitoxin.[7] They had first tested antitoxin production in goats, sheep, dogs, and a cow, but after Roux's success in producing antitoxin in horses, this animal was used exclusively.

During 1896, at which time there were 12 professionals in the Department of Health Laboratory, Anna Williams made a series of unsuccessful attempts to obtain a streptococcus toxin and curative antiserum by the inoculation of rabbits, sheep, and horses. The results were inconclusive as they were with antisera against cholera vibrio and the typhoid bacillus with which she also experimented. Late in May of that year she went to the Pasteur Institute in Paris and worked with Emile Roux to perfect herself in laboratory diagnosis of rabies. While there she also worked with Dr. A. Marmorek on streptococci since he too was attempting to produce a streptococcus antitoxin. He also spoke German, which was more congenial for her than French. However, she made an effort to perfect her French as well as her laboratory skills. Living in a pension where only French was spoken, she also took daily lessons in French. Dr. Biggs was again in Europe that summer and visited the Pasteur Institute. He obtained some samples of Marmorek's streptococcus serum and entered into a discussion with Roux and others about the skin rash that sometimes followed the injection of diphtheria antitoxin, the first inkling of serum sickness.

Dr. Biggs wrote to Dr. Park at the laboratory in New York that the city of Paris had furnished 40 horses and a stable for Dr. Marmorek's streptococcus research and that the streptococcus antiserum was used in France in conjunction with diphtheria antitoxin and was thought to be useful in cases of puerperal fever. Anna Williams brought back with her tissue blocks from animals treated with Marmorek's anti-streptococcus serum which she planned to section and study back at the New York City laboratory. On her return, however, all thought of continuing this research had to be deferred because of the volume of laboratory work at hand. In May of the following year (1897), a fire in the Blackwell Medical College, where her tissues had been stored, destroyed all of the samples.

Dr. Williams had left Paris for home late in August of 1896. At about that time Dr. Park became critically ill with typhoid fever. He was unable to return to work at the laboratory until November. Thus the heavy burden of routine work fell to Dr. Williams on her return, although by then there were three additional assistant bacteriologists, an assistant pathologist, and an assistant chemist in the regular Division of Bacteriology. Working with Dr. Alexander Lambert, Williams developed procedures for standardization of the Widal serological test for typhoid fever, a diagnostic test which had first been made available to physicians in October of 1896.[8]

A Rabies Breakthrough

The diagnosis of rabies in animals, under Dr. Anna Williams' direction, was another service made available to physicians by the New York City Board of Health Laboratory in the fall of 1896. This was seven years before the discovery of Negri bodies. The diagnosis of rabies was made at that time by injection of rabbits with brain medulla from the dog suspected of being rabid, then waiting for the rabbits to develop symptoms of the disease. In November of 1896 the production of antirabies serum commenced. This antiserum was produced in rabbits with a fixed rabies virus, i.e., rabies virus that had been successively passed through rabbits until its virulence was stabilized and the disease appeared after a constant incubation period. The rabies vaccine itself was prepared according to the Pasteur method from dried spinal cords of the infected rabbits.

In addition, Williams was busy during 1898 studying the cause of measles and smallpox, studies started soon after her arrival at the laboratory. She inoculated the cornea and skin of rabbits with smallpox virus, then studied the microscopic appearance of lesions in different stages of development to determine the time of appearance and disappearance of the so-called "vaccine bodies" (Guarnieri bodies). She also continued her efforts toward the development of a protective antiserum against streptococci, maintaining the virulence of stock strains by frequent passage through a broth culture medium. She continued to immunize horses and sheep with streptococci and was always looking for a more virulent strain, hoping thereby to produce a more effective vaccine, or antiserum. The City Department of Health issued 456 bottles of anti-streptococcus serum in 1898 in addition to 526 bottles of tetanus anti-toxin, and 1,703 bottles of tuberculin. The laboratory produced enough smallpox vaccine to vaccinate 157,411 persons against smallpox. Diphtheria antitoxin was administered to 3,300 persons. Yet 1,778 deaths from diphtheria occurred, and in 1899 the number increased to 1,924 deaths from this disease.[9]

Anna Williams was obliged to leave the laboratory in the spring of 1899 to care for her brother Harry who was dying of tuberculosis in a sanatorium at Saranac Lake. There she continued work with streptococci in the Trudeau laboratory.

During the years 1902–4 an increasing volume of routine diagnostic tests was handled in the research laboratory, yet some very fruitful research was also pursued. It was during these years that Anna Williams missed the opportunity that might have raised her to the pinnacle of scientific fame. It was she who first observed the bodies characteristic of rabies in the brain smears of rabid animals. While she was carefully accumulating evidence to satisfy herself that the "bodies" were indeed diagnostic of rabies, Negri, a worker in Golgi's laboratory in Italy, published a series of papers on the etiology of hydrophobia (rabies). He suggested that these bodies might be protozoa, the cause of the disease. There followed a communication from Anna Williams in the Report of the Board of Health of the Department of Health Reports. She confirmed his results and described quicker diagnostic procedures by diagnosing rabies in smears rather than sections of tissue, a procedure that made diagnosis possible within half an hour rather than the usual one to several days. The procedure also eliminated the need for animal inoculation. The Williams' technique soon became a standard method for diagnosis of rabies. In her report she stated, "It was found that the Negri bodies, studied previously only in sections which had been proven by us as well as by others to be diagnostic of hydrophobia, could be stained even more characteristically as well as more quickly in smears than in sections."[10] Pasteur had used rabbit inoculation which meant waiting ten to 15 days before it was known whether or not the anti-rabies treatment was necessary. R. J. Wilson in the New York City Laboratory shortened the time to about nine days by using guinea pigs. Then Negri suggested the use of stained tissue sections of suspected brain tissue, a method that required two to three days. Now Anna Williams had reduced the time to half an hour.[11]

In 1904 a paper was presented to the New York Pathological Society by Dr. D. W. Poor, who was in charge of the Pasteur treatments for rabies at the City Research Laboratory. Dr. Williams, one of the discussants of the paper, expressed the opinion that the inclusions seen in the brains of rabid animals were organisms, possibly protozoa, but since the organism would pass through a Berkfeld filter, it was probable that they were viruses. In the following year (1905) Williams presented a paper before the society in which she described a modification of the staining technique used to demonstrate Negri bodies: fixation with Zenker fluid followed by Giemsa staining. She carefully described the controls that had been employed in the confirmation: tissue sections from animals inoculated with rabies, with tetanus, with diphtheria, and with meningitis organisms, as well as uninoculated controls. She concluded her presentation by stating that it seemed reasonable to make the positive statement that the bodies seen in smears and tissue sections from rabid animals are specific to hydrophobia (rabies).[12]

The New York City Laboratory was continually involved in testing hypotheses of other researchers for confirmation or disproof. In 1902 Williams read a paper at the Second Annual Meeting of the American Association of Pathologists and Bacteriologists held in Cleveland, Ohio. She reported her inability to confirm the inference of others that the diphtheria bacillus readily transmutes in the throat to a different form which can then revert to true diphtheria bacilli. She asserted that only the morphologically typical diphtheria bacillus is of concern in laboratory diagnosis. In a second paper she reported on the etiology of vaccinia (cowpox) and variola (smallpox) noting that the clearest "vaccine bodies" could be seen in epithelial cells from the cornea of rabbits after inoculation with active vaccine.[13]

Groundbreaking Work in Pneumonia

Following the devastating epidemic of cerebrospinal meningitis and pneumonia in 1904, a Commission on Acute Respiratory Diseases was established by the mayor. Among its nine members were William Osler and William H. Welch of Johns Hopkins University, Theobald Smith of Harvard University, and Frank Billings, dean of Rush Medical College in Chicago. A study of the organisms having a relationship to pneumonia was undertaken in many laboratories. The commissions' 30-page report was published in the *Journal of Experimental Medicine* of 1905.[14] Park's and Williams' studies led off the report. They reported that they had examined 200 people, some normal and others suffering from acute upper respiratory infection, for the presence of pneumococci by culture and animal inoculation. They noted that the organism could be found in throats of healthy individuals, though the organisms isolated from those suffering from pneumonia were more virulent. They also reported the development of an anti-serum specific for the homologous strain of the organism. But one of the discouraging conclusions of the commission's report was that little new had been added to what had already been known about pneumonia, that a "curative serum" was still needed. There was no immediate follow-up on Park and Williams' report. It was, in fact, twelve years later when the monograph on the pneumococcus and lobar pneumonia by Avery and coworkers at the Rockefeller Institute appeared.[15]

Dr. Williams was made assistant director of the Research Laboratory in 1906. She published in that year a more detailed description of her work on the diagnosis of rabies with illustrations and documentation of her experiments, presenting the time course of appearance of the diagnostic bodies, demonstrable before the appearance of symptoms in laboratory animals, on the fourth day with fixed virus and seventh day with street virus.[16]

During Park's absence in the summer of 1907, while he vacationed in Europe, letters from Anna Williams kept him informed about the laboratory. She noted that tests were being made on specimens collected from a cook suspected of carrying typhoid fever. An investigative committee on typhoid, appointed in 1905, had recommended[17] that water supplies be isolated and protected from sewage, that filter systems be introduced, and that the medical profession and the public should be educated to the necessity for sterilizing all excreta from typhoid patients. Yet typhoid persisted as a major health problem in New York City. A paper on the role of ice in transmission of typhoid had been published in 1907 by Park.[18] He stated that harvesting ice from contaminated rivers such as the Hudson should be condemned. Later in this same year the dramatic capture and laboratory confirmation of "Typhoid Mary" as a carrier occurred. There was abundant circumstantial evidence against the cook, Mary Mallon: seven typhoid outbreaks in seven households where she had worked. In one of Anna Williams' letters to Dr. Park that summer, she mentioned that the typhoid work was going slowly, typhoid bacilli had been isolated in three cases and no bacilli had been found in the last three specimens from "the cook." Whether the cook referred to in the letter was Mary Mallon is not certain, but it is known that typhoid bacilli were, in fact, cultured from most of her specimens for the rest of her life.

No matter what urgent bacteriological problems demanded Anna Williams' immediate attention, she never abandoned her research on streptococci, always returning to those studies whenever possible. The Annual Report of 1907 includes a paper by Williams (later published in *American Journal of Obstetrics* of 1908),[19] on the etiology of scarlet fever.

The first evidence of her interest in amoebiasis appeared in the annual reports of 1908. Somewhat later, 1911 and 1912, she reported on her attempts to culture amoebae from cases of human amoebic dysentery. She did succeed in culturing some amoebae which she at first thought to be the true etiologic agent of the disease. She also published investigative work on gonorrhea, including both clinical and laboratory studies which had been started in 1910 in the Contagious Diseases Hospital of the New York City Health Department.

Trachoma Study Undertaken

During this same period she became involved in studies on trachoma, another area where she made astute observations. As a consequence of the evidence that some cases diagnosed as trachoma were not trachoma at all, an investigation was initiated at the Research Laboratory in which she became engaged. The results of this study under her direction were published in 1912–13,[20] "A Study of Trachoma and Allied Conditions in the Public School Children of New York City," which she had presented at the Congress on Hygiene and Demography, the fifteenth meeting of the International Congress, but the first to be held in the United States. At this congress she reported on both the amoebae and on trachoma.

Dr. Williams and her associates had continued the trachoma study for four years in cooperation with the Division of Child Hygiene, established in 1908 with Dr. S. Josephine Baker as director. Williams reported that among the children of 60 public schools in the crowded lower East Side district of New York, which was said to be a hotbed of trachoma, she had, during the past four years, found no cases of conjunctival affections with the classic descriptions of trachoma. In view of the fact that nearly half of the more than 33,000 cases of acute contagious conjunctivitis reported during 1912 had been diagnosed as trachoma, the Williams' report was a bombshell. She showed, however, that none of the 3,000 cases examined at the Health Department Laboratory had developed cicatricial changes due to infection, that the great majority of the infections had resolved, and at the time of her report presented normal conjunctivas. She also noted that bacilli indistinguishable from *Bacillus influenzae* were found in a large proportion of the cases and that these organisms were found coincidentally with the so-called "trachoma inclusions." A paper was published, "Chronic Conjunctival Afflictions in

Childhood" in *Archives Pediatrics* of 1914.[21] As a consequence of her thorough study, the trachoma clinics in the city were closed.

During World War I, the city laboratory was overwhelmed with production of vaccines and antisera, antimeningococcus antiserum and tetanus antitoxin in particular. Anna Williams and her staff were occupied during 1917–18 with detection of meningococcus carriers, since at that time attempts were made to segregate healthy carriers. Earlier, before the United States' entry into the war, during the summer of 1916, New York had suffered a severe polio epidemic. Williams became involved in studies on the etiology of poliomyelitis. That summer saw thousands of unfortunate children crippled. Early in June an unusual number of cases of infantile paralysis were reported in Brooklyn. By mid-June physicians were alerted and the alert was reported in the newspapers. Additional nurses were assigned to the Board of Health and on June 22nd a supplementary corps of medical inspectors was brought in. By the end of June the Board of Health took the unusual step of publishing daily the names of all true cases reported during the previous twenty-four hours. This practice continued until September 9, after which lists were published at less frequent intervals. Beginning on the first of July 1916, public lectures on polio were held for physicians; special polio clinics were opened in several hospitals and early in July all theaters were closed to children under 16 years of age. The United States Public Health Service came to the assistance of the city, making available all eleven officers to assist with the statistical and epidemiological studies. Committees were appointed to advise the mayor on handling the disease. Even interstate transportation was controlled by the Public Health Service in an effort to prevent the spread of the disease. The greatest number of cases occurred on August 3, 1916; 217 cases were reported to the Department of Health on that day. In the following week the greatest weekly total occurred, 1,151 cases and 301 deaths were reported.[22] Anna Williams, who had in some measure been involved in the laboratory studies on poliomyelitis published a paper on the etiology of poliomyelitis in the *Collected Studies of the Research Laboratory.*[23]

War Brings New Demands

After the United States entered the war, workers were needed for war service in medical laboratories. Anna Williams was put in charge of a course at New York University, where Park was then a member of the faculty, to train laboratory technicians in bacteriological techniques of diagnosis, a three-month course in which Dr. Park participated. At the City Laboratory problems were encountered in obtaining supplies, especially glassware, during the war. Loss of staff to enlistment in military service or from recruitment by other laboratories where opportunities appeared greater was another severe problem.

During these war years Anna Williams published few papers. Teaching and the routine demands of the laboratory consumed her time. However, an indication of the broad scale of her involvement is evident in the few papers which did appear: on the etiology of polio (inconclusive), on meningitis carriers, and on influenza. If 1916 was the "polio year," 1918 was the beginning of the "flu years." The great pandemic which had been sweeping through the army camps in Europe became an undeniable presence in the United States in 1918. In New York City, September 15, 1918, marked the first evidence of a significant increase in reported cases of influenza. The city had experienced influenza epidemics in the past but since 1891 the number of deaths reported annually had ranged from 100 to 500. However, from September 15 to November 16, 1918, there were recorded 10,886 deaths from influenza and 9,722 deaths from pneumonia in New York City.[24]

At the City Laboratory, as in other laboratories, endeavors were underway to decipher the cause of influenza. Unfortunately, at the City Laboratory the question of a filterable agent was not seriously considered. Enormous efforts were directed toward a study of possible bacterial agents. Anna Williams and her collaborators, Hazel Hatfield, Alice Mann, and Helena Hussey commenced the study in mid-September 1918 at the first indication of a mounting problem. They reported that the earlier the case was cultured, the more constantly did they find large numbers of influenza bacilli in the naso-pharynx.[25] Many other bacteria were found in their cultures, notably pneumococci and streptococci in a high percentage of cases. Dr. Williams' summary was straightforward, though inconclusive, ". . . the influenza bacillus was found more frequently than any other organism. But whether or not it was the initiating cause of the disease or only a more frequent invader . . . we cannot say." In a second paper on the subject she made reference to the conceptual difficulties of a search for a possible virus.[26] She concluded that a study of the existence of a filterable virus, to be worth anything, involved such controlled handling of human tests that it could best be done in (army) camps with volunteers.

Tests for a possible epidemic strain of the influenza bacillus, using antisera produced with nine separate isolates, only indicated nine separate strains with no cross-agglutination among them. These nine strains had all been obtained at autopsy. That raised the question of whether the initiating strain had been missed. So Williams and her assistants studied 200 strains from early cases and were able to add only that a single individual continues to harbor the same strain throughout the illness but that they had found many individual strains and no master strain—and in some cases no influenza bacilli at all. Their conclusion was that the organism causing the epidemic had not yet been identified.[27]

Following up the recommendations of the conference between the Influenza Commission, formed in 1919, and the New York Research Laboratory,[28] the New York City Laboratory undertook a study of the bacterial and viral flora of the upper respiratory tract in otherwise healthy individuals suffering from the common cold or influenza. The study entailed a trial of vaccines on healthy individuals, on individuals with colds, and on those with influenza and pneumonia. Most of the test specimens were collected from employees of the Metropolitan Life Insurance Company. Vaccines were tested on 1,600 volunteers from this organization. Reporting in 1921[29] on the results, Anna Williams described the change in bacterial flora from health to disease. She noted that her efforts to demonstrate a virus in influenza had been without success. In the same year,[30] Williams reported on her study of strains of *Streptococcus viridans* implicated in upper respiratory disease. She had in this case, as with influenza, collected strains of the organism in an attempt to detect an epidemic strain. In this effort too she was unsuccessful since a multiplicity of serological types had been found. Altogether, she authored or co-authored five reports dealing with investigations related to the influenza epidemic.

Another claim that Williams undertook to disprove was that an alpha hemolytic streptococcus, i.e., *S. viridans,* was the etiologic agent of measles.[31] Aided by a grant from the Milbank Memorial Fund, she demonstrated that the putative agent could not be the cause of the disease since it was found too irregularly in patients with measles and found too frequently in normal, healthy individuals. It was further demonstrated at the Department of Health Laboratory that the so-called toxin produced by the streptococci could not serve, like a Schick test, to demonstrate the state of immunity in children with respect to measles. Hundreds of young children had been tested and the test results were variable and non-predictive.

Beginning in 1924 extensive studies on scarlet fever were carried out over the next few years. A number of papers by Anna Williams and collaborators were published on use of the Dick test (on more than 21,000 school children) and clinical studies were made on over 400 scarlet fever cases treated with scarlatinal antitoxin. This was, in fact, a very quick follow-up on the publication by George and Gladys Dick[32] only six months earlier. Anna Williams was at the time investigating the streptococci which cause scarlet fever. Her particular contribution was her discovery that toxin producing hemolytic streptococci could be isolated from cases of erysipelas, from some infected wounds and sometimes from the throats of healthy people.[33] She among others demonstrated the complexity of scarlet fever toxin, that it was not a single homogeneous toxin, but a complex group of toxins and that this discovery could in fact explain the re-occurrence of scarlet fever in individuals who had previously recovered from the disease. She reported that the toxin was strain specific.[34] She showed that immunization against scarlet fever was not as effective nor as long lasting as was immunization against diphtheria and that streptococcal antitoxin was more likely to produce a reaction then recognized as serum sickness, an allergic reaction to the antiserum, than was diphtheria antitoxin.[35]

Since Park never lost his interest in diphtheria, when the Schick test was first described in 1913 it was immediately tested in the Department of Health Laboratory and the skin test antigen was made available to physicians the following year. Research on diphtheria was continued when not pre-empted by emergencies. Anna Williams undertook an immunological study of the types of *Corynebacterium diphtheriae,* the causative agent of diphtheria, to find out whether there was any detectable difference in the toxin, and subsequent anti-toxin produced by the five different types studied. This was found not to be the case; a monovalent antitoxin was found suitable for protection against all diphtheria strains.[36] However, in the early 1920s there were still many deaths from diphtheria, the majority among pre-school age children. The testing of diphtheria toxoid began in 1924 with some trial injections in a few nurses in Bellevue Hospital.[37] By January 1927, the New York City Bureau of Child Hygiene began immunizing children against diphtheria, in the schools, in the Baby Health Stations, and in institutions housing children. Up to this time the Bureau of Laboratories had been responsible for conducting immunizations of this sort. A real decline in mortality and morbidity from diphtheria followed these procedures.[38]

In 1929 the book, *Who's Who Among the Microbes* by Park and Williams, appeared.[39] These sketches grew out of a series of radio talks on communicable diseases and their microbes, as the preface indicates. The authors endeavored to show why some microbes are harmful to man, others harmless, and others helpful. There are chapters on the discoveries in bacteriology, on the use of the microscope to study "microbes," on "How Microbes Live and Act" and their reactions on culture media. Several chapters are devoted to the tribes and families of bacteria, e.g., "Blood Thirsty Tribe (Hemophileae)," "The Resistant Family (Bacillaceae)," and "The Coiled-Hair Family (Spirochaetaceae)," which speaks of "The pale spirochaete and the immoral disease." Consideration was also given to sanitation: clean water, milk, and food.

Three years later, in 1932, Anna Williams (sole author) published a compilation of her work on streptococci, *Streptococci in Relation to Man in Health and Disease.*[40] This publication was referred to as a definitive treatise at the time. Beginning with her early work with Marmorek at the Pasteur Institute in 1895, she described her attempts to bring order into this complex group of organisms, always with the objective of more accurate diagnosis and more effective means of treatment. The book, like *Who's Who Among the Microbes,* was to a large extent written for the lay public.

Some years later, in 1940, Dr. Williams was honored by inclusion in a radio broadcast on "Women in Science" presented by the Office of Education, then part of the Federal Security Agency.[41] The script presented not only a profile of their lives and accomplishments but detailed the ridicule and hardships they had endured as women scientists. Dr. Williams helped to prepare the material on some of the other women. She was herself honored for her work on rabies and on streptococcal infections.

Dr. Park was due to retire in 1935 at age 70 but was granted an extension to remain until September 1936.[42] In the following month, October 6, 1936, to be exact, a new $700,000 laboratory named in his honor, The William Hallock Park Laboratory, was dedicated. It provided the occasion for tributes to Park on his retirement and, in return, an opportunity for him to distribute compliments to his staff. Among those praising him were the

New York commissioner of health, Dr. John L. Rice; the mayor, Fiorello LaGuardia; and Anna Williams. She said, "I have been asked by one in authority to speak, for three minutes, on the work of women in our laboratories. I refused, not because of the three minutes, but because in all my 40 years' experience in these laboratories I never had to consider women as women in the work; it was always the worker, man or woman. . . . It is true—shall I tell it—Dr. Park did confess, once upon a time, that if a man and a woman, both equally competent, applied at the same time for a laboratory position, he would choose the man every time. He gave several reasons for this stand. His chief one seemed to be that he thought the man needed the work more than the woman. And the times and customs being what they were, and are, he had public opinion on his side. He did say something about the work being more balanced—whatever that may mean—if we were to have a more nearly equal number of men and women. Fortunately for Dr. Park, an opportunity seldom arose, because women applied in such numbers that naturally there were some superior ones among them, and the result was women, and more women, were appointed. A superior man did slip in now and then . . . [but] our laboratories have always had more women than men workers. And in spite of that hypothetic unbalance they have done such good work under Dr. Park's inspiring direction and active aid that it does not need to be described; it is too well known."[43]

Forced Retirement

Anna Williams had not been as fortunate as Park in extension of retirement when she reached 70 years of age. Despite a petition to Mayor LaGuardia from the Physicians and Allied Professions Political League and one from Dr. Park himself, the principle of obligatory retirement at age 70 was upheld. Anna Williams retired in 1934.

The heavy responsibilities at the Department of Health Laboratory did not prevent Dr. Williams from active participation in professional organizations. In 1907 she established the Women's Medical Society of New York which she served as president in 1915. She was an active member of the Society of American Bacteriologists, the Association of Pathologists and Bacteriologists, American Medical Association, the Society of Experimental Biology and Medicine, the New York Academy of Medicine, and the American Public Health Association (APHA), where she was the first woman to be named a committee chairman. In 1909 she was appointed to chair the Committee on Standard Methods for the Diagnosis of Rabies. She became an elected Fellow of the APHA and was also the first woman to be given full recognition by the Laboratory Section, becoming vice-chairman in 1931–34 and in the following year the first woman to be elected chairman of that section (1932–33).[44] In 1936, in recognition of her pioneering work in advancing the cause of women physicians, a testimonial scroll as presented to her by the Women's Medical Society of New York.

Through the years Anna Williams maintained close contact with her family. In 1893 she and her mother visited the Chicago World's Fair, then traveled to Portland, Oregon, where Amelia and her husband, Dr. Robert H. Wilson, were living. A few years later when the Wilsons had moved back east, the four of them, Anna, her mother, and the two Wilsons, lived together in a rented flat on Riverside Drive and 127th Street in New York City. In 1908 Anna built a home in New Rochelle, New York, where her mother lived with her until her death in 1915. After retirement Dr. Williams went to live with her sister Amelia in Woodcliff, New Jersey, where she died in 1954 at age 91.

FLORENCE RENA SABIN 1871-1953
DOCTOR OF MEDICINE

CHAPTER III

Florence Rena Sabin

". . . . A distinguished career of 'firsts';
a crusader in Colorado."

Although tuberculosis was at one time viewed romantically as increasing aesthetic sensitivity, it was actually one of the great killers, taking a particularly heavy toll of the young who should have been in the prime of their energies. After Robert Koch's 1882 discovery that a bacterium, *Mycobacterium tuberculosis,* was the cause of the disease, earlier diagnosis became possible. It became evident that there was considerable individual variation in susceptibility to the infection; therefore, much of the early research dealt with susceptibility and immunity to tuberculosis. One of the investigators who spent many years at the Rockefeller Institute (later Rockefeller University) studying the role of tissue macrophages, which ingest tubercle bacilli in the response to infection, was Dr. Florence Sabin. It was her second career and she spent 35 years there following her distinguished tenure at the Johns Hopkins University School of Medicine. After retirement Dr. Sabin launched a third career battling the Colorado state legislature for passage of laws to improve public health.

Colorado Beginnings

Florence Rena Sabin was born in Central City, Colorado, on November 9, 1871, to George Kimball Sabin and Serena Miner Sabin. Her father, a Vermont farmer, was the descendant of a Huguenot, William Sabin, who came to Rehoboth, Massachusetts, in 1643. George Sabin's father had practiced medicine in Vermont and his son was inclined to follow the same profession, but in 1860 gave up the idea and left for Colorado to become a mining engineer. At that time Serena Miner was teaching school in the south, but during the Civil War she moved west to teach school in Blackhawk, Colorado. It was there she met and married George Sabin in 1868. Florence Rena Sabin was their second child; Mary was the first. The family lived in a small, two-story house built on the side of a hill so steep that a retaining wall was necessary in front. A stairway led up from the dining room to a door that opened onto a bridge extending from the upper story to the hill where the barn was located. Life there was primitive; water was peddled from door to door and stored in large barrels; there was no plumbing. In 1875 the family moved to Denver where the children could attend school. The west was still wild in those days: Indians were feared as they came into town.

In 1878 Florence's mother died and both the children were placed in a boarding school, Wolfe Hall. Some years later their father took them to the home of his brother in Illinois where they attended a private school for two years. Summers were spent with their grandmother in Vermont on a farm near Saxton's River. When she was 12 Florence was left with grandparents while her sister Mary returned to Illinois. But in 1885, both sisters were placed in a boarding school, Vermont Academy, in Saxton's River. Four years later Florence entered Smith College where her older sister had been enrolled for two years. The two sisters lived together in a house near the college.

Florence graduated from Smith in 1893 with a Bachelor of Science degree. Mathematics and zoology had been her particular interests. After graduating, she returned to Wolfe Hall in Denver to teach mathematics for two years. She then became a substitute instructor in zoology and spent the summer at Woods Hole in Massachusetts. Medical school was her objective, so during her two years of teaching she saved money for that purpose.

A First for Johns Hopkins

Women were not accepted into the medical schools of the great universities in those days but Florence Sabin had a great determination. She was involved with efforts to obtain equal rights for women. It was her good fortune that a group of women, headed by M. Carey Thomas—later to become president of Bryn Mawr College—and Mary Garrett, both daughters of Johns Hopkins University trustees, had by 1893 raised sufficient funds for a medical school. Nearly half a million dollars was donated with the stipulation that the Johns Hopkins medical school be open to women as well as men. This opportunity was seized by Florence Sabin who entered the Johns Hopkins University School of Medicine in 1896. Her excellent scholastic record, training in mathematics and zoology, and her teaching all helped to qualify her as an "equal" of the male applicants.

Her future course was set early in medical school. Her first class, anatomy, was taught by Franklin Paine Mall, the school's first professor of anatomy. He was an outstanding teacher with the unusual philosophy that students should be treated as fully responsible, independent adults. He inspired exceptional students with investigative spirit but he never pushed them to such a degree as to deprive them of the excitement of original discovery.[1] Florence was encouraged to pursue research in anatomy, then an imperfectly understood science. Franklin Mall influenced her greatly throughout this period in medical school and during her internship at Johns Hopkins. She flourished in research and did not care to become a practicing physician. There were no staff positions open for her at the time but again the Baltimore ladies facilitated her aspirations by creating a fellowship for her to work with Dr. Mall. Thus she was enabled to continue her investigation of the brain and the lymphatic system. Sabin had great admiration for Mall and some years later (1934) wrote a biographical memoir entitled *Franklin Paine Mall: The Story of a Mind,*[2] in which she stated "The writer worked for 20 years under Mall; four as a student, one as a Fellow, and fifteen years on his staff. Her start in research as a medical student and her opportunity for a career in scientific medicine she owes wholly to him."[3]

While still a student, her first investigations concerned the structure and function of the medulla and mid-brain. She constructed models from serial sections of a newborn infant. These models were used for many years in teaching at the medical school. Her first publication in 1897 was "On the Anatomical Relations of the Nuclei of Reception of the Cochlear and Vestibular Nerves,"[4] and her first publication after graduation (she received her M.D. in 1900) was *An Atlas of the Medulla and Midbrain"* published in 1901.[5] Despite her investigative work, she did well in her classes and was said never to expect any favors as a woman but rather to wish to be treated as an equal to the men.

A Dedication to Lymphatics

As a fellow in Dr. Mall's department, she began a study that was to engage her for many years: the development and structure of the lymphatics. At that time the anatomy of the lymphatics was poorly understood and embryologists were in disagreement about their development. Sabin wrote some years later, "When I began my work, it was the accepted theory that lymphatics arose from tissue spaces, then grew toward the veins."[6] She acknowledged that Wangert and Ranvier had presented some evidence to the contrary with late, relatively large pig embryos (90mm in length), but the evidence was not conclusive nor generally accepted. Employing very small pig embryos (20–25mm), she injected the lymph vessels with colored (Prussian blue) or black (India ink) material. These preparations indicated to her that the lymph vessels arise as buds from the veins and grow outward as continuous channels by a process of further budding, much as Wangert and Ranvier had suggested. She also clarified the apparent discrepancy between the evidence for continuous channels in injected materials by comparing them with an uninjected contralateral side in which serial sections appeared to display discontinuous lymphatic channels. Reconstructions from the serial sections of the injected side (via jugular lymphatic sac) showed lymph channels connecting with each other. She further showed that the peripheral ends of the lymphatics are closed and that they neither open into the tissue spaces nor are derived from them. Her findings were confirmed by others using the transparent tails of tadpoles. A considerable controversy amongst anatomists ensued. Her views were opposed by those who held to the view that the tissue spaces developed into lymphatics. Dr. Sabin was firm in upholding her results. She put it forcefully in a paper defending her work against her critics: "The facts are correct and have been verified, the reasoning was correct and has been justified."[7]

Her first papers on the lymphatics, "On the Origin of the Lymphatic System from Veins and the Development of the Lymph Hearts and Thoracic Duct in the Pig," obtained for her the prize of the Naples Table Association (1903), which maintained in the Zoological Station at Naples a position or "Table" for the promotion of scientific work by women. The prize was given for the best scientific thesis written by a woman based on independent laboratory research.

After the termination of her fellowship in Naples and her return to Johns Hopkins, Sabin was made an assistant, then an associate, and in 1905 an associate professor of anatomy. In 1917 she became professor of histology, the first woman to hold this rank at the Johns Hopkins University. During this period her published papers brought her to the attention of medical scientists throughout the world and established her reputation as an investigator of the first rank. As a logical corollary of her studies, she became interested in development of blood vessels and blood cells from endothelium. For this work she employed early methods of tissue culture. She was able to watch growth in the hanging drop preparations and see development of the earliest blood cells in explanted chick embryo blastoderm. During this period she made one of her many trips to Europe, spending some time in Leipzig and other German university laboratories. Upon her return she developed methods of staining cells, while alive, with innocuous dyes.[8] By this means she was able to differentiate certain types of cells not distinguishable in the living state without stain. In 1924 she received a grant from the National Tuberculosis Association to study host defense against tubercle bacilli. In publication of her results she noted in particular the monocytes which were involved in tissue reactions against infectious organisms, notably the tubercle bacillus.[9]

Called to Rockefeller

By this time she had received several honors. Smith College had awarded her an honorary Sc.D. in 1910. In 1924 she was elected president of the American Association of Anatomists, the first woman to hold the office. In the following year, 1925, she was elected to the National Academy of Sciences, the only woman then so honored. In the same year she was invited by Dr. Simon

Flexner, director of the Rockefeller Institute, to become a full member of the institute. Flexner had known Sabin as a student at Johns Hopkins and had followed her career through his friend Franklin Mall.[10] A front page column announcement of Sabin's planned departure from Johns Hopkins appeared in a May 1925 Baltimore newspaper.

At the Rockefeller Institute in New York, Sabin launched a new career of full-time investigation, a study of the pathology of tuberculosis. She directed a group of investigators, one of whom, Charles Doan, had accompanied her from Johns Hopkins University. At first she continued her research on the role of the monocyte in tubercle formation. It was not long, however, before she became involved with chemical fractionation of the tubercle bacillus as a member of the Research Committee of the National Tuberculosis Association. This Committee had been initiated by Esmond R. Long of Philadelphia and Treat B. Johnson of Yale with the aim of integrating research on tuberculosis ongoing in several laboratories. Sabin directed the group in biological, chemical, and bacteriological investigations, an inter-institutional program involving state and privately endowed universities and two pharmaceutical companies.

She and her group at Rockefeller Institute demonstrated that many of the lesions characteristic of tuberculosis could be induced by one of the chemical fractions of the bacilli.[11] It had long been known that dead tubercle bacilli injected into tissues would elicit tubercles. The question was to determine which chemical constituent of the organisms was responsible. Enormous quantities of tubercle bacilli were grown by the two pharmaceutical firms, H. K. Mulford Company and Parke Davis and Company. Chemical fractionation of the organisms was carried out by Johnson and R. J. Anderson at Yale and Long and Florence Seibert at University of Chicago.[12] Anderson worked with the water-insoluble substances which Sabin tested in animals. She found that one of the lipids, a phosphatide, when injected intraperitoneally into rabbits, would induce typical tubercles. Using the method of vital staining which she had developed at Johns Hopkins, she could observe the transformation of monocytes into epithelioid cells and the subsequent development of a tubercle, even, in a few experiments, the caseous degeneration typical of the late pathology of human tuberculosis.[13]

Sabin and others also demonstrated that the tuberculo-protein sensitizes the host.[14] Thus it was that Sabin became involved with a study of antibody formation. It had been observed that injected particles and bacteria were taken up by cells lining the blood vessels and by phagocytes of the reticuloendothelial system, and it was supposed that the cells taking up antigen produced the antibody. Sabin found that a tracer antigen injected into animals appeared in reticuloendothelial cells, especially in phagocytic macrophages. She noted that after a few days the tracer dye became separated from the protein, the cells shed their antigen, and, at about the same time, antibody appeared in the blood. She also noted that leukocytes might take up the tracer antigen, then in turn be engulfed by macrophages.[15] Many other of her acute observations meticulously recorded, stand unchallenged today, although the interpretation of some of these phenomena may differ.[16]

Many of the younger workers associated with Sabin during the 13 years she spent at the Rockefeller Institute later became well known research investigators. They were all impressed by her great energy, her enormous enthusiasm, and intellectual integrity. One of them has said, "The great joy and pleasure she derived from her work was like a contagion among those around her. . . ."[17]

Honors Abound

Many honors accrued to her during this New York period. In 1929 she received the $5,000 Annual Achievement Award of the magazine *Pictorial Review* and in the same year an Sc.D. from Mount Holyoke College. She was named one of America's twelve most eminent living women by a poll conducted by *Good Housekeeping* magazine in 1931. She received the National Achievement Award of the Chi Omega Sorority in 1932; two Sc.D.s, from New York University and from Wilson College, in 1933; Sc.D. from Syracuse University in 1934; two Sc.D.s in 1935, one from Oglethorpe University and the other from the University of Colorado. In that same year she received the $5,000 M. Carey Thomas Award in Science at the 50th Anniversary of Bryn Mawr College, and was named on Mrs. Carrie Chapman Catt's annual list of the country's ten outstanding women. The year 1937 brought her Sc.D.s from the University of Pennsylvania and Oberlin College, and in the next year an Sc.D. from Russell Sage College. In that year, 1938, she retired from the Rockefeller Institute at age 67.

Sabin published some 50 reported of her research, in addition to her biography of Franklin Paine Mall,[18] and a paper on "Women in Science."[19] She had few doubts about the feasibility of business or professional careers for women. However, as she grew older she came to understand the complexities of a career woman's life, the conflicting claims of home life and profession, and eventually she came to recognize her own life as an exception. The numerous honors she received helped to emphasize her unique position. Some honors came to her because of her work on behalf of the advancement of women's rights. In fact, the first two awards she received were for promotion of women: the fellowship of the Baltimore Association for Promotion of University Education of Women, the second from the Naples Table Association.

During her years as a teacher at Johns Hopkins, Dr. Sabin enjoyed stimulating discussions with students or faculty on almost any intellectual topic—but especially those concerning equal rights for women. She backed the suffragettes but was not considered a reformer. She stood firm for the independence of all persons and an equal opportunity for women. "Because of her later scientific eminence and integrity, because of the fact that she later became so well known as an exponent of new methods of teaching, because still later, she became such an excellent public health officer and a proponent of new public health laws, . . . her influence for the improvement of the lot of women was immense. She accomplished much more by the example of her work than she could have as a mere advocate of reform."[20]

As she became older she enjoyed social entertainment in her home, particularly for students, and was renowned for her cooking. Despite her warmth of friendship, she always maintained a certain reserve. First names were never used with students. She considered herself on an equal footing with the men of the faculty, and by her forthrightness confirmed it. When in 1950 she was asked to address the graduating class of the Women's Medical College of Philadelphia, she chose the topic "The Extension of the Full-Time Plan of Teaching to Chemical Medicine"[21] in which she affirmed her faith in the fitness of women as physicians and scientific investigators, even if married. She also urged a shift "in interest by the leaders of the medical profession from application of knowledge to the cure of disease to the study of the problems of disease." In her view research could lift teaching to a higher plane, yet she well understood that only a certain percentage of medical students needed training in experimentation itself.[22] For those who showed an interest in research she freely gave her time and encouragement.

Before her retirement from Rockefeller Institute, about 40 of Dr. Sabin's friends and colleagues arranged a surprise dinner for her in the famous Rainbow Room of the Rockefeller Center, a restaurant she had never seen. It was arranged so that there were six tables, each with an empty chair, and Dr. Sabin took one course at each. Tributes were offered her by Isaiah Bowman, then president of Johns Hopkins, and others.

Life After Rockefeller: A Return to Roots

After retirement from Rockefeller Institute for Medical Research in 1938, Florence Sabin returned to Colorado to live with her sister Mary, who by then had retired from teaching mathematics in Denver high schools in order to receive her pension. Sabin frequently returned to the east during her service as member of the Advisory Board of the John Simon Guggenheim Memorial Foundation (1939–1947) and the Advisory Committee of United China Relief (1941–1953). In Colorado she was soon made an honorary member of the Denver Tuberculosis Society and appointed to the Board of Directors of the Children's Hospital (1942). Through these activities and her associations with researchers at the medical school, she became acutely aware of the archaic nature of Colorado's laws as they related to public health at that time, and the primitive methods of enforcement of such laws.[23] Sabin still had great energy and a clarity of vision to recognize what needed to be done. Allying herself with a group of public-spirited citizens led by Dr. Lloyd Florio—who had unsuccessfully (as late as 1945) sought support from the Colorado legislature—Sabin took up the cause. Her appointment to the Governor Vivian's Post-War Planning Committee and to a subcommittee on Public Health, which she chaired, gave her a vantage point. When W. Lee Knous became governor, Florence Sabin acquired his active support. Gov. Knous is said to have called her "Florence the atom bomb." The Sabin committee, aided by

Mark Henry Harrington, then president of the Denver Tuberculosis Society, William McGlone, later chairman of the State Board of Health, and Hubert Henry, all lawyers, drew up a legislative program consisting of six bills. The measures 1) provided for reorganization of State Health Department, 2) allowed adjoining counties with limited resources to receive federal, state, or local funds in order to organize district health services, 3) set up a State Tuberculosis Hospital, 4) increased per diem allowance for hospitalized indigent tuberculosis patients, 5) established for the first time a strict control of brucellosis, then rampant among the cattle of Colorado and consequently a serious problem in public health, and 6) authorized the State Health Department to receive funds under the Hill-Burton Act for hospital construction.[24]

A long battle ensued during which Dr. Sabin went to every one of the 63 counties of the state, campaigning for the program. Weather was no obstacle. It is reported that on one such occasion her car was forced to turn back for tire chains because of a blizzard, but she insisted on persevering and reached her destination in time to make the principal address. Florence Sabin, famous, elderly, indomitable character that she was, stirred public interest and served to dramatize the campaign. The newspapers carried picturesque stories of its heroine; many supported her fight for passage of the public health laws. In 1946 many opponents of the laws were defeated in election, and Knous became governor. From then on Sabin lobbied directly with legislators. Some lawmakers were said to fear her dauntless, direct approach, but many became her supporters. In 1947 four of the bills were passed. The bill to establish a Tuberculosis Hospital failed, as did the bill for control of brucellosis. The latter Sabin continued to work on against the stubborn resistance of cattlemen and the dairy industry. Then, in 1949, a compromise bill was passed that improved the situation with respect to brucellosis. However, in 1947 Florence Sabin was appointed chairman of an Interim Board of Health and Hospitals of Denver by Mayor Newton. She later resigned from that board and was named by the mayor as manager of the more prestigious and powerful Denver Department of Health and Welfare. She donated her $4,000 annual salary to the University of Colorado Medical School for research. In 1951 she was named chairman of the newly formed Board of Health and Hospitals but resigned as chairman the following year at age 81. According to the *Rocky Mountain News* of March 1, 1951,[25] she had during her short tenure marshalled forces behind a proposed water pollution control act aimed at attacking the filth and stench of Colorado's sewage-laden streams.

In 1951 she was a recipient of the Lasker Award, referred to as the "Oscar of Medicine" by the *Denver Post* of October 9, 1951.[26] On November 9, 1951, Florence Sabin celebrated her 80th birthday. On December first of that year the School of Medicine of the University of Colorado dedicated its new Florence R. Sabin Building for Research in Cellular Biology. Florence's sister was quite ill at the time and absorbed much of Florence's energies. That may have contributed to a severe illness (cardiac decompensation, pneumonia, and other complications) that Florence suffered early in 1953. She seemed to be making a satisfactory recovery when on the third of October, while watching a World Series baseball game, she suffered a fatal heart attack.

In her will she characteristically left her estate, after her sister's death, to the Medical School at the University of Colorado. The *Denver Post* termed her the "First Lady of American Science." A Sabin School, named for the two sisters, was established in Denver. A bronze bas-relief of Florence Sabin was placed in the Denver General Hospital and her figure is included among 17 women in a wooden panel, "Pioneers of Progress" carved by John Rood. In recognition of her versatility and courage, the State of Colorado chose Florence Sabin as one of its two representatives in the National Statuary Hall in the Capitol at Washington, D.C. The bronze statue by Mrs. Joy Buba was formally presented to the United States on February 26, 1959. In the same year the Colorado centennial year, the University of Colorado Press published a comprehensive biography entitled, *Florence Sabin: Colorado Woman of the Century* by Elinor Bluemel.[27] The *Rocky Mountain News* of June 18, 1959,[28] announced that Florence Sabin's personal and professional papers were to become part of the Sophia Smith Collection at Smith College.

In his book on the Rockefeller Institute,[29] Corner states that Florence Sabin seemed to consider her last professional undertaking merely incidental for she did not list it in *Who's Who in America,* esteeming membership in the Rockefeller Institute the climax of her career. He added that to her scientific associates, her work at the institute seemed less characteristic than her teaching and research at Johns Hopkins University in Baltimore and her public service in Denver. "Her talents," he stated, "were more fully displayed to her medical students and in public life than in a relatively cloistered environment like that of the Institute laboratories of her day. Teaching and inspiring a score of her country's best young histologists and hematologists and guiding the people of Colorado toward higher standards of public health, she was a great scientific leader."[30]

Florence Seibert receiving
National Achievement
award from First Lady
Eleanor Roosevelt, 1944.

CHAPTER IV

Florence Barbara Seibert

*". . . . Overcame crippling polio to make
dramatic advances against tuberculosis."*

While tuberculosis was still raging, before specific drug therapy had closed the sanatoriums, one of the controls exerted against the disease was a skin test survey to determine where the cases were in order to treat the infected and protect the uninfected. A positive skin test provided evidence of infection, previous or present, and x-ray diagnosis presented a picture of the current condition; the skin test helped to identify the specific disease. The first skin test antigen, known as old tuberculin, was a crude product. A purified protein derivative (PPD) was later developed, yet research efforts continued for many decades to make the skin test antigen more sensitive and more specific so that no cases would be missed and no other infections would give a false positive reaction. One who spent many fruitful years of her life in perfecting a purified protein derivative standard, PPD-S, was Dr. Florence Seibert whose strenuous efforts are the more remarkable for the fact that as a child she suffered poliomyelitis.

Overcoming Polio

On October 6, 1897, in Easton, Pennsylvania, Florence Barbara Seibert was born, the second of the three children (Russell, Florence, and Mabel) of

Barbara Memmert Seibert and George Peter Seibert. Her father carried on the family rug business while his brothers went through medical school. At age three Florence and her four-year-old brother Russell both became victims of the polio epidemic then rampant in their town of 20,000. Later, it was to be recorded as the first epidemic of polio in the United States to be so recognized. The younger child, Mabel, quickly removed from the environment, escaped the infection. After the tragedy the family moved closer to the school so the afflicted children could attend. Through their mother's patient ministrations and the medical assistance from their two physician uncles, the children regained the ability to walk. When the children were in high school the family moved to a two-story apartment over the father's store. The parents did all they could to make the two youngsters stand at play, walk, and use their legs without the aid of braces.

Florence was an eager student and developed a great interest in mathematics in high school. She suffered typhoid fever in her junior year, but recovered to graduate with her class. She longed to go on to college; however, it was questioned whether she would be physically able to accomplish it. The parental opposition was overcome when she was offered a scholarship to Goucher College. This provided the first opportunity for Florence to be away from home on her own.

It proved to be a permanent separation from the town as a resident; after college she returned only for family visits, to receive an award from her high school as an honorary member, and in 1947 to receive an honorary Sc.D. degree from Lafayette College at the same occasion as General George Marshall's receipt of an honorary degree from the same college.

The extent of her parents' reluctance to "abandon" her at college was evident when her father accompanied her to Goucher College and waited a week to take her back home, so convinced was he that she would find college too much for her. But she had no inclination to return home; she made friends readily and in her senior year was asked to serve as president of one of the freshman dormitories. Starting out with mathematics as her major, in time she discovered biology which she found even more intriguing. She was fortunate to spend the summer before her senior year at Woods Hole, Massachusetts. There her summer roommate was Lucy Graves, who married one of the instructors, George Taliaferro, and became part of the eventually famous Taliaferro team at the University of Chicago, which contributed so much to knowledge of immunology of parasitic diseases.

On Her Own at Last

Florence Seibert was inclined to study medicine so she prepared herself with the recommended prerequisites. These included organic chemistry which was taught by Dr. Jessie Minor, who played a significant role and influence in Florence's life. The course in physiology and hygiene was taught by Dr. Lillian Welsh, one of the famous pioneer medical women in Baltimore, who discouraged Florence Seibert from the pursuit of medicine. An eager and omnivorous student, Florence also found the study of history fascinating and returned to teach the subject in her old high school in Easton, Pennsylvania, during one summer vacation. Florence also studied philosophy and religion. College was a happy and fulfilling experience for her about which she has said, "Above all I learned . . . that I was not an invalid but was able to stand on my own two feet with a chance to make a contribution to the world."[1]

Many years after her graduation from Goucher College, Seibert became a member of the Board of Trustees as alumna trustee and urged the construction of a new science building. When the building was completed she took part in the dedication. In 1938, on the 50th anniversary of the college, she received an honorary L.L.D. from Goucher.

After graduation from college in 1918, Florence Seibert was caught up in the atmosphere of sacrifice for the war effort. Women were taking the places of men who had left for military service. One of these women was Dr. Jessie Minor, Florence's chemistry teacher, who had become head of the chemistry laboratory of Hammersley Paper Mill Company. Florence accepted an invitation to work there with Dr. Minor. Located in Garfield, New Jersey, the mill was close enough to New York City for Florence to make trips to meetings of the Chemists Club and to the public library. She learned how to write scientific papers, and, with Dr. Minor, published her first three papers dealing with the reactions of cellulose.

Seibert and Minor shared in a cooperative household of local school teachers and some from Goucher College, organized by Dr. Minor. They took meals together and kept house on a rotating schedule. Minor and Seibert had rooms in a house next door but participated in the arrangement. It proved to be a stimulating environment and served as a forum. Through these discussions Florence firmed up her religious convictions which served as her strength throughout the rest of her life.

After the war, as men returned to take up their jobs, women became expendable, they were no longer needed and were in general resented where they kept men out of work. However, Minor stayed on for several years and Seibert might have continued, but she recognized the limits of the job and her own limitations as well. Encouraged by Dr. Minor, she decided to advance her education, for research attracted her and she knew she needed more training.

She had saved some money and was determined to go to Yale for advanced study of biochemistry. Her former biology teacher, William Longley of Goucher College, arranged for her to work with Professor Lafayette B. Mendel, head of the Physiological Chemistry Department and one of the discoverers of vitamin A. She obtained a Yale scholarship to supplement her meager savings.

Graduate Work at Yale

In 1923, women were accepted only in the graduate school at Yale and were openly resented by the undergraduates. Mendel's laboratory was then located in the old "2 Hill-House" residence with a tower, a large brownstone mansion transformed into laboratories. His office was at the top of a "palatially bannistered" winding stairway and the main lecture room was located in the converted old parlor with a lecture table in front of an open fireplace and mantle. Florence Seibert had her office here just off the old dining room, a room she shared with P. Mabel Nelson who later became dean of home economics at Iowa State College. Laboratory animals were housed in the tower at the top of a stepladder-like stairway.

At that time research on vitamins and on proteins was underway in the laboratories. Florence decided upon the latter for her dissertation research, specifically protein fevers. It was already recognized that intravenously injected proteins tended to produce fever and chills in the recipient. While presenting a problem, the phenomenon also was taken advantage of in therapy. Called "protein therapy," it was for a time employed for treatment of arthritis.

Seibert undertook to determine what proteins produced fever and why they did so. Starting with 22 purified proteins prepared by Dr. Thomas B. Osborne at the Connecticut Agricultural Station, she immediately discovered that the phenomenon was not consistent; of the proteins injected into rabbits all produced fever on some occasions but not always. This suggested to her that it might not be the protein itself which caused the fever. Her advisor suggested that she first test the physical and chemical variables such as pH, rate of injection, temperature of protein solution, and the suspending medium. Following through on his advice, she discovered in her controls that some so-called pure distilled water would produce fever. Thus this problem took precedence over other matters, for unless a distilled water could be produced which was reliably non-pyrogenic none of the other variables could be tested. She found that glass distilled water produced in an apparatus with a baffle to prevent droplets of undistilled water from becoming entrapped in the steam never produced fever. From this experience she recognized that the fever-producing substance was heat stable. Using the term pyrogen, from the early literature, for this substance, she sought to find out what was removed in distillation. She observed that pyrogenic waters could be boiled or even filtered through bacterial filters without removing the pyrogen. Typically in a department of physiological chemistry, this whole problem had been approached by chemical analysis, but it finally occurred to them that bacterial contamination might be involved, since it had been noted that properly distilled water which was non-pyrogenic after distillation might become so after standing a few days. To quote Dr. Seibert, "I believe this must have bacteria in it. I have tried everything else." A few experiments were sufficient to prove that there were indeed bacteria present in the water which became pyrogenic.

Although she was interested in pursuing the bacteriological problem, she was reminded by her mentor, Professor Mendel, that her thesis problem dealt with "protein fevers." So commencing with casein isolated by bacteriological technique from milk that she obtained with sterile gloves from thoroughly cleaned udders, she determined that fever was not induced by casein so isolated and suspended in freshly distilled water, nor were egg or serum proteins per se pyrogenic. It was therefore concluded that the reactive protein solutions, like the distilled water, had been contaminated by bacteria.

Florence Seibert received her doctorate from Yale in 1923 but was allowed to remain during the summer to work on the bacteriological aspects of the problem. In collaboration with Dr. Seibert, Dr. Janet Bourn, a bacteriologist, assisted in isolating and identifying the pyrogen producing organisms.[2] It was demonstrated that the pyrogenic products produced by the bacteria were indeed heat stable. Following this clear demonstration of the causes of "protein fever," it became standard practice in research laboratories and in industry to use sterilized materials in preparation of biologics. Years later, in 1962, Dr. Seibert received the John Elliott Memorial Award from the American Association of Blood Banks for her work with pyrogens.

Upon receipt of her degree, Dr. Seibert wrote Dr. H. Gideon Wells, professor of pathology at the University of Chicago, asking to work on chemical pathology, a field in which Dr. Wells was an authority, having written *Chemical Pathology* and, later, *Chemical Aspects of Immunity.* To her great gratification, she was offered a fellowship. She also received a renewal of the American Physiological Society fellowship she had held at Yale. Living economically in a women's dormitory, she was thus able to continue her pyrogen research at the University of Chicago. She worked in the nearby Ricketts Laboratory and was able to take additional courses in immunology and pharmacology at the University of Chicago. She also attended seminars where she met Dr. Esmond Long, with whom she later worked for twenty-one years in tuberculosis research. She remained at Chicago until 1932, when, as an assistant professor in biochemistry and associate in Sprague Memorial Institute, she left to take up a position at the Henry Phipps Institute in Philadelphia with Esmond Long.

In 1924 while at the University of Chicago, she received the Ricketts Prize for work with pyrogens, a prize accompanied by $300, a considerable sum at the time. Seibert had no problem deciding what to do with the prize money. She bought a secondhand car, a black Chevrolet Coupé specially adjusted for use with her stronger foot. This car opened a new dimension in her life, for up to that time she had been severely restricted by her disability. About that time she also acquired a dog which accompanied her on drives and to the lab. While still at the University of Chicago, Long recruited Seibert to work on his research which concerned an analysis of tuberculin, to isolate the active substance from the crude product. He arranged for her to work part-time on his project and to continue part-time at the Otho S. A. Sprague Memorial Institute with Dr. Wells, the director. Thus started her most important research activity, an association with tuberculosis research which lasted for 35 years.

Beginning a Lasting Commitment

Her first step was to crystallize proteins from the crude tuberculin. This material was active in skin tests but so too was the remaining fluid. It was therefore decided to precipitate out larger quantities of the material although it obviously was not homogeneous. The first successful product was TPT or tuberculin protein trichloracetic acid precipitated. This was prepared in sufficient quantities for practical diagnostic use in skin testing.

In 1930 Florence enjoyed a sabbatical leave in Europe. Traveling with her sister Mabel by ocean liner, she arrived in London in mid-June where she spent some time at the Wellcome Laboratories, where England's tuberculin was prepared. In France she visited the Pasteur Institute and there talked with Drs. Bouquet, Calmette, and Guerin, who had developed the attenuated bovine strain of *Mycobacterium tuberculosis* used in the live vaccine, BCG (Bacillus Calmette, Guerin). She made a stop in Frankfort and at Hoechst, where she had been invited by Professor Dr. Karl Lautenschlager of the I. G. Farben Industrie, who had recently crystallized tuberculoprotein by Seibert's method. In Geneva the sisters were met by Dr. Arnold Klebs, a friend of Dr. Long and son of Dr. Edwin Klebs, for whom the Klebs-Loeffler bacillus *Corynebacterium diphtheriae* was named. They had letters of introduction to Dr. and Mrs. Ernst Loewenstein, whom they visited at the renowned Krankenhaus in Vienna. Before leaving, they made two stops in Berlin, one to visit Dr. Emmy Pinner, sister of Dr. Max Pinner, who was well known for his lifelong work on tuberculosis, the second stop to visit the Robert Koch Institute, named for the discoverer of the tubercle bacillus.

In 1932 Dr. Esmond Long accepted an invitation to go to the Henry Phipps Institute in Philadelphia and took with him his most valued assistant, Dr. Florence Seibert. By the time she left for the Phipps Institute, Seibert had published 34 papers—five of them dealing with protein fevers (through 1925), and 18 of them dealing with tuberculin, perhaps the most famous of which is the publication describing her crystallization of tuberculo-protein.[3]

The Phipps Institute had been founded in 1903 through the joint efforts of Henry Phipps, a wealthy partner of Andrew Carnegie, who wanted a charitable outlet for his wealth, and Dr. Lawrence F. Flick, a physician who envisioned a hospital and clinic for the study, treatment, and prevention of tuberculosis—"even though most doctors at that time thought tuberculosis inevitable and incurable."[4] The institute, which became a part of the University of Pennsylvania in 1910, offered clinical services as well as research opportunities. Dr. Long at first directed the research laboratory, but in time became director of the Phipps Institute.

Inevitably the research at the institute turned to a study of OT (Old Tuberculin), which had been used for skin test diagnosis since the time of Robert Koch. Prepared by extracting tuberculo-protein substances from cultures of *M. tuberculosis* boiled in the culture broth, the extract after filtration became the crude OT. This product was then used for separation of tuberculo-protein by precipitation with trichloracetic acid. The product was called PPD, purified protein derivative, because it represented protein possibly degraded by heat. PPD was found to be specific in that uninfected individuals gave negative reactions to skin tests; individuals known to have tuberculosis all gave positive reactions.

Large quantities of PPD were prepared by two drug companies under support of the National Tuberculosis Association. Seibert served as consultant in the production.

During the early years at Phipps Institute, Dr. Seibert was called upon to lecture at her old school, Goucher College, and at the Johns Hopkins University. She made frequent trips to Rockefeller Institute for consultation with Dr. Florence Sabin, then chairman of the National Tuberculosis Association (NTA) Committee on Tuberculin. In her memoirs Seibert notes that Sabin was particularly kind and thoughtful to her, the only other woman attending the NTA meetings, and it was through Dr. Sabin's efforts as a member of the Guggenheim Board, that Florence Seibert was awarded a Guggenheim fellowship for a year's study in Sweden.

Dr. Seibert had been much impressed with Svedborg's separation of proteins using an ultracentrifuge of his own design—for which he had received a Nobel Prize. This time, 1937–38, Florence Seibert took her car with her and it served her well in getting to Uppsala and in exploring the country.

At the Fysikalisk-Kemiska Institutionen she met Dr. Arne Tiselius, who had just developed a new apparatus and method which he called electrophoresis, for which he in turn received a Nobel Prize. With this method molecules were separated by electrical charge, in contrast to Svedborg's ultracentrifuge which separated them by size. During 1937–38 Elvin Kabat, who had just finished his doctorate at Columbia University, visited the laboratory, as did Professor J. B. Sumner from Ithaca, who had been the first to crystallize an enzyme, urease, for which he later shared a Nobel Prize. Later, after Sumner left, Dr. Frank Horsfall, Jr., of the Rockefeller Institute, took his place at the laboratory.

Using Svedborg's ultracentrifuge Dr. Seibert determined that there were tuberculo-protein molecules of different sizes. Following this with electrophoresis of the crude concentrated tuberculin, she discovered first that there was a quantity which moved rather rapidly like proteins and also a considerable amount of material that hardly moved at all. This latter component was found to be a complex carbohydrate of the tubercle bacillus. Next she examined PPD by electrophoresis and found a very fast moving component identified as a nucleic acid.[5] Her research there also included work with animals with which it was demonstrated that only the protein fractions of tuberculin gave positive tuberculin skin test reactions.[6]

One misfortune marred her stay in Sweden and impeded her progress in research. She fell in the laboratory, injuring her poor foot which was at first thought to be broken, but later proved to be only sprained. During her enforced absence from the laboratory, she reviewed her notes and realized she had been discarding perhaps the most important part of the broth cultures, the filtrates. When she returned to the laboratory she soon verified this and thereafter obtained one good preparation after another.

Dr. Seibert's experiences in Sweden included many happy occasions, Christmas with a Swedish family, a Swedish wedding, the Nobel Fest at which

Dr. Albert Szent-Gyorgi, then of Hungary, received one of the prizes. Of her year there, she has said that it was one of the most wonderful years of her life.

On the return trip to the United States she was able to stop in Copenhagen to visit the laboratory of Dr. K. Linderstrom-Lang at the Carlsberg Laboratories. After her return to Phipps Institute, Dr. Seibert was pleased to have a Tiselius electrophoretic apparatus for her own laboratory. Sent from Sweden and assembled at Phipps from memory, the apparatus proved quite a challenge for Seibert to assemble.

While still in Sweden, Seibert received an invitation to present a paper at the National Tuberculosis Association meeting in Los Angeles. She had intended to decline the invitation, but on return to Phipps Institute found that Dr. Long had made arrangements for her to attend and report on her research in Sweden. This was her first trip west so she took her sister Mabel with her and they visited some of the national parks. At the NTA meeting Seibert was surprised to receive the Trudeau Medal. She was the first woman to receive this honor. The Second World War came along then, preventing an exchange of visits, but after it ended a succession of Swedish friends visited Dr. Seibert at the Phipps Institute.

After Europe

Work continued on purification of PPD. For this work large volumes of the cultures were required. Through the NTA it was arranged that Seibert, as an NTA grantee, would prepare the PPD in the laboratories of Sharpe and Dohme at Glenholden, Pennsylvania. She grew the organisms in flat sided liter bottles of liquid medium at 37°C for eight to ten weeks, until the organisms covered the entire surface of the medium. The incubator had the capacity for 600–700 bottles at one time. This operation was repeated six times in order to obtain the 4,000 cultures required to produce 100 grams of PPD powder, sufficient to last many years since it represented about five billion doses of low-dose skin tests. This new product was designated PPD-S, the standard product was adopted by the United States Bureau of Biologics in 1941.

After tests on guinea pigs proved satisfactory, about a thousand junior and senior high school students were tested with the material (PPD-S), first with a minimal dose 0.00002 milligram in 0.1 milliliter buffer solution injected intradermally. Then the non-reactors were tested with a stronger dose, 0.005 milligram in 0.1 milliliter buffer solution. These tests proved the safety of PPD-S. The product was made available commercially through drug companies for over ten years after which they started production of PPD-S themselves.

Not all was well however. Complaints about PPD-S arose from Copenhagen, from the World Health Organization (WHO) laboratory, where they were promoting a product they themselves made, by the old original method, as the International Standard.

During the war years, work on the International Standard was deferred. Changes in personnel occurred everywhere and Dr. Seibert lost her good assistant Walter Nelson to the Air Force. Her sister Mabel was brought in to learn techniques and thereafter became Florence's best all-around assistant. After the war, when normal business was resumed, Dr. Long, back from his Washington war assignment, took up the issue of the International Standard, as did the British, represented by Henry H. Green, chief of the Weybridge Laboratory, for preparation of PPD. Florence Seibert had known Dr. Green as a Commonwealth Fellow from South Africa, when she was a graduate student at Yale. In 1949 Dr. Green visited Seibert's laboratory thereby initiating a valuable cooperation between the two laboratories. In 1952 Seibert visited the Weybridge Laboratories and in that same year PPD-S was selected as the International Standard by the Expert Committee on Tuberculosis of the World Health Organization. However, the question was not settled until 1966, when Seibert travelled to a World Health Organization meeting in Geneva, Switzerland, for a conference on Standardization of Tuberculin, where she and Dr. Jablovka from Russia were the only women in the assemblage. At the end of the week the committee recommended to the Expert Committee of All World Biologics that PPD-S be made the official standard for purified tuberculins.

In 1955 Esmond Long retired from the Phipps Institute, but just before his departure he and Florence Seibert were made full professors at the University of Pennsylvania. A new director was named at the institute (Dr. Julius Wilson) and the institute moved into the new University of Pennsylvania Science Building in 1958. In that year Florence Seibert retired to her new home in Florida and most of her equipment (purchased with National Tuberculosis Association funds) was transferred to the Centers for Disease Control (CDC) laboratory in Atlanta, Georgia.

During these 26 years at Phipps, Seibert had published some 70 papers dealing largely with her research on tuberculin, special methods for its production, and special media for growth of *Mycobacterium tuberculosis*. Some publications dealt with the effects of purified fractions of tuberculin on tuberculin-sensitive tissue.[7]

Retirement in Name Only

After retirement from the University of Pennsylvania and the move to Clearwater, Florida, Seibert continued to serve as a consultant on tuberculosis at CDC. She also took up some research she had become involved with while still at Phipps Institute. Around 1955 Dr. Irene Diller at Phipps engaged Florence Seibert's interest by asking her advice concerning acid fast organisms found repeatedly in rat sarcomas. Over a period of 12 years Dr. Diller followed mice of the ICR strain and was apparently able to fulfill Koch's postulates by production of tumors with cultured organisms and with recovery of the acid fast organisms from the experimental tumors. She also noted that such acid fast organisms could be recovered from the blood of very young mice of a high tumor incidence strain long before tumors appeared, and as the animals died from their tumors it was confirmed that those in which organisms were demonstrated in early life were the ones which developed tumors.[8]

Seibert, motivated by Diller's studies and by the death of several close friends from cancer, commenced a serious study of bacteria associated with malignancies, working in her own home laboratory equipped with her own apparatus brought from the Philadelphia laboratory. At first she was supported by grants from the American Cancer Society, and the Leukemia Society, but she was later unable to obtain support when she resumed research in 1964 after a five-year hiatus. However, through her determination and efforts, gifts were donated to her from lesser known sources, such as Gulf Coast Leukemia Foundation, Beta Sigma Phi Sorority, The Cooms Memorial, The Page Foundation, The Sower's Coins for Cancer, The Wolfe Memorial, and a number of personal contributions from individuals. She obtained volunteer assistants in the laboratory and her faithful sister Mabel carried on the work. They were successful in finding the same pleomorphic organisms found by Diller from tumor specimens supplied to them, and they cultured the organisms from the blood of cancer patients. Dr. Seibert published her findings in 1967.[9] Others attempted to classify the organisms and found them different from the recognized groups of atypical mycobacteria and remarkably pleomorphic, even able to pass bacterial filters and thereafter be cultured on bacteriological media. Seibert continued to study this enigmatic problem as long as she retained a laboratory.

The home Florence and Mabel Seibert retired to was built for them by their brother, Russell, an architect, on land he owned between Clearwater and St. Petersburg, Florida. It was here that Florence Seibert set up her home laboratory, acquired some cats, and entertained visitors and collaborators.

In 1963 Florence and her sister moved to an apartment in Carlton Towers in St. Petersburg with a view of Tampa Bay. Her laboratory equipment was stored for a time, then was moved to Mound Park Hospital in 1964. Later she transferred her activities and equipment to Bay Pines Veterans Administration Hospital and there continued for some time her research under Beta Sigma Phi support.

For her accomplishments Seibert received the First Achievement Award given by the American Association of University Women (AAUW) in 1943, a $2,500 stipend, and later (1964) was honored by that organization with a named fellowship, the Florence B. Seibert Endowed Fellowship of the AAUW. In 1944 she received the National Achievement Award of Chi Omega. The Gimbel Award (1945) was accompanied by $1,000. The John Scott Award (1946), a medal and $1,000, was presented by the trustees of the city of Philadelphia from the income accumulated from a fund created by a chemist, John Scott of Edinburgh, Scotland, who out of admiration for Ben Franklin, bequeathed funds in 1816 to the city of Philadelphia, to be used for awards to "ingenious men and women who make useful inventions." In 1950, Seibert was named a Distinguished Daughter of Philadelphia, which automatically made her a member of a board of distinguished women who selected future awardees of Philadelphia, based on their humanitarian or creative activities. In 1962 Seibert was honored by receipt of the John Elliott Award from the American Association of Blood Banks for her early work on pyrogens.

Seibert's early discovery that distilled water was frequently contaminated by pyrogenic bacteria proved to be of vital importance in intravenous medication. She is best known for her characterization and refinement of tuberculin which led to more precise diagnosis of tuberculosis. Her interest in the etiology of cancer motivated her to continue research long after retirement. She received many awards and tributes for research accomplishments. A vigorous woman all her life, despite her handicap, she retained great vitality and continued to speak as an invited lecturer well into her eighties. A scientist of remarkable fortitude, she was deeply involved with research and was an inspiration to many others. In the preface to her autobiography, *Pebbles on the Hill of a Scientist,* she wrote that she hoped that the great satisfaction she had experienced in her work would tempt young workers to pursue their dreams with all their energy, for nowhere would they find a more rewarding endeavor.

Alice Evans and Rebecca Lancefield at Annual Meeting of American Society for Microbiology, 1964.

CHAPTER V

Rebecca Craighill Lancefield

". . . . Established ground-breaking classification of streptococci; recorded advances against rheumatic fever."

The streptococci would appear to be quite versatile organisms for they can produce such diverse illnesses as septic sore throat, scarlet fever, erysipelas and puerperal fever. Microscopically they appear as a chain of cocci (spheres) and they are ubiquitous, widely distributed. However, though they all look much the same under the microscope, they are not the same in their potential for causing disease. Dr. Rebecca Lancefield at the Rockefeller University approached this complex field with the objective of differentiating the types of streptococci which can produce disease in humans. She was so successful in her efforts that one now categorizes these organisms by the Lancefield classification of streptococci. She clarified a confusing problem and made many contributions to the study of rheumatic fever.

A Nomadic Childhood

Dr. Lancefield was born Rebecca Price Craighill in 1895 at Fort Wadsworth, Staten Island, New York, on the army post where her father was stationed. A West Post graduate like his father before him, her father spent his career in the army moving the family to his assigned posts and providing his daughters with a varied geographic and educational background. His own family, the Craighills, came from Virginia where his forebears had settled in the early 1700s. Rebecca Craighill's maternal forebears had also settled in Virginia, but moved as pioneers to Mississippi. Her mother, Mary Wortley Montague Byram, a direct descendant of Lady Mary Wortley Montague, a promoter of vaccination and other public health measures,[1] married William Edward Craighill, a West Point classmate of her brother, both assigned to the Corps of Engineers.

Dr. Lancefield was educated at many schools; public schools when satisfactory and convenient to the army base, otherwise, she studied with governesses or went to private schools. She entered Wellesley College in the fall of 1912 with vague intentions of majoring in French and English, but her interest was aroused by her roommate's freshman course in zoology. She then changed her major to zoology and took as many other courses in biology as could be fitted in with the college requirements for the B.A. degree. This included an elementary course in bacteriology, the only bacteriology course given at the college at that time. When she discovered that she should have a good background in chemistry, it was almost too late. However, she devoted her last two years at Wellesley to remedying this deficiency as much as possible, graduating in 1916.

At that time the expectation was that graduates not immediately getting married would teach. Rebecca followed the conventional pattern and started out teaching science and mathematics at a girls' boarding school (Hopkins Hall) in Burlington, Vermont. The science turned out to be physical geography, but this did not disconcert her. Her annual salary was a splendid $500 plus room and board. Out of this she saved $200 to go to graduate school.

She was offered a scholarship with graduate tuition at Teachers' College at Columbia University. This scholarship was established by the Daughters of the Cincinnati for daughters of army or navy officers. She wished to do her graduate work in either bacteriology or genetics, yet on studying the catalogue, she could not find courses suited to her program. However, her adviser assured her that the scholarship did not require that she take courses at Teachers' College; it was only necessary to matriculate there; she might take any course offered at Columbia.

A Beginning in Bacteriology

So while registered at Teachers' College, she studied bacteriology in the department of the great bacteriologist Hans Zinsser. Graduate and medical bacteriology classes were then given in an old ramshackle building at 59th Street and Amsterdam Avenue, the College of Physicians and Surgeons of Columbia University. She spent a year there studying all the bacteriology and related subjects available. Zinsser was then (1918) away in Europe involved with World War I, and A. K. Balls, an enzyme chemist, served as head of the department. Following the Zinsser tradition, Balls expected his students to spend all of their waking hours in class or in the laboratory. At the end of the year Rebecca Craighill received the degree of Master of Arts from Columbia and then married Donald Lancefield, whom she met as a graduate student at Columbia in the drosophila genetics course of Dr. T. H. Morgan. Donald Lancefield was called into service at this time during World War I. At the beginning of his service, while still a private, he was stationed with the Sanitary Corps Unit at the Rockefeller Institute for Medical Research to attend a special course conducted in part by Dr. O. T. Avery and Dr. A. R. Dochez. These two eminent investigators found time in their pneumonia research program at the Rockefeller Institute Hospital to lend their services to a study of streptococci isolated from bronchopneumonia which was rife in military camps.

Dochez and Avery, returning from a trip with a medical commission sent by the surgeon general to visit Texas army camps, brought back about 120 cultures of streptococci. Rebecca Lancefield, having just finished her year of graduate work in Zinsser's department at Columbia, applied to the Rockefeller Institute for a position. In June 1918 she was assigned as a technician for the streptococcus study at the Rockefeller Hospital. So, for a time, both Lancefields worked at the institute.

Streptococcal classification and related pathogenicity were in a very confused state at that time. However, using the most difficult, and at the same time the most trustworthy method for typing, that is, mouse protection tests, the group studying streptococci at the Rockefeller Institute were able during the ensuing winter to identify at least four immunologically specific types of streptococci among their 120 or so cultures. This finding was accepted at the time and has been subsequently confirmed in numerous laboratories by several different approaches. These studies, published in 1919,[2] were interrupted soon after by termination of funds from the surgeon general's office. Avery and Dochez returned wholeheartedly to research on pneumococci, partly interrupted by the war.

In the summer of 1919 the Lancefields went to Woods Hole, Massachusetts, with the Columbia University zoology group on their annual three-month stay at the Marine Biological Laboratory. On their return to New York, Rebecca Lancefield worked as a research assistant for Dr. C. W. Metz to work in his genetics laboratory at Columbia. He wished to add genetic and cytological studies of *Drosophilia willistoni* and of other species he was already studying to the findings of the Morgan laboratory. Three publications on *Drosophila willistoni*, both cytological and genetic, resulted from Lancefield's work with Metz in the next two years in his laboratory at Columbia.

To Oregon and Back

In 1921 Donald Lancefield had finished the work for his Ph.D. and was offered a position at the University of Oregon. His home had been in Amity, Oregon, in the Willamette Valley, and he was a member of the first class to graduate from Reed College in Portland, Oregon. Thus, after careful consideration, he accepted the position in Oregon. Rebecca Lancefield also found a position at the University of Oregon, teaching bacteriology. During that year she also became acquainted with the state where Donald Lancefield's parents had been pioneers, his mother having arrived by covered wagon at the age of ten. At the end of the school year the Lancefields were ready to return to New York and to Columbia University, Donald Lancefield to join Morgan's department, and Rebecca Lancefield to finish her degree with Zinsser.

She has said that Zinsser didn't much care for women working around his laboratory, but he knew of her previous work and that she had taken almost all the courses offered in his department. So he agreed to accept her as a candidate for the Ph.D. degree and suggested that she might like to consider an opening then available at the Rockefeller Institute Hospital, where she had worked before. Dr. Homer Swift was starting a study of rheumatic fever at the institute, and Rebecca Lancefield was glad to accept a position with him.

She remained at this institute for the rest of her professional life. Thus it was her great good fortune to see the Rockefeller Institute in one of its great periods and also to live through the heyday of Morgan's research group in the Department of Zoology at Columbia University, where her husband remained on the faculty for many years prior to becoming chairman of the Department of Zoology at Queens College.

Professional Frustrations

When Rebecca Lancefield commenced work on rheumatic fever, about 1922, the medical community associated the disease with the "green" streptococcus, *Streptococcus viridans.* Lancefield worked in Swift's department with the "green" streptococci for two years, attempting to extract a satisfactory polysaccharide or other antigen from the organisms that would react specifically with rheumatic fever patients' sera for a diagnostic test. Her three publications on *S. viridans* bear witness to the frustration she felt after working two years and finding that the nucleoprotein antigen finally decided on as a laboratory test for rheumatic fever was unsuitable. It exhibited a broad range of activity in tests with sera of animals immunized with streptococcal preparations, but this antigenic fraction reacted strongly not only with sera from rheumatic fever patients, but equally well with 50 percent of the sera from control subjects.

She expected to accomplish her other objective, that of differentiating specific types of *S. viridans,* in much the same way that the pneumococcus investigators had found so successful for pneumococcal types, but Lancefield had only one strain that reacted the same as one of Swift's four original individual strains, hardly sufficient to create a type! It seemed that each strain of *S. viridans* was law unto itself, quite unlike the hemolytic streptococci from the Texas army camps previously studied with Avery and Dochez, with which many serologically similar or identical strains were found in each of the four types identified from the wartime epidemic.

Lancefield received her doctorate in bacteriology at Columbia University in 1925 with this work on streptococci used for her dissertation. Frederick

P. Gay had by that time succeeded to the chairmanship of the Columbia department. Lancefield's thesis based on the *S. viridans* study made in Dr. Swift's laboratory at the Rockefeller Hospital was entitled, "The Immunological Relationships of *Streptococcus viridans* and Certain of its Chemical Fractions." Two publications in the *Journal of Experimental Medicine,* Volume 42, resulted from the work.[3]

New Directions

After receiving the doctorate, Lancefield returned to work full-time at the Rockefeller Institute taking up again the work with hemolytic streptococci, obviously important in rheumatic fever and so much more rewarding than *S. viridans* for her work in rheumatic fever. She had, with Avery and Dochez, already obtained proof of the existence of immunologically specific types of hemolytic streptococci. By then it was becoming clear that hemolytic streptococci were highly pathogenic to man. Avery and his group, located at the opposite end of the floor from Lancefield, were at the height of their research on pneumococcus polysaccharides, and frequent discussions took place among them.

Lancefield found a polysaccharide common to all streptococci studied at that time from acute human infections. She later found this polysaccharide characteristic of the serological group A; this "C" carbohydrate has been employed to classify all group A strains. Separate type-specific substances isolated from the individual and serologically specific types found within group A were discovered to be proteins, a distinct, so-called, M substance for each type. The finding that antibodies to the M antigen determine the immunity of the host against infection with specific streptococci, prompted the designation of the M antigens as the basis of type specificity. The nomenclature of these group A types is therefore referred to as the M antigens.

In 1928 she published a series of five papers on the antigen complex of *Streptococcus haemolyticus,* all appearing in volume 47 of the *Journal of Experimental Medicine,*[4] in which she describes and characterizes the type M substance, its chemical (protein) and immunological properties, the chemical and immunological properties of the species-specific C substance, a polysaccharide. She also reported that the nucleoprotein fraction P, widely cross-reactive among gram-positive cocci, is a true antigen, capable of stimulating antibody production in rabbits and producing anaphylactic shock in guinea pigs actively or passively sensitized; whereas the purified polysaccharide C substance does not give rise to circulating antibodies in rabbits but does produce passive anaphylactic shock in guinea pigs sensitized with antibacterial sera against whole organisms. Similar results were obtained with the type-specific M substance; both were considered partial antigens or haptens.[5]

Two additional publications in collaboration with E. W. Todd in 1928 concerned correlation of cultural variants of streptococci and virulence. She found matt colonies of these variants contained the M antigen and were capable of being virulent. In the year which Todd spent in the Rockefeller Rheumatic Fever Department in 1926 as a British Medical Research Council Fellow, he and Lancefield found that their individual interpretations of his matt and glossy colonies on the one hand and of her type-specific M antigens (named for his matt colonies) meshed with extraordinary precision, and resulted in a delightful collaboration and lifelong friendship. In 1933 Lancefield published one of her most significant papers, "A Serological Differentiation of Human and Other Groups of Hemolytic Streptococci."[6] In this paper she describes her methods of producing streptococcal antigens and antisera for use in precipitin tests and she notes that "the results of this study are of interest not only from the theoretical viewpoint of establishing an orderly grouping of these microorganisms but also from an epidemiological aspect in providing means of identifying the probable origin of a given strain." She discussed the results of the biochemical (metabolic) tests then available and mentioned differential tests in use, such as hydrolysis of sodium hippurate, which were consistent with her serological classification. Using 106 strains of hemolytic streptococci from various sources (human, other animals, dairy products), she demonstrated that the streptococci could be classified by precipitin test into five distinct groups. The first streptococcal strains studied earlier with Avery and Dochez were all of human origin. These strains she designated as group A and distinct groups discovered later were assigned succeeding letters of the alphabet.

Lancefield's next publication in 1934[7] dealt with group B streptococci. Most of the strains studied were from bovine sources but for one series isolated by Hare and Colbrook from patients in a large London Maternity Hospital.[8] The latter series pointed out the fairly common occurrence of group B streptococci from human sources.

The next nine of Lancefield's publications refined and extended her basic discoveries and further characterized the streptococcal antigens. In 1936 Dr. Swift, in collaboration with her, presented a paper on problems encountered in typing streptococci at the Second International Congress for Microbiology in London, England.

Scientific Collaboration

In the preceding five or ten years the results of her work concerned with classifying streptococci serologically had converged with that of Fred Griffith in London who had approached the problem with different methods specially developed by him and with a somewhat different point of view suited to his epidemiological studies. Both investigators needed exact identification of the streptococci encountered in their studies. Griffith, with his famous slide agglutination technique and careful work, was able to classify hemolytic streptococci (1926–1934) from his London laboratory into 30 accurately defined types in his studies of streptococcal epidemics in schools. When this classification was published in 1934 he agreed at once to Lancefield's request to send representative type strains to her so that she could correlate the Griffith types identified by agglutination with those collected in her work and identified by the tests she employed, i.e., precipitin reactions, test tube agglutinations, and mouse protection tests. He supposed that his slide agglutination method of typing was probably dependent on the same M antigen prepared by Lancefield as the type-specific substance in her experiments. This was substantiated when they exchanged not only his type strains but also samples of his unabsorbed sera which could be tested by the M precipitin method. Both absorbed and unabsorbed undiluted anti-M sera crossed the Atlantic to Dr. Griffith from Dr. Lancefield's laboratory. With very few exceptions, the agreement of types was so satisfactory that Lancefield then adopted Griffith's type numbers instead of the patients' names she had been using as type-identification. These types were restricted to Group A.

The protein T antigen, studied in detail serologically and described (1946) chemically with Dr. Dole[9] in connection with the correlation of Griffith's types with the results of M and T reactions, was considered inadequate as the basis of type classification because of cross-reactions both in agglutination and in the lack of protective properties. Griffith's antigens and antibodies for each type had been prepared in such a way that cross-reactions due to the T antigen-antibody system were eliminated except in special unusual cases. In current usage the slide agglutination reaction is used to advantage for preliminary broad classification known to depend upon T reactions.

When the nomenclature subcommittee of the International Congress of Microbiology sanctioned the use of the M antigen as the basis for the serological typing of group A streptococci, it resolved the confusion in referring to streptococci in research projects and in epidemiological studies.

In 1940 Rebecca Lancefield was selected to present the Harvey Lecture. Her presentation was entitled "Specific Relationships of Cell Composition to Biological Activity of Hemolytic Streptococci."[10] It provided an exposition and summary of her own contributions to the field. It begins with a historical review from the earliest descriptions by Pasteur in 1879, who saw streptococci as a chain of beads in the blood of a patient dying of puerperal sepsis, to Schottmüller, who characterized (in 1903) streptococci by their effect on blood agar; distinguishing hemolytic, viridans, and the indifferent or non-hemolytic streptococci. Lancefield pointed out that it was the so-called streptolysin described by Besredka (in 1901) that was the first useful distinction in classification of these organisms.

In the Harvey Lecture Lancefield also referred to early attempts to bring order into classification of streptococci by means of fermentation reactions and other biochemical tests. Although some progress had been made using such tests, there was always overlapping among the classes differentiated and the results were difficult or impossible to interpret. She mentioned the first efforts at serological classification, using agglutination tests, and the technical difficulties encountered. Lancefield's publication with Avery and Dochez[11] presented the first reliable methods of serological typing of streptococci using agglutination, precipitation, and mouse protection tests, followed in later studies by other immunological tests. By the time of this lecture (1940) Lancefield had characterized, or been consulted about, groups A through H and K (later dropped), L, and M.

Back to the Basics

When antibiotics burst upon the scene around 1936, one of her colleagues, needling her, said, "What are you going to work on now?" She replied that she was glad to be freed of the many practical responsibilities connected with streptococcal research, and could pursue her principal objective which was to determine the connection, if any, between group A streptococci and rheumatic fever, before leaving this field.

One concern that she and her collaborators and others studying rheumatic fever encountered was the type-specificity of streptococci found in recurring attacks of rheumatic fever. They came to the conclusion before the availability of antibiotics that a strain of different type-specificity initiated each recurrent attack. After the introduction of antibiotics this was no longer found to be true; the same type strain could be found repeatedly. Antibiotic therapy had interfered with antibody production by early elimination of the infecting streptococcus.

Closely though informally associated with the Rockefeller Hospital Rheumatic Fever Department was Dr. Ann G. Kuttner, who was much interested in the recurrent attacks of rheumatic fever patients. She contributed greatly to laboratory and clinical investigations in this area of work. She was joint author with Markowitz of the first edition (1965) of *Rheumatic Fever: Diagnosis, Management and Treatment.*[12] To the second edition (1972), dedicated to Dr. Kuttner after her death, Lancefield provided the preface.

Puzzling strains of streptococci were sent to Lancefield from far and near. Her study of streptococci from an epizootic in guinea pigs at Saranac Lake in the 1930s led to her characterization of group C streptococci and suggested to her that serological groups of this sort existed among strains from other sources.

Later, in 1960, she studied, in collaboration with Hook and Wagner,[13] organisms from a strange epizootic in Swiss mice at Johns Hopkins University. A similar epizootic occurred in Memorial Hospital laboratories at about the same time. In both instances the important finding was that these animals were infected by a group A streptococcus of the newly designated type 50. This organism was found to be the same as that isolated in 1935 from a mouse colony at Cornell University. This strain was identified by Lancefield in 1960 from dried cultures which she had stored in her collection. The more recent epizootics occurred in animals obtained from a single breeder.

During the decade of World War II, several of Lancefield's publications were collaborative efforts by most members of the Rheumatic Fever Department at the Rockefeller Institute. Their results were published in a series of papers delineating the effort to identify antigens in group A streptococci which might be involved in preventing pharyngitis and associated sequellae in military personnel. Their endeavors included supplying type-specific antisera to military laboratories and, at times, typing large numbers of strains for military hospitals. During these large-scale studies it was found in many laboratories that the dominant strain of streptococcus varied from year to year, and that the streptococci found in complications following scarlet fever may differ from the strain initiating the disease. This latter finding led to a study of the persistence of type-specific antibodies which might prevent reinfection with the homologous type streptococcus.[14] Other studies resulted in characterization of the cell wall polysaccharide of group A streptococci by chemical analysis (McCarty)[15] and structurally by electron mycroscopy (Swanson).[16] Curtis and Krause (in St. Louis)[17] performed the same service for the group B cell wall determinitive polysaccharide.[18]

During the 1950s Lancefield and others investigated the confusing R antigen. First thought to be the specific M antigen of type 28 streptococcus of group A, it was found by immunological analysis to be a protein present fairly widely within A streptococci and present as well in other groups. It was concurrently discovered that this R antigen, so similar in many characteristics to the M antigen, was not related to virulence of an organism nor was it protective against streptococcal infection.

In later years Lancefield returned to study the group B streptococci, partly from purely theoretical considerations of the chemical and immunological nature of the type-specific antigens in this serological group, and partly to elucidate the occurrence and prevalence of group B streptococcus meningitis in newborn infants. This question was of particular interest to pediatricians and gynecologists who had been engaged with perinatal infections. Dr. Lancefield encouraged several younger investigators whose curiosity had been aroused about the prevalence of group B organism and by their clinical implications. Her publication of 1975 with McCarty and Everly in the *Journal of Experimental Medicine*[19] is concerned with the question of the significance of the polysaccharide and protein antigens of group B streptococci in virulence and protection. The strains studied were isolated from newborns. One of the interesting findings to emerge from the study was the evidence that antibody against either polysaccharide or protein antigen of a single strain of group B streptococci could be protective against that strain. Multiple mouse protective antibodies were found in the sera of immunized animals for all group B strains investigated, i.e., from three to possibly four distinct antibodies could be found in serum raised against a single strain.

In 1943–44, as president of the Society of American Bacteriologists, Rebecca Lancefield was spared the work and distractions of a national meeting; the National War Travel Act made it impossible for society members to travel for that purpose. No such encumbrance hindered her performance of duties and rituals when she became first woman president of the American Association of Immunologists in 1960–61.

In 1968 the Lancefields took their sabbatical leaves in England. They spent five to six months at Cambridge, then travelled on the continent. Several other visits were made later to England, combining scientific meetings with pleasure. Customarily, their summers were spent at Woods Hole near their daughter and grandchildren.

Lancefield was supportive of women seeking equal rights but she remarked that they sometimes expect too much. She said that it is not easy to have both a scientific career and a family without compromising one or both—despite the fact that she managed it quite well herself.

Passing the Torch

Rebecca Lancefield was generous with her talents and time. She trained young scientists and for many years served as the Scotland Yard of streptococcal mysteries. A lingering disappointment to her was the unresolved question of the undoubted, but largely unexplained, role of group A streptococci in rheumatic fever. She was a guest speaker throughout the land, at home and abroad, and she received many honors. In 1960 she received the T. Duckett Jones Memorial Award. She was honored with the American Heart Association Achievement Award in 1964, and, in 1965, she was selected to present the T. Duckett Jones Memorial Lecture at the General Meeting of the Society for General Microbiology in England. Later in the same year, she presented the Armine T. Wilson Memorial Oration. In 1970, she was elected to membership in the National Academy of Sciences which up to that time had elected only ten women to membership. She received the New York Academy of Medicine Medal in April 1973 and Research Achievement Awards from the journal *Medicine* and from the Alumnae Association of Wellesley College, also in 1973.

In June of 1973 she received the highest recognition from the institution where she had spent most of her professional life, the Rockefeller University, which awarded her a Doctor of Science (Honoris Causa) degree. Of her scientific contributions they said, "That our knowledge of hemolytic streptococci has reached its present well-ordered state is due in large part to the work of Dr. Lancefield. The major portion of the conceptual schemes, methodology and detailed experimental analysis which form the basis for understanding the composition of this important group of organisms has come from her laboratory." The name Lancefield is associated throughout the world with the grouping and typing of streptococci.

Rebecca Lancefield lived to age 86. An obituary appearing in the American Society for Microbiology *News* for December 1981,[20] pays tribute to her as a major contributor to the field of streptococcal research, pursuing her research with unceasing devotion to the end of her life.

CHAPTER VI

Gladys Lounsbury Hobby

". . . . Pioneer in antibiotics —
the 'miracle drugs.'"

The magic bullet against syphilis, the arsenical chemicals, was discovered by Paul Ehrlich in 1904. It brought forth hope and a long search for other specific drug treatment. But it was not until the discovery of the sulfa drugs in the 1930s that the hope was extended. With the discovery soon after of the usefulness of antibiotics (antimicrobial agents of microbial origin) the hope was fulfilled and a golden age of medicine initiated. Dr. Gladys Hobby has been involved from the first in critical research on antibiotics. She made definitive studies on penicillin. Her subsequent research with streptomycin, viomycin, and the broad spectrum antibiotics, her contributions to the discovery and development of oxytetracycline (Terramycin[R]), and her extensive studies on the chemotherapy of tuberculosis, established her as an authority in the field.

Early Influences

Gladys Lounsbury Hobby was born in Washington Heights in New York City in 1910. She obtained her early schooling in New York City, attended the upper grades and high school in White Plains, New York, and graduated from Vassar College in 1931. Although primarily interested in science, she acquired an appreciation of art from her mother, Flora Lounsbury Hobby, who taught in the New York City public school system, and from her father, Theodore Y. Hobby, who, initially in the retail dry goods business, became a close associate of Benjamin Altman while Altman was making his collection of porcelains, paintings, and other works of art which ultimately comprised the Altman Collection at the Metropolitan Museum of Art in New York City. Mr. Hobby travelled extensively in Europe with Mr. Altman, and on the latter's death became "keeper" of the Altman Collection at the Museum. He later became associate curator of Far Eastern Art, as well, and assisted John D. Rockefeller II in collecting the Japanese and Chinese porcelains now a part of the Rockefeller Collection at the Metropolitan Museum of Art.

Gladys Hobby began her training in bacteriology with Dr. Anne Benton Riebeth at Vassar College, and worked for a time—while still in college—at the New York City Department of Health Laboratories, under Dr. Anna Williams and Dr. Annis Thomson. Following graduation, she continued the study of bacteriology at the College of Physicians and Surgeons (P&S) at Columbia University in New York. Working initially on *Corynebacterium diphtheriae,* she applied the phenomenon of microbial variation as described by Arkwright, Frederick Griffith, Martin Henry Dawson, and others, to diphtheria bacilli, and received an M.S. degree in 1932, a Ph.D. degree in 1935. In 1934 Gladys Hobby moved from the bacteriology department at P&S to the Department of Medicine, to work with Henry Dawson, who was then engaged in research on the morphological, serological, and disease-producing properties of hemolytic streptococci. Hobby worked closely with Dawson for ten years and collaborated with Rebecca Lancefield at the Rockefeller University and with Fred Griffith in England. Dawson's interest in rheumatic diseases brought them in contact with many patients with subacute bacterial endocarditis, a disease then uniformly fatal to 100 percent of patients. Their interest in bacterial endocarditis and their desire to find a remedy for the disease, led them to experimental chemotherapeutic studies with gold salts, the sulfonamides, and finally penicillin. With Dawson and Karl Meyer, a chemist at P&S, Hobby prepared the first penicillin made in the United States and, in 1940, Dawson initiated the first clinical trials of its action, testing it in patients with subacute bacterial endocarditis. For Gladys Hobby, this was the start of many years of research on antimicrobial drugs.

A New Age

Hobby, Dawson, and Meyer clearly demonstrated the chemotherapeutic potential of penicillin, demonstrated the relation of size of infecting dose to the amount of penicillin required to protect experimentally infected animals, and, importantly, demonstrated also that penicillin is effective only against actively multiplying microbial cells.[1] Dawson and Hobby in addition made a detailed study of the clinical effectiveness of penicillin, reporting the therapeutic effects of the drug in 100 patients treated between 1940 and 1944.[2] In 1944, due to failing health, Dawson was forced to curtail his research, and

Gladys Hobby moved to Pfizer, Inc. Early in 1945 Dawson published, with Dr. Thomas Hunter[3] of the College of Physicians and Surgeons in New York, a report on the treatment of 20 patients with subacute bacterial endocarditis. Therapy was apparently successful in 15 of the 20. Dawson had achieved what he sought when he started, with Gladys Hobby and Karl Meyer, to study penicillin in 1940. He died in March of 1945.

Hobby continued her research on antimicrobial agents for 15 years at Pfizer, Inc. In 1950 she was co-discoverer of oxytetracycline (Terramycin[R]),[4] organized its experimental evaluation, and later its clinical trials, prepared the New Drug Application for its approval by the U. S. Food and Drug Administration, and helped to promote it widely in hospitals throughout the United States, Canada, the British Isles, Europe, Central and South America. During the early years at Pfizer, Inc., Hobby continued to retain an academic appointment at Columbia University where she taught bacteriology, but with the extensive travel required for promotion of Terramycin[R] she relinquished her academic position. Shortly after leaving Pfizer, Inc., she was appointed clinical instructor (later clinical assistant professor) of public health at Cornell Medical College in New York.

In 1959 she moved to the Veterans Administration as chief of the Veteran's Administration Special Research Laboratory for the Study of Chronic Infectious Disease, and there continued research for yet another 18 years. She devoted her attention primarily to the control of tuberculosis, studying each of the many antituberculosis drugs that were introduced, evaluating the extent and significance of the emergence of resistance of tubercle bacilli to the antimicrobial agents, and showing clearly that streptomycin with or without para aminosalicylic acid was not sufficient to eradicate viable tubercle bacilli from tuberculous lesions in humans.[5]

Penicillin Led the Way

In 1951 Hobby published a historical review of microbiology in relation to antibiotics[6] in which she pointed out that medical therapy until the end of the nineteenth century was largely a body of empirical knowledge. Some of the herbal remedies known to the Greeks and Romans, and even earlier peoples, were still in use. In the closing decades of the nineteenth century a few discoveries provided great impetus to the search for the active component in herbs and plants and to a search for new remedies with specific action against the etiologic agents of infectious diseases that were rapidly being discovered during the same period. Many antagonistic substances were discovered and tested, but until 1929, when Fleming discovered penicillin, none proved efficacious. Hobby pointed out the serendipity in Fleming's observations, also how fortuitous a discovery it was that penicillin was the first antibiotic studied: its availability, its spectrum of action, its bactericidal effect on sensitive organisms, and its low toxicity leading to its development for clinical use.

Gladys Hobby's output in publications on her research matches her extensive input. Starting in 1934 with the publication of her doctoral thesis, she had to her credit by 1978 more than 125 articles in reviewed journals, and had made contributions to six books. She prepared the chapter on "The Mode of Action of Streptomycin," in *Streptomycin*, edited by S. A. Waksman (1949),[7] and the chapter "Terramycin" in *Therapeutics in Internal Medicine* (1950).[8] In 1954 she contributed the section on "Synergism, Antagonism and Hormesis" in *Antibiotic Therapy*, edited by H. Welch,[9] in 1960, "Antibiotics" in *Encyclopedia of Science and Technology*,[10] "Viomycin,"[11] and in 1963, "Antimicrobial Susceptibility Tests" in *Diagnostic Procedures and Reagents, Fourth Edition*.[12]

She has been an active member of many professional organizations, served as vice president and chairman of the Long Range Planning Committee of the American Thoracic Society from 1968 to 1969; vice president of the New York Trudeau Society (1966–1967); president of the New York Lung Association (1963–1965); for many years chairman of the Laboratory Committee of the Veterans Administration Cooperative Study of Chemotherapy of Tuberculosis; and from 1975 to 1979 vice president and member of the Executive Committee of the International Society of Chemotherapy. She has served as a member of the editorial boards of *Applied Microbiology* (1952–1958), *American Review of Respiratory Diseases* (1965–1968), and the *Journal of Infectious Diseases* (1965–1972). In 1968, Hobby served as a consultant to Mayor John Lindsay's Task Force on Tuberculosis in New York City. Earlier (1962–1966), she had represented the Veteran's Administration on a study section of the National Institute of Allergy and Infectious Diseases, National Institutes of Health, Bethesda, Maryland.

Gladys Hobby has also been active in church work, being a member of the Madison Avenue Presbyterian Church in New York City, a member of the Board of Trustees of the Church (1971–1977) and a co-chairman of the church's endowment fund campaign (1974–1978). She has travelled widely, through the United States, Canada, Europe, the British Isles, Japan, Central and South America—in part for personal pleasure and in part for professional purposes. In 1951, she received the Mademoiselle Award in Science, and in the same year received, for the team of investigators at Pfizer, Inc., who had discovered oxytetracycline, the Commercial Solvents Award in Antibiotics. She is a charter fellow, American Academy of Microbiology; a fellow, New York Academy of Sciences; a fellow of the American Public Health Association and also of the American Association for the Advancement of Science. She is an associate fellow of the New York Academy of Medicine; honorary member of the American Society for Microbiology; honorary member of the American Thoracic Society; emeritus member of various other scientific organizations. In 1977 she received from the New York Lung Association an honorary award for 20 years of outstanding service toward improving community health in the fight against tuberculosis and other lung diseases. She is listed in the major biographical references, e.g., *American Men and Women of Science* (since 1955), *Who's Who of American Women, World Who's Who of Women*, and others.

Gladys Hobby, always a professional, is a meticulous research scientist, highly valued for her scientific expertise. Through her broad experience in science and publishing, she has made major contributions to the understanding and treatment of infectious diseases. A woman of distinction, she is much admired by her colleagues.

Rhoda Benham and assistant, 1930.

CHAPTER VII

Rhoda Williams Benham

*". . . . Pathfinder in mycology; differentiated
the pathogenic from the harmless."*

Ringworm is a skin disease familiar enough to those who have experienced it and not unknown to the few who escape it, while coccidioidomycosis, known in California and the southwestern United States as valley fever or desert rheumatism, is not so widely appreciated. Both conditions are caused by fungi: ringworm, an annoying infection which can be quite persistent but is rarely life-threatening, and coccidioidomycosis, a systemic disease of many scenarios, ranging from an inapparent, silent infection to a raging, fatal condition. Of the hundreds of thousands of fungi in the world, only a very few—100 or so—are pathogenic for humans, but it took mycologists many decades to substantiate the fact, to sort out the culprits from the innocent multitude. Dr. Rhoda Benham was one of the diligent mycologists who made the distinctions more precise for the scientist, the decisions easier for the physician.

Rhoda Williams Benham was born in 1894, in Cedarhurst, Long Island, New York, to Sarah Brower Benham and James Tyler Benham. Her father was an independent corn product broker who had established his own company. Rhoda had three younger brothers and a younger sister. Her brother George eventually took over his father's business; James Tyler Benham, Jr., was in the textile business, and Victor Benham, like his father and brother George, was a broker, but a sugar broker; he too established his own business. Edith, the youngest of the children became Mrs. Edith Benham Johnson and named one of her children for her older sister, Rhoda Benham Johnson, who is an artist and photographer.

Rhoda Benham was valedictorian of her class at Lawrence High School in Cedarhurst. She then attended Barnard College of Columbia University, where, in 1917, she received a B.A. degree in Botany. She remained at Barnard for the next eight years, until 1925, serving there as a teaching assistant, then as a graduate student until she received an M.A. in Botany in 1919.

A New Direction

There were at that time several prominent botanists on the Columbia University faculty who provided Rhoda with an excellent background in botany and stimulated her interest in mycology. Four of her professors were mycologists: Dr. B. O. Dodge, Professor Henry M. Richards, Professor R. A. Harper, and Dr. Tracey Hazen. She studied with Professor Richards for her Ph.D. degree, working out the mineral requirements of the fungus, *Aspergillus niger.* However, her work was interrupted by an intriguing request from Dr. J. Gardner Hopkins, newly appointed professor of dermatology at Columbia University School of Medicine. Hopkins recognized the importance of fungous diseases in dermatology and wished to establish a mycology laboratory. Dr. Dodge had recommended Miss Benham to him as a well-trained, suitable assistant. Hopkins made her an assistant in dermatology. Thus began a most fruitful collaboration.

As a consequence of her new orientation toward medical mycology and pathogenic fungi, Rhoda Benham changed the direction of her doctoral dissertation research; when completed, the thesis was titled "Certain Monilias Parasitic on Man; Their Identification by Morphology and by Agglutination." She received her Ph.D. degree in 1931 in botany. The paper prepared from her thesis[1] became a classic. It was the first example of the application of immunologic principles, serology, in diagnostic and taxonomic procedures involving fungi. Her careful studies reduced to synonomy many yeasts and showed that most of the "monilias" infectious for humans were found in a single species, *Monilia* (later *Candida*) *albicans.*

Benham developed cornmeal agar for use in rapid induction of chlamydospores, a technique that became part of the standard diagnostic procedures. Two publications had preceded this paper (both with J. G. Hopkins), her first one on monilia infections of the hands and feet, and the second on asthma due to the fungus *Alternaria.*

Dr. Benham soon extended her taxonomic studies with pathogenic yeast to include the cryptococci "Monilias, Yeasts and Cryptococci; Their Pathogenicity, Classification and Identification" published in 1932.[2] Again using serological methods for differentiation, she isolated yeasts from a variety of clinical conditions and classified the monilias into eight types, but found that isolates from clinical conditions recognized as thrush, infection of mucous membranes, were all *Monilia albicans.* She described the pathogenicity of this species for rabbits, the method of producing the characteristic chlamydospores on cornmeal agar, the typical fermentations, and gave a microscopic description of the yeast and pseudomycelium. Cryptococcus she described as producing no mycelium, reproducing by buds only and being non-pathogenic for rabbits. She included descriptions of some of the common yeasts non-pathogenic for humans such as Saccharomyces, Willia, and Mycoderma.

Lure of the Laboratory

These early studies established Rhoda Benham as an authority on laboratory diagnosis of yeast infections. But her studies of pathogenic fungi truly included all known pathogens, for her laboratory became a center for graduate students and visiting scientists who wished to learn about pathogenic fungi. Supported initially by a grant from the Rockefeller Foundation, the laboratory attained world-wide renown. At the start Drs. Hopkins and Dodge recruited students to the laboratory, but it soon became unnecessary to recruit; the problem was to accommodate the numbers who wished to study there.

Another accomplishment to Rhoda Benham's credit was the development of a course in medical mycology, the first in this country. With assistance from Drs. Hopkins and Dodge, Benham developed a course organized for postgraduate students at the College of Physicians and Surgeons of Columbia University. An academic credit course, it was sponsored by the Department of Dermatology and Microbiology.

As an aid to teaching, a large number of fungi were collected by Rhoda Benham. Prepared slides and cultures of fungi, sections of infected tissue, as well as photographs were assembled by her for use with lectures or for reference. Photography became one of her hobbies which she pursued at the laboratory, at home, and on vacation. Some of her photographs of trees won prizes at photographic exhibits of the medical center personnel at Columbia University. Dr. Benham's photographs of clinical-laboratory specimens added greatly to the mycological exhibits she prepared for the American Medical Association and the American Public Health Association. Her exhibits were also displayed at meetings of the Society of American Bacteriologists (now American Society for Microbiology), and the Dermatology International Congress in Budapest, 1935. The exhibits included photographs of patients with mycotic infections as well as gross and histologic sections of tissue from mycotic infections. These photographs, in addition to her fungus culture collection and slides, form part of the legacy left to the Mycology Laboratory at the College of Physicians and Surgeons of Columbia University. Some of her exhibits won awards and gold medals for excellence.

As Rhoda Benham's expertise became better known she was frequently called upon to serve as consultant. She served on the Committee on Medical Mycology, which prepared proposals on nomenclature for the International Botanical Congress in Stockholm in 1950. It was at this congress that her proposal to conserve the generic name "Candida" was accepted. From 1948 to 1953, she served as consultant on mycology to the commissioner of health for the State of New York, Dr. Hilleboe. She contributed the chapter "Pathogenic Fungi" in Gay et al., *Agents of Disease and Host Resistance.*[3] She also edited the chapter on "Pathogenic Fungi" for the fourth edition of *Diagnostic Procedures and Reagents* of the American Public Health Association.

Dr. Benham was active in professional organizations, a member of the Mycological Society of America, Society of Investigative Dermatology, The Harvey Society, the Microbiological Section of the New York Academy of Medicine, Society of American Bacteriologists, New York Academy of Science, and the American Association for the Advancement of Science. She was one of the original editors of the journal *Mycopathologia.*

Her activities were curtailed and her productivity diminished when at age 54 she suffered a heart attack which incapacitated her for nearly a year. However, she did return to professional pursuits and for most of the next seven years was active in research, teaching, and consulting, and, even in retirement at home in poor health, continued writing. She completed the manuscripts for her last two papers before her death in Cedarhurst in 1957.

Dr. Benham's research was always significant, for she was pioneering a field little known to most physicians and scientists and in considerable confusion among those few who had given their attention to the study of pathogenic fungi. It remained for Rhoda Benham, Norman F. Conant at Duke University,[4] and others[5] to bring order into this chaos and to devise reliable procedures for laboratory diagnosis suitable for general use.

Master Tools of the Trade

Principally a taxonomist, Dr. Benham utilized all the known tools of the trade, serological tests, metabolic (nutritional) studies, cultural and morphological descriptions. Her first papers on yeast exemplify this well, for she successfully used serological tests to differentiate species. Her publications on sporotrichosis involved a broader study since the route of transmission includes plants.[6] She described the two types of disease that occur in humans: the lymphatic, originating at a point of injury and producing a chain of nodules along the lymphatics but rarely involving the regional lymph nodes; and the disseminated gummatous disease characterized by subcutaneous lesions in scattered areas, apparently by hematic distribution from an undetected port of entry. She noted that contagion from another human case had never been proven but that contagion from infected animals was suspected in several cases involving animal bites. She suggested that both man and animals could possibly be infected from a plant source, noting that many cases occurred among gardeners and nursery workers who had been injured by a wood splinter or a thorn. A species of Sporotrichum isolated from beech tree bark by Gougerot in France was identified by him as *Sporotrichum beurmanii.* Benham questioned the validity of the species as distinct from *S. schenckii.*

Her study of blastomycosis and coccidioidal granuloma in 1934[7] resulted from the need to differentiate the tissue forms of these organisms from yeasts found in tissue, a natural interest following her work with Candida and Cryptococcus. She described *Blastomyces dermatitidis* as producing mycelium and conidia on cultures at room temperature and yeasts with typical broad-based buds in the tissue of animals innoculated with the mycelial form. *Coccidioides immitis* she described as mycelial on culture, producing in experimentally infected guinea pigs "thick wall spherical cells with endospore formation." In summary she stated that each organism produced a distinct disease.

Work with Parasites

In 1938 Benham began publishing her studies with dermatophytes, research which engaged her interest to the end of her life. The first two papers, published with E. D. DeLamater, concerned experimental studies with dermatophytes in rabbits. They described the development of the primary disease in these animals[8] and the state of immunity and hypersensitivity resulting from infection.[9] They reported the development of lesions in guinea pigs infected by a suspension of fungi rubbed into a shaved and scarified area. Typically the time course was four to six-day incubation, seven to ten-day spread of the lesion, with a climax at 12–15 days and clearing of the lesion by 30–35 days. *Trichophyton gypseum* and *Achorion quinckeanum* (as then designated; they were later reduced to synonymy as *T. mentagrophytes* whose perfect state is *Arthroderma benhamae*) were used for study of the time course of the infection. Several other species of Trichophyton were tested as were *Microsporum felineum* (*M. canis*), *M. audouinii,* and *Epidermophyton floccosum*. It was found that the time course differed somewhat among the various dermatophyte infections but eventually all regressed and the lesions healed. With intravenous injections of fungus suspensions results were even more varied. Some animals developed lesions in previously scarified areas, then the infection involuted; other animals had a more prolonged course with fungi demonstrable in multiple lesions for as long as six weeks. Three of their pregnant guinea pigs aborted after the intravenous infection but recovered rapidly from the fungus infection. Lesions produced in rabbits involuted but kittens had prolonged infections; when infected with *M. felineum,* infected hairs in the fur were found to be fluorescent 85 days after infection. With reinfection the animal lesions cleared faster, most by 20 days.[9] Rabbits developed a hypersensitivity, reacting positively to a skin test. Neither the hypersensitivity nor the rapid clearing from reinfection were species specific, i.e., one dermatophyte sensitized an animal to the other dermatophytes.

A total of ten papers appeared between 1938 and 1955 on dermatophytes. These dealt with pigment production by dermatophytes; nutritional requirements of these fungi, and treatment of onychomycosis due to *Trichophyton rubrum*. A critical review of infections caused by *T. rubrum,* a clinical, mycologic, and experimental study, was the last of Benham's publications in this series on dermatophytes and the third paper to be co-authored by Dr. Margarita Silva-Hutner, who succeeded Dr. Benham as director of the Laboratory of Mycology of the College of Physicians and Surgeons at Columbia University and carried forward the mycological investigations.[10]

Benham devoted several years to a study of *Pityrosporum ovale,* a lypophilic yeast whose unusual metabolism provided a challenging study. The results of Dr. Benham's studies appeared in a number of papers published between 1939 and 1945. Chapter four on the "Biology of *Pityrosporum ovale*" in *Biology of Pathogenic Fungi,* edited by Walter Nickerson,[11] was prepared by Rhoda Benham.

Case reports of infections or allergies at the time thought to be unusual were also reported by Benham. For example in 1930, "Asthma Due to a Fungus Alternaria" with J. G. Hopkins and B. M. Kesten;[12] "*Phoma condiogena, an Excitant in Asthma;*"[13] "*Allescheria Boydii,* Causative Agent in a Case of Meningitis," published with Lucille Georg in 1948;[14] and "Maduromycosis of the Central Nervous System" published in 1953.[15]

Final Studies

Interestingly enough, Benham returned to the study of the yeasts of the genus Candida and Cryptococcus in the 1950s. Her last three papers on these organisms extend the research with which she began. In 1956 she published a review of the literature on Cryptococcus including her own investigations and laboratory experience.[16] The review includes the botanical background for the family Cryptococcaceae, and describes tests for demonstrating the virulence of *Cryptococcus neoformans* in mice as well as the use of India ink preparations for demonstrating the capsule of *C. neoformans.*

The last two of Benham's publications dealt with the most frequently isolated species of Candida[17] and the chlamydospores typical of *C. albicans,*[18] which was published posthumously. She remarked on the difficulties that had arisen in preparing a cornmeal agar which was reliable for use in inducing chlamydospore production by *C. albicans.* The cornmeal varied regionally and so did the results. She noted that there were two media new at that time which had advantages over cornmeal agar—purified polysaccharide agar of Nickerson & Mankowski and soluble starch agar, though she had tested these two media she had found cornmeal agar still the best and gave explicit directions for preparation. Following the introduction of tetracycline antibiotics with broad spectrum activity against bacteria, the incidence and seriousness of infections with Candida increased. Species of Candida were isolated which, at the time of Rhoda Benham's early work with these organisms in 1931 were infrequent and generally innocuous, were now isolated from serious infections. She reported isolating *C. parapsilosis* from 24 percent of the clinical specimens sent to her laboratory, *C. guillermondii* 1.6 percent, *C. tropicalis* in 2.8 percent and *C. albicans,* still most prominent, in 63 percent of the cases, plus some nonfilamentous yeasts of genus other than Cryptococcus.

A lasting tribute to Rhoda Benham and her contributions to medical mycology was established by the Medical Mycological Society of the Americas in 1967, a year after the founding of the society by Dr. Lorraine Friedman and other mycologists. The Rhoda Benham Award was set up in her honor. It is given each year to an outstanding mycologist who delivers the Rhoda Benham Lecture at the annual meeting of the society. Some of the outstanding women mycologists have received the award: Elizabeth Hazen along with Rachel Brown in 1972 (Dr. Hazen of the State Laboratory in New York City was a close associate of Dr. Benham.); Lucille Georg in 1974 (Dr. Georg was a student of Dr. Benham's and became an associate director of the Mycology Laboratory at the Centers for Disease Control in Atlanta); and Dr. Charlotte C. Campbell in 1978 (Dr. Campbell worked at Walter Reed Army Institute for Research during the 1940s and 1950s and later, 1960s, at Harvard University School of Public Health).

Rhoda Benham became an associate professor of dermatology at the College of Physicians and Surgeons, Columbia University, and an internationally recognized expert on fungi. She was a pioneer in the study of pathogenic fungi and in establishing with Dr. J. G. Hopkins the first laboratory for research and teaching of medical mycology in this country. Later she developed the first graduate school course on the subject. Great as were her accomplishments during her lifetime, they are far exceeded by her influence on her own and subsequent generations of mycologists.[19]

Elizabeth Hazen and Rachel Brown.

CHAPTER VIII

Elizabeth Lee Hazen

*". . . A private life in pursuit
of important discoveries."*

Discoveries and inventions, like seeds, must fall upon fertile ground to be productive. The time must be right for a discovery to be useful. The antibiotic era began with a search for new organisms producing new antibiotics; the chemists came later, modifying antibiotics of known chemical structure. When Elizabeth Hazen began her work, the search was still on. New soils from new places were tested for antimicrobial activity and old antibiotics were rediscovered again and again. But Dr. Hazen did discover a new one— Nystatin, an antifungal antibiotic. It was chemically characterized by her colleague Rachel Brown at the New York State Department of Health Laboratory, produced commercially, patented, and provided support for mycological research for the many years of the patent.

Born August 24, 1885, on a farm in Rich, Mississippi,[1] Elizabeth Lee Hazen was orphaned at an early age and taken with her sister to live with relatives in Lula, Mississippi. She attended the public schools of Coahoma County, Mississippi, and graduated with a bachelor's degree in 1910 from the State College for Women (now Mississippi University for Women). For the next six years she taught science at a Jackson, Mississippi, high school, spending her summers at the University of Tennessee and University of Virginia. In

1916 she matriculated at Columbia University to study bacteriology, receiving an M.A. degree in 1917. She immediately became involved in World War I, serving in the Army diagnostic laboratories and subsequently in the laboratory of a West Virginia hospital. After this four-year period she returned to Columbia University to study for a doctorate in Microbiology, which she earned in 1927 at age 42.

A Career Begins

She remained at Columbia for four years as an instructor in the College of Physicians and Surgeons, then joined the Division of Laboratories and Research of the New York State Department of Health. Assigned to the New York City Branch Laboratory, she was responsible for special problems of bacterial diagnosis.

She traced an outbreak of anthrax to a brush factory in Westchester County, uncovered unsuspected sources of tularemia in New York, and was the first in North America to identify and incriminate *Clostridium botulinum* type E toxin in deaths due to imported canned seafood.[2] She collaborated with Dr. Ruth Gilbert, then assistant director of diagnostic laboratories of the Division of Laboratories and Research, in a pioneering study of moniliasis (candidiasis). The experience of working with fungi was influential in directing her attention to the widespread need for assistance in laboratory diagnosis of mycotic diseases. Under her direction the Branch Laboratory undertook this responsibility in 1944, receiving cultures isolated at the Central Laboratory in Albany in addition to cultures and specimens submitted locally.

Dr. Hazen's contacts with Columbia University served her well in this new venture for she could benefit from the research, teaching, and service laboratory which had been established by Dr. J. Gardner Hopkins and Dr. Rhoda W. Benham. A fruitful collaboration continued for many years between the New York Branch Laboratory of the New York State Department of Health and the Mycology Laboratory of the Department of Dermatology at Columbia Presbyterian Hospital. Hazen participated in the collection, direct examination, and identification of superficial fungi, and later of systemic fungi obtained from hospitalized patients. She acquired cultures of fungi for study and for reference from Dr. Benham's stock culture collection. From her studies at Columbia University and from her extensive experience in the Branch Laboratory, Hazen prepared a collection of cultures and slides of fungi pathogenic for humans which formed the basis of her book *Laboratory Identification of Pathogenic Fungi Simplified.*[3] In preparing the book she had the assistance of Frank C. Reed, an illustrator in the Division of Laboratory and Research, who coauthored the first edition published in 1955. A second edition was published in 1960, with Reed, and in 1970 a third edition with Dr. Morris A. Gordon as coauthor.

In 1945, Elizabeth Hazen and Rhoda Benham organized a conference of the New York State Association of Public Health Laboratories at which Dr. Hazen contributed "Notes on the Examination of Specimens for Evidence of

Mycotic Infections." Shortly thereafter Hazen was encouraged by J. Gardner Hopkins at Columbia University to study the nutritional requirements of *Microsporum audouini*, which was then producing an epidemic of tinea capitis among school children. Part of the study revolved around the unanswered question, why *Bacillus weidmaniensis* seemed to induce macroconidia formation in *M. audouini*. Macroconidia, an aid to identification of the organism, were difficult to obtain on culture media then in use. Her results published in Mycologia of 1947[4] discussed not only the effect of the bacterium on colony characteristics and macroconidial formation but included the effects of yeast extract, thiamine and pyridoxine. She found that yeast extract added to honey agar increased production of macrospores, that all 18 strains tested (all fresh isolates) were positive for production of macroconidia on rice medium to which pure cultures of *B. wiedmaniensis* was added.

She extended this work in 1951 with a publication[5] in which she referred to the work of Dr. Lucille Georg at the Communicable Diseases Center (now Centers for Disease Control). Georg had demonstrated that *B. weidmaniensis* produces thiamine and inositol in culture but no pyridoxine.[6] Dr. Hazen's experience with addition of single vitamin supplements to culture medium for growth of *M. audouini* was not encouraging, nor were her tests with various nitrogen sources definitive. She demonstrated that *M. audouini* could use an ammonium salt as a nitrogen source but no single nitrogen source nor vitamin supplement induced macroconidia production in all strains tested.

Later, after the Mycology Laboratory at Columbia had moved to a new location, she found that some of these earlier methods of inducing macroconidia failed in the new laboratory. She recognized that the temperature of incubation (usually room temperature) might be a factor. Tests with duplicate cultures at two temperatures 29–32°C and 25–27°C confirmed her suspicion. At the lower temperature more abundant macrospore production occurred, some strains of *M. audouini* grown at the higher temperature produced none. In 1957 she reported her discovery that *M. audouini* will not form macroconidia at temperatures above 25°C.[7]

Intrigued with the study of this fungus, Hazen returned after her retirement to the Mycology Laboratory at Columbia University to continue research with the organism. She made many attempts at crossing strains of *M. audouini* in an effort to demonstrate a sexual state in the fungus. She was herself never successful but she seemed to be on the right track because compatible mating of other species of Microsporum (e.g., *M. canis* and *M. gypseum*) had been shown by other investigators to belong to the genus *Nanizzia*.

An Added Impetus

When, in 1945, Dr. Gilbert Dalldorf became director of the Division of Laboratories of the State of New York Department of Health, the service of medical mycology was given increased impetus. As diagnosis of human mycotic diseases improved and the information was disseminated, it became increasingly evident that the problem of mycoses was not insignificant and that superficial fungous infections were widespread, at times occurring in epidemic proportions among school children in New York City. Concurrently, the recognition that treatment of many mycoses was ineffective spurred the Central Laboratory at Albany to join the search for antibiotics which would be useful in the treatment of infectious diseases. Thus the stage was set for Dr. Hazen's search for actinomycetes with antifungal activity. Her endeavors began at a time when she had increased responsibility at the State Laboratory as part of the service for analyzing serum samples for antibodies against fungi, as well as providing a consulting service to physicians all over New York State, a service made available through the Division of Laboratories and Research.

Because of the pressures of routine work and her perseverance in the research, she developed stomach ulcers. However, her stubbornness and good humor prevailed. She screened soil samples from many parts of the country, a good many of which she and Rachel Brown collected themselves. Dr. Brown, a chemist in the Albany laboratory, prepared extracts from the cultures sent her by Dr. Hazen from New York. The testing protocol set up by Hazen required that each extract be tested against two fungi, *Candida albicans* and *Cryptococcus neoformans*. This precaution proved to be crucial in the discovery of Nystatin.

In 1948 Hazen collected a soil sample near Warrenton, Virginia, where she was vacationing. From this sample a streptomyces was isolated which was later named *Streptomyces noursei* in honor of her host, William B. Nourse. The culture was given the number 48240. Isolated by Hazen in the New York City Branch Laboratory, the culture was shipped to Albany for chemical fractionation by Brown. The extracts returned to Dr. Hazen in New York showed activity right away but the activity was irregular. Because they were using two to four test organisms, the irregularity was soon explained when it was shown that *Streptomyces noursei* produces two antibiotics, one the previously discovered actidione, a water soluble antibiotic which is excreted into the medium, and the other a new antibiotic obtained from the surface growth, the mycelium and spores, by alcohol fractionation and sodium acetate precipitation. Drs. Hazen and Brown reported their findings at a meeting of the National Academy of Science in Schenectady, New York, in October of 1950, then published a brief paragraph in *Science*[8] stating only that one, extractable from the culture fluid, resembled actidione and the other, antibiotic extractable with alcohol from the surface growth, "differs from other antibiotics within our knowledge." At first designated fungicidin, the new antibiotic was later given the proprietary designation Nystatin by agreement with the commercial producers of the antibiotic. By then the antibiotic (fungicidin/Nystatin) had been tested against all the major pathogenic fungi and had been found to inhibit growth *in vitro*. It had been tested in mice infected with *C. neoformans* and found to prolong survival. Among the fungi tested were a number of plant pathogens, such as *Ceratostomella ulmi,* the scourge of the elm trees, as well as *Aspergillus fumigatus* which can produce a fatal pneumonitis in turkeys. Nystatin proved to be useful in protecting elms, even in treatment of trees not yet seriously damaged; it proved useful in protecting poultry and also useful in protecting stored fruit, such as green bananas, from adventitious fungus destruction.

A critical evaluation of Nystatin was made by E. R. Squibb and Sons, division of Olin Mathiesson Chemical Corporation, from the culture of *S. noursei* made available to them by Hazen and Brown. Later they tested a pure crystalline sample of the active agent isolated by Rachel Brown. The success of the testing led to patenting and licensing the antibiotic through the Research Corporation of New York. Drs. Hazen and Brown specified that only half of the royalties from sale of Nystatin should go into a fund, later named the Brown-Hazen Fund, for grants in biological sciences of interest to the inventors, notably research on mycotic diseases and their etiologic agents. Initially the remainder of the royalties was made available to the Research Corporation grant programs for research in other areas, primarily in the physical sciences, but eventually all royalties were restricted for biological sciences. The sales of Nystatin, released commercially in 1954 by Squibb and Lederle Laboratories, produced over the 17-year life of the patent more than $13 million in royalties.[9]

Nystatin: The Versatile Antibiotic

Nystatin has been used as a specific for oral, vaginal, and cutaneous infections caused by *Candida albicans* and other Candida species. It has also been used in combination with some of the broad spectrum antibiotics (oxytetracycline, for example) which tend when used alone to enhance the opportunities for Candida infections to become established and to spread. The addition of Nystatin to these antibiotics for clinical use prevented such opportunistic infections. In addition to its usefulness in human and veterinary medicine, Nystatin was used to rescue priceless paintings and frescoes in the Uffizi Gallery in Florence, Italy, following the devastating floods of 1966.

Dr. Hazen was honored by the Squibb Award bestowed in 1955 which she shared with Dr. Brown. They were in great demand as speakers in symposia dealing with antibiotics. One invitation they accepted was to discuss their research at the International Symposium on Antibiotics held in Prague, Czechoslovakia in 1959. Earlier they had presented two papers at a symposium on therapy of fungus diseases (in *Therapy of Fungus Diseases. An International Symposium,* of 1966).[10]

In 1954 the Branch Laboratory in New York City was disbanded and Dr. Hazen returned to the Central Laboratory in Albany. It was at this time that she completed the book *Laboratory Identification of Pathogenic Fungi Simplified* while continuing to carry out her responsibilities in the diagnostic mycological laboratory.

She contributed to publications on *Histoplasma capsulatum,* publishing with François Mariat of the Pasteur Institute in Paris in 1955.[11] She and co-workers reported two cases of histoplasmosis acquired in felling a decayed tree in the Mohawk Valley of New York.[12] She also contributed to some of the early work on ultrastructure of *H. capsulatum* done by the Edwards at the State Laboratory.[13]

In 1958 Hazen accepted an associate professorship at Albany Medical College where she served as lecturer and consultant on medical mycology. At the time of her retirement in 1960 she relinquished both the professorship and her position at the state laboratory. She returned to New York City, where she had retained her apartment, long her home, and became a guest investigator at Columbia University Medical Mycology Laboratory, then under the direction of Dr. Margarita Silva-Hutner, a protégé and successor to Dr. Rhoda Benham. Hazen served in the laboratory as teacher and tutor and assisted with diagnostic mycology. She continued research on her own, attempting to mate strains of *M. audouini* in an effort to produce sexual spores. Furthermore she started an investigation of the possible relationship between *Sporotrichum schenckii* and the ascomycete *Ceratostomella ulmi,* both organisms found in wood, one a human pathogen (Sporotrichum) and the other a plant pathogen. All of this work was left uncompleted when in 1973 she left the laboratory to visit her sister in Seattle, there was taken ill, and later died.

Elizabeth Hazen received the Rhoda Benham Award from the Medical Mycological Society of the Americas along with Rachel Brown in 1972. She was given honorary degrees by Hobart College and by William Smith College. In a break with tradition, the American Institute of Chemists gave Elizabeth Hazen the Chemical Pioneer Award, changing their rules to do so, since she was not a chemist but a microbiologist. This last award came to her only one month before her death on June 24, 1975, in Seattle, Washington.

Dr. Elizabeth Lee Hazen was a very private person. Reserved and modest, she eschewed publicity and notoriety and avoided photographers. Intensely involved in her research, she expended immense energy in her work with a stubborn perseverance in pursuit of a goal. Her discovery of Nystatin was far more than a fortuitous accident and it has yielded far more than the antibiotic potential. Many owe their research and career opportunities to Elizabeth Hazen. Through her efforts many lives have been saved and many more enriched.

Leona Baumgartner at Friday
Harbor, Washington, 1908.

CHAPTER IX

Leona Baumgartner

*". . . An unparalleled depth of understanding
for public health problems."*

Leona Baumgartner became a celebrity in the field of public health. She
served as commissioner of health in New York City, appearing frequently on
radio and television during that period. She received a veritable bouquet of
honorary degrees, she served as president of the American Public Health
Association, and she was a faculty member of Cornell University Medical
School, Columbia University College of Physicians and Surgeons, and Harvard University School of Medicine. She was elected to the Institute of
Medicine of the National Academy of Science. After retirement she continued to serve as consultant to the World Health Organization and to travel in
its behalf to India, to Sudan, and wherever critical public health problems
might take her. Her illustrious career is based upon her beginnings as a
microbiologist.

Born in 1902 in Chicago where her father, William J. Baumgartner,
was a graduate student at the University of Chicago, Leona Baumgartner
grew up in Lawrence, Kansas, where her father became a member of the
faculty in the Department of Zoology at the University of Kansas. He came
from a studious Mennonite family whose progenitor, Reverend David Baumgartner, had been sent by his father, Abraham, to Bethel College, a Mennonite

college, in Newton, Kansas. There he met and married Olga E. Leisy, whose father had emigrated at age seven to America from Friedisheim, Germany. Leona was the first child of William and Olga Baumgartner; a son born three years later died in infancy. Thus Leona received the full attention of her parents. She travelled with them summers to Friday Harbor Marine Station of the University of Washington, a week's journey by pullman from Kansas. For many summers Mr. Baumgartner took a group of teachers and students from the University of Kansas to study at the Marine Station. These summers made a great impression on Leona and remained a fond memory of her childhood. The family was not well-to-do but, by community standards, was comfortably situated. It was a warm and secure childhood. In retrospect, Leona recognized security as a major factor in her early years, opening the way for development of self confidence and imagination, one of the major differences between her childhood and that of children today: not only was the immediate present safe but the future of the world also seemed secure in those days.

During these years Leona sometimes visited her maternal great grandmother Baehr, who on the death of her husband took over and successfully managed the family brewery in Cleveland. Her mother too was a dynamic woman with great executive ability and boundless energy in her youth. These family members and the faculty members from the University of Kansas, who were frequent visitors, all served as models of success to Leona.

In 1920 Leona was graduated from high school in Lawrence and went on to the University of Kansas, where she majored in bacteriology. At the university, she came into contact with Dr. Cora Downs, who was an old family friend. Downs nurtured her students, and Leona Baumgartner remembers her with great fondness and respect as one of the great influences in her early career development. Downs taught her, as her father had by example, to observe minutely and to analyze thoroughly; she emphasized the value of evidence. She exerted a strong stimulus on Leona, was in part responsible for her choice of bacteriology as a major, and became her lifelong friend.

Teaching: A Beginning

After receiving her B.S. degree in 1923 from the University of Kansas, Leona spent a year teaching in Colby, Kansas, in order to be near home since at the time her mother was not well. The next year she returned to the university to take a master's degree, nominally with Dr. Noble P. Sherwood, but actually with Cora Downs. Clara Nigg, who later attained prominence for her work in immunology (with Landsteiner) at the Rockefeller Institute, at Fort Detrick, and at the Office of Naval Research Laboratory in Berkeley, California, was then a graduate student in the same department. She too became a long-time friend of Leona's.

Baumgartner's research problem for the master's degree dealt with the supposed immunity of American Indians to scarlet fever. She collected serum samples at the nearby Indian residential school. Serological tests were evaluated in conjunction with a Dick test, a skin test using the streptococcus erythrogenic toxin as antigen. The survey revealed that the supposition was not correct. The skin tests were negative, indicating that the toxin was neutralized by antibody; antibodies were also demonstrated in the sera. Following up this information, physicians found that, in fact, recognizable scarlet fever did occur among the Indians, though in a less severe form than the classical description of the disease. These studies formed the basis of her first publications.[1]

Several positions were offered Baumgartner after she received her M.A. degree in immunology (1925). The position that held the most attraction for her was at the University of Montana in Missoula, in part because of its distance from her home and family. Pleased at last to get away where (she thought) she would not be known, she was greeted with "Aren't you the daughter of Professor Baumgartner?" on her first encounter registering at a hotel in Missoula.

At the University of Montana she taught bacteriology, immunology, and physiology, which left her no time for research. Nevertheless her interest in research continued and on many occasions she visited the Rocky Mountain Laboratory of Rickettsial Research, then a recent venture under minimal federal support housed in rather shabby quarters, quite inappropriate, she thought, for the research undertaken there. Here in Montana she again came into contact with the American Indians, both informally and in her professional capacity, since she had been selected to deal with an elderly Indian chief who came to the university periodically with his correspondence. His procedure was to give Miss Baumgartner cotton plugs for her ears to use while she read a letter to the chief, after which she removed the plugs to hear his instructions for answering the letter or be told what he considered proper for her to know.

During her second year in Montana she began to consider continuing her education, to work for a doctorate degree. She found that teaching without the opportunity for research left her dissatisfied, unfulfilled. She still felt committed to research. However, her plans were deferred by her father's sabbatical and the invitation to accompany her parents to Munich.

Her father had been denied his doctorate degree at the University of Chicago, where he had worked under Frank Lillie for three years, because he was scooped on his research a few months before his final examination. He had for many years intended to complete the degree and Mrs. Baumgartner had for as many years been urging him to do so. Now, some twenty-six years later, he was at last taking a sabbatical in Munich with Professor Karl von Frisch.

Broadening Horizons

After two years of independence Leona had some reservations about returning to the confines of the family, but the reservations were easily overcome by the attraction of spending a year in Germany. Furthermore, it occurred to her that she might take some courses toward the doctorate. After arrival in Munich, she found that she had already taken all the courses offered there. Thus for a while she accompanied her mother sightseeing and explored the city by bicycle, seeking such American foods as cornflakes and peanut butter. Soon she met Dr. Irving Page and this changed the tenor of the year for her. Dr. Page was a visiting American scientist in the chemistry section within the Deutsche Forschungsanstalt für Psychiatrie of the Kaiser Wilhelm Institute. He offered Leona the opportunity to work in his laboratory. This fortuitous event transformed her year there to a second order learning experience. Her credentials, a master's degree, placed her above the usual laboratory strata in the hierarchy. She chose to do her own laboratory experiments (dieners performed much of the benchwork for the senior staff), and was allowed to attend seminars and teas with the faculty. Her contacts were further expanded by Dr. Felix Plaut's (the director) need for an interpreter fluent in both English and German. Leona met the requirements perfectly and was frequently asked to meet with British and American scientists and escort them around the institute and to meetings.

Dr. Page permitted Leona to choose her own research problem. Vitamin D (ergosterol), under study there at the time, was known to promote calcification. So she sought to find out whether ergosterol would promote calcification in tuberculosis. In her very first experiment she broke the leg of an animal about to be examined. Blaming herself, she proceeded more cautiously with the next animal, but the same thing happened. She then became suspicious and reported the unexpected events. A careful study of the condition followed and revealed widespread calcification of soft tissue and bone demineralization mediated by phosphatase and excess vitamin D. Leona was included among the authors of the published work.[2] She discussed her research with a visiting scientist from Canada, Dr. Frederick Banting, who invited her to work in his laboratory on her return from Germany.

After her father completed his studies for the doctorate in zoology (awarded 1929), the family travelled to Italy before returning to the United States. Leona remained in New York with an uncle for a visit and, while there, developed an appendicitis and was hospitalized for surgery. During her recuperation she read the biography of Sir William Osler. This book stimulated her interest in medical history and biography and led to her own publication of several historical papers. When she left New York she returned home briefly to consider graduate schools. Her particular preference was Harvard, where Hans Zinsser was then professor of bacteriology.

An interview was arranged and she discussed with Zinsser her wish, among other things, to take gross pathology, the study of diseased organs. He pointed out that gross anatomy, the study of normal human body structure, was a prerequisite. Leona was agreeable to taking the prerequisite. Zinsser hesitated, then said he probably could arrange to have a cadaver issued to her. "To take home?" she said. He explained that women were not allowed in the gross anatomy laboratory. Thus it was that she went to Yale where she was allowed to take gross pathology without any prerequisites and would be allowed to dissect a cadaver in the school laboratory.

At Yale she worked on an immunological problem involving the aging process, "Age and Antibody Production." Her experience there was pivotal in her career. She made lifelong friendships with Dean Winternitz, John Fulton, and C. E. A. Winslow, among others. During the course of her studies for the Ph.D. she was persuaded by her Yale advisors, strongly backed by her father, to take an M.D. as well as a Ph.D. degree.

Medical Historian

While a student at Yale (1930–34), Baumgartner wrote four articles on medical history. The first, on Leonardo da Vinci as a physiologist, was published in the Annals of Medical History.[3] It drew some criticism from a Dr. Arnold C. Klebs, a Swiss bacteriologist and historian, who pointed out similarities between her work and an earlier work of his own on da Vinci. She wrote Dr. Klebs assuring him that her conclusions were her own and in the course of the correspondence and meetings with him she became so interested in Dr. Klebs' father, Dr. Edwin Klebs, who had discovered the diphtheria bacillus, that he became the subject of a later biographical sketch, "Edwin Klebs, A Centennial Note," published in 1935.[4] Prior to that she had written and published with John Fulton a bibliography of Giralamo Fracastors's poem "Syphilis Sive Morbus Gallicus," which first appeared as a handlist[5] and was later produced as a book by Yale University Press (1935). Her fourth biographical publication, on Johann Peter Frank,[6] brought out her developing interest in public health policy. It dealt with an eighteenth century physician who had written a monumental treatise on public health policy which influenced European public health practice for nearly a century.

Leona Baumgartner never lost her interest in medical and public health history and in reformers. She continued for some time to produce articles on related subjects. In 1937 she published a paper on "John Howard and the Public Health Movement,"[7] also in 1939, a bibliography entitled "John Howard (1726–1790), Hospital and Prison Reformer."[8] These articles were later published as a book by Johns Hopkins University Press in 1939. "Harvey Cushing as Book Collector and Litterateur" was published in 1940.[9] In 1943 an obituary profile of Arnold Klebs appeared in the *Bulletin of the History of Medicine* of 1943,[10] and in the following year a further publication on Klebs as a humanistic scholar appeared in the *Bulletin of the Medical Library Association.*[11] Earlier, in 1938, she had produced "Old Dog and New Tricks, the Story of Ivan Pavlov."[12]

For her doctoral dissertation research at Yale, Baumgartner worked on immunological maturation and age as factors in the host immunological response. Exposing young (four- to six-week old) and adult (six- to 13-month old) rabbits to invasive bacteria (*Bacterium [Salmonella] enteritidis*) and to foreign (sheep) red blood cells, in another test, she found greater antibody avidity for antigen in young animals than in the adults. Her adviser, George H. Smith, allowed her to proceed with the research fairly independently and undisturbed, but when she presented him with the statistically analyzed results he encouraged her to publish the research. The paper appeared in the *Journal of Immunology* of 1934.[13] The literature review on the subject was published separately in the *Yale Journal of Biology and Medicine*.[14] This latter publication won her the John Lovett Morse prize of the New England Pediatric Society in 1935.

During this same period she began writing on medical subjects, e.g., "Pituitary Basophilism, Pituitary Tumors and Hypertension," her M.D. thesis.[15] In 1936 a paper on lipoid pneumonia and the conditions which may favor its occurrence was published.[16] One further paper on her immunological research appeared in 1937,[17] a quantitative study on the precipitin reaction with antisera produced in young and adult rabbits.

After receiving the Ph.D. degree in 1932 and an M.D. degree in 1934, Baumgartner was much inclined to continue with laboratory research. However, her father and her professors at Yale encouraged her to complete a medical residency and prepare herself to practice medicine even though she had no intention of doing so. Thus she interned at Cornell University Medical School in pediatrics and simultaneously continued research in immunology with Jules Freund. At Cornell she came into contact with the medical and public health problems of New York City. After completion of her residency, she gave serious consideration to some of the opportunities available to her in medical research. It was at this point that she became aware of the serious problem of ingrained sexual discrimination. Interviewed for a research position at the Rockefeller Institute, for which she had been recommended by her adviser without reference to her gender, she was immediately confronted with the professor's statement that he would not hire a woman for the job no matter what her credentials. Soon word got back to her that the professor had laughingly told his colleagues that he might have hired "that woman" if she did not have such cute feet and ankles. This infuriated Baumgartner and put her on her guard. She could plainly see the fate of the women at the Rockefeller Institute, where only Florence Sabin had become a full member of the staff. Therefore she declined the offer of a position with Thomas Rivers at the Rockefeller Institute. Recommended by C. E. A. Winslow of Yale for a position in the New York City Health Department, she was interviewed by the commissioner of health, John L. Rice. He offered her a choice of positions, saying that there was not a single pediatrician in the Bureau of Child Health nor a single immunologist in the section on syphilis control; she could fill either position. So with minimal regret for her laboratory research and her clinical practice she accepted a position in the Bureau of Child Health and embarked on a career in public health.[18]

Being a civil service position, the appointment was for several months in advance. This left her a free interval during which she worked with Alice Evans on a brucellosis survey in Kansas, investigating an alleged outbreak of the disease. She also examined patients referred for possible chronic brucellosis. Serological tests and skin tests of the individuals examined showed a close correlation between a positive skin test and exposure to unpasteurized milk. Two publications resulted from this work with Evans.[19]

Beginning a Career in Public Health

In 1937 Baumgartner joined the New York City Health Department as medical instructor in child and school hygiene. In that year she published the first in a series of papers on public health training. Six papers related to this topic appeared over the next seven years.

Her appointment followed the election of Fiorello LaGuardia as mayor of New York. He greatly expanded the New York City Health Department. Baumgartner immediately began efforts to improve and strengthen the Bureau of Child Hygiene and the School of Hygiene. She recognized that instruction and persuasion were required to promote the acceptance by public health personnel of new skills and knowledge. Her tact and ingenuity were immediately evident. The training was called a research project. In 1938 she was named director of public health training, a position which provided her with ample opportunity to reach the public health personnel through speeches, demonstration projects, and publications. Also in 1938 she became a lecturer in nursing education at Teachers College of Columbia University, a position she held until 1942. With the public health staff she organized noon-hour discussions and wrote a weekly newsletter which they received with their paychecks. Her concerns extended to the foodhandlers, from the farmers through the restaurants, the milk inspectors and the Sanitary Corps.

During 1938 the Edinburgh International Congress on Women invited Baumgartner to address them on the subject of "Recent Advances in Public Health," an invitation which she accepted. She sailed on the same ship with Harvey Cushing, whose autobiography had so profoundly influenced her some years before. After the conference she travelled to France, where she visited public health facilities and libraries. She also payed a visit to Arnold Klebs in Switzerland. Altogether it was a pleasant and profitable trip for her, though sad, for the portents of war were by then so obvious.

The following year, 1939, Commissioner Rice offered Baumgartner the position of district health officer in the Kips Bay-Yorkville Health Center. When she accepted the position, reluctantly at first, she also took on an instructorship in the Department of Pediatrics of the New York Hospital of Cornell University, where she had so recently been a resident. Despite her reluctance to accept the position, she typically took up the work energetically and assumed responsibility for the ongoing programs of the District. These included the tuberculosis and venereal diseases clinics, public health nursing, a dental clinic, school health, health education, and well baby care. In this position she developed her natural abilities in administration. The experience as a district health officer served her well when she later became commissioner of health. She learned firsthand the limitations of the decentralized district facilities, yet at the same time observed where they could be particularly effective.

In 1940 Baumgartner was deeply grieved by the death of her mother. She returned to Lawrence, Kansas, and spent several weeks with her father.

The Move Upward

Later in that year she was promoted to the position of director of the Bureau of Child Hygiene. Following in the tradition of Josephine Baker, who headed the bureau from its inception in 1915 through 1923, Baumgartner established good relations with New York's philanthropic and voluntary service agencies, consulting with them on new programs in order to strengthen and expand the services of the bureau. The heads of these agencies provided not only funds and services but also served as a powerful constituency supporting Baumgartner in her dealings with the city and state government. Her easy speaking style made her much in demand as a speaker to many sorts of organizations all over the city. This was an activity she willingly undertook since it augmented her efforts at educating the public in health and hygiene.

During her tenure as director of the Bureau of Child Health, she took on the problem of providing services and rehabilitation for handicapped children. At the time of the Second World War she sponsored day care centers for children of mothers working in defense industry. With the centers she ran into the problem of opposition from private child care agencies who resented "government interference" with their enterprise. Some of their complaints she found to be justified so she discussed these problems with Mayor LaGuardia. Other objections she confronted in court. Winning the cases she thus cleared the way for the bureau to enforce standards in all day care units.

She was also involved with a program sponsored by the Children's Bureau of the United States Department of Labor, that of providing health care for dependents of servicemen, a service authorized by Congress in 1943. No sooner was the program announced than the New York Bureau of Child Health was deluged with phone calls from wives, widows, and lovers of servicemen. Baumgartner set up a special telephone switchboard to handle the calls and, as rapidly as possible, put into operation the Emergency Maternal and Infant Care (EMIC) program. During the six years that the bureau administered the program, six million dollars was disbursed to New York City hospitals. The records of these years provided hitherto unobtainable data on the average cost of maternal care and on the frequency of unusual cases requiring extraordinary services.

In the course of the war activities Leona Baumgartner met and married Nathaniel B. Elias, a chemical engineer and a widower with two adolescent children. As a consultant in Washington, D.C., he was subject to summons to duty, and soon after the marriage he was in fact called to Washington, stationed there a few months, then sent overseas. Fortunately, he returned safely about a year later. Their marriage lasted 22 years, until his death in 1964. He gave her great moral support and companionship—and enjoyed her successes. He was interested in social and political affairs and had, as a student at Columbia University marched for women's suffrage. Her career was enriched by her marriage.

After the war ended Baumgartner made a study, at the request of Dr. Louis I. Dublin of the American Red Cross, of the nutritional needs of French children, taking six months leave of absence from the Department of Health to make the survey. She and Dublin found the nutritional status of the children not to be so bad as had been feared. However, she was then dispatched to Germany, where the aftermath of the war was a shattering experience for her, as for the Germans. Nevertheless, this trip to Europe re-awakened her interest in international affairs.

On her return, a program for premature babies was established in the New York City Bureau of Child Health. As part of the program the department sought to prevent premature births by encouraging women to seek prenatal care. A counselling service and psychiatric service were later offered in the well baby clinics.

For her achievements at the bureau Baumgartner received in 1946 the American Design Award "for creative work in designs for living for children." The following year the University of Kansas honored her with a distinguished service award. The Elizabeth Blackwell Citation was presented to her in 1950 for her work in maternal and child health. Later, in 1954, she received the Albert Lasker Award for "distinguished achievement in public health administration."

In 1948 the New York Department of Health was reorganized and Baumgartner was named assistant Commissioner in charge of maternal and child health services. The very next year she was persuaded to assume the position of associate chief of the Children's Bureau in the United States Department of Labor, replacing her friend Martha Eliot with whom she had long been in close contact regarding work with handicapped children, the day care program and the EMIC program. Dr. Eliot was taking a year's leave to accept a position with the World Health Organization in Geneva. In anticipation of the passage by the Congress of a fourteen million dollar bill for school health programs, Baumgartner agreed to come to Washington. The bill failed to pass and she was assigned to other programs such as the 1950 White House Conference on Children.

Confronting Destiny

She returned to her position in New York in 1951, but in 1953 resigned from the New York City Department of Health to take a position as executive director of the New York Foundation, a philanthropic organization. However, politics that fall changed many things. Robert Wagner became mayor of New York and persuaded Baumgartner to return to the Department of Health as commissioner of health. Thus she enjoyed only a short respite from public service, returning to the department in 1954. By agreement with Mayor Wagner, she was relieved of the duties of political speech making. She continued her efforts to educate the public in matters of health by radio and television. She appeared weekly on the Arlene Francis television show (National Broadcasting Company) to discuss topics of general interest such as: "New drugs in mental illness"; "Baby's first bath"; and "Father's place in the home today." The success of this show led in 1958 to the creation within the Bureau of Health Education of a radio and television unit. In this situation her being a woman seemed to help, to lend credibility to the more serious problems handled by the department. She was, for example, very successful in the campaign for polio vaccine. She made skillful choices for her deputies, which facilitated matters.

In the course of her administration as commissioner of health of New York City, Leona Baumgartner revised the by then badly outmoded 1914 sanitary code. She brought in a lawyer, Frank Grad, to direct the project which took four years to complete. Public hearings held during the process were skillfully handled so that in 1958 when the new code went into effect, it was well accepted.

She encouraged public health research which had been one of the functions of the department since the early days when William H. Park and Anna W. Williams pioneered in diphtheria antitoxin production and so many other preventive health measures. The Public Health Research Institute was created in 1941 by Mayor LaGuardia but had not been well supported in the interim. In 1961 ground was broken for a new building to be erected across the street from Bellevue Hospital and Leona Baumgartner officiated at the ceremony. This building, completed in 1967, houses both the Public Health Laboratories of the Department of Health and the Public Health Research Institute.

Baumgartner also promoted research in hospitals under city support by the newly created (1950) Health Research Council. Philanthropists Mary Lasker and Anna Rosenberg contributed advice and assistance on building up the research fund. The city appropriated $600,000 in 1958 and four million dollars in 1961, funds that were matched by the state for support of research and fellowships.

In 1955 Baumgartner took a leave of absence from the health department to undertake a mission for the Ford and Rockefeller foundations. At the invitation of India she was sent by the foundations to assist the minister of health with family planning in India. Before leaving, Baumgartner consulted with her neighbor, Eleanor Roosevelt, whom she had long known socially, regarding matters of diplomacy. After completing the mission, she travelled with her husband and friend Dr. Gertrude van Wagenen of Yale to Ceylon, Nepal, Thailand, Bali, Hong Kong, and Japan.

Upon return to New York City she became involved with the arguments for and against fluoridation of water (an issue that was not resolved until 1965), with control of radiation, particularly in physicians' and dentists' offices where improperly installed equipment produced a radiation hazard. She set up a poison control center to deal with accidental poisoning. Carbon monoxide poisoning from gas heaters was also a great problem at that time. The City Health Department was concerned with rodent control and with water and air pollution.

Fighting on Another Front

Because of the marked decrease in deaths from infectious diseases in the 1940s and 1950s, chronic diseases became more evident. Baumgartner engaged in the fight for preventive medicine and early detection of disorders such as diabetes, heart disease, and cancer, both for humane and for economic reasons, as the cost of health care escalated with the increasing sophistication of technology. The Bureau of Adult Hygiene, established in 1948 and directed by Alice Waterhouse, prospered during Baumgartner's term of office. As commissioner, she attended meetings of the County Medical Society as often as possible in order to promote cooperation among private practitioners in public health care. Her presence at these meetings also had the effect of reducing fear of the bureaucracy among the practitioners as they observed municipal and governmental programs for care of the public in city clinics. Through her experience with the Bureau of Adult Hygiene, Baumgartner became aware of the need for advance planning; a task force was set up for this purpose, she herself serving with the group.

Consultant to the World

In 1958 she was sent by the United States Department of State with a delegation of women to visit Russia. This was one of the first cultural exchange missions that the United States State Department and the Russians agreed upon during the "Cold War." While in Russia she visited nurseries, hospitals, and universities. On her return she was eagerly sought for radio and television programs because of the great curiosity of Americans about Russia. She was able to dispel many misconceptions about Russia. The Russian mission had also made it possible for her to expand her international horizons by a tour with her husband of many European and Asian countries.

Leona Baumgartner served on many national committees and commissions, e.g., United States Labor Department, Advisory Committee on Young Workers (1951–1953); Department of Health, Education and Welfare, as a member of various advisory committees to the secretary; the National Institutes of Health; and the Public Health Service. She was active in professional societies such as the American Public Health Association, which she served as president in 1959. She collected a great diversity of awards and honors: the Lord and Taylor Award to Outstanding Leaders of New York City, 1955; a Citation for Distinguished Work in Promotion of Health from the Royal Society of Health in England, 1956. In 1957 she was named Outstanding Professional Woman of the Year by New York State. Also in 1960 she received the William J. Schiffelein Public Service Award of the Citizen's Union of New York City. In 1961 the Elizabeth Blackwell Award of Hobart and William Smith Colleges was bestowed upon her. Baumgartner continued to accumulate honors after she left the New York City Health Department; these included the Herman M. Biggs Award of the New York State Public Health Society of the American Public Health Association and the Albert Einstein Award for Distinguished Service to Humanity, 1964.

A Lifetime Honored

She received 14 honorary degrees from universities and colleges: Sc.D. from Women's Medical College, 1950; New York University, 1954; Russell Sage

College, 1955; Smith College, 1956; Western College for Women, 1960; University of Massachusetts, 1963; University of Michigan, 1967; McMurray University, 1967; New York Medical College, 1968; Clark University, 1969: an L.H.D. from Keuka College, 1963; L.L.D. from Skidmore, 1959; Oberlin, 1965; and from Yale in 1970.

Leona Baumgartner resigned as commissioner of health for New York City in 1962. She had been commissioner for nine years. President Kennedy had urged her to accept an appointment to a post within the Department of State with the Agency for International Development, where she would be responsible for guiding the United States foreign aid dealing with health, food, agriculture, and jobs. Fowler Hamilton, director of the agency asked her, on behalf of the President, to join his staff with the rank of assistant Secretary of State. Her mission involved the development of a program of technical assistance to underdeveloped nations. She accepted the position and remained with the agency until 1965. During her term of office she also served with the World Health Organization and headed a delegation to Thailand, India, and Pakistan. She was closely associated with the movement to change the policy of the United States government on population control. President Eisenhower had insisted that no federal funds could be used for support of family planning, but Baumgartner, with others who helped, got that policy changed.

In 1964 her husband, Nathaniel Elias, became seriously ill and she took leave from the State Department to be with him. After his death in 1964, she moved to Harvard University as visiting professor of social medicine at the Medical School. From 1968 to 1972 she served as executive director of the Medical Care and Education Foundation of Massachusetts. In 1970 she married a friend from her internship days at Cornell, Alexander Langmuir, a former director of the epidemiology program at the Centers for Disease Control in Atlanta, Georgia. At the time of their marriage he was a professor of epidemiology at Harvard.

Leona Baumgartner was elected to the Institute of medicine of the National Academy of Science in 1969 and received the Public Welfare Award of the Academy, its highest award. She had been an officer of the Child Welfare League and the National Health Council. In 1974 she retired from her Harvard post. However, she did not retire completely from professional activities for she was continually called upon to serve as a consultant to the World Health Organization, among others.

Leona Baumgartner's stable early background provided her with the confidence and flexibility which served her so well in seeking out new experiences and in developing the extraordinary opportunities which were opened to her extraordinary talents. Her intense interest in research and her production of medical biographies provided her with a depth of understanding for public health problems unusual in a scientist so adept in politics. An outstanding leader in the field of public health and an accomplished administrator, she cut through the thickets of bureaucracy, making progress wherever she led. She advanced the state of health care for millions in New York City, modernized and made understandable the sanitary code, and motivated her staff to extraordinary accomplishment and remarkable honesty. She made an asset of being a woman. As such she was newsworthy and she turned publicity to good account in educating the lay public and the medical establishment.

The
National Institutes
of
Health

CHAPTER X

Ida Albertina Bengston

*". . . Despite some years of fruitless research,
heralded for work on tick borne infections and
botulism and related diseases."*

Much that now is taken for granted in diagnostic laboratory testing once had
to be worked out from the beginning. All the aids in diagnosis and guides to
proper therapy had to be devised. Before the first prototype, the first example of
its kind, much trial and error went into laboratory investigation. Through
serendipity and arduous efforts, Dr. Ida Bengston laid the groundwork for her
successors. The first woman of science to serve on the staff of the United States
Public Health Service Bureau of Hygiene, the forerunner of the National Institutes of Health, she made a prolonged study of three subjects: pathogenic anaerobes and their toxins; the eye affliction, trachoma; and rickettsial diseases.

Ida Albertina Bengston was born in Harvard, Nebraska, on January
17, 1881, of Swedish immigrant parents. She obtained her early education
there and in 1903 received an A.B. degree from the University of Nebraska.
Science had not yet claimed her attention; she majored in languages and
mathematics and was elected to Phi Beta Kappa.

Not long after graduation she went to Washington, D.C., to be a cataloguer in the United States Geological Survey. There she became acquainted
with one of the few women then working in a Federal Civil Service position in

science. From this chance meeting she decided that the life of a scientist could be more interesting than that of a cataloguer of records. Consequently, in 1911, she resigned from her position with the United States Geological Survey and went to the University of Chicago to study bacteriology with chemistry and physiology as minor subjects. In 1913 she received an M.S. degree. She continued at the university for two additional years under a university scholarship and was then appointed assistant bacteriologist in the Chicago Department of Health, where she remained only one year. In 1916 she was appointed assistant bacteriologist at the Hygienic Laboratory of the United States Public Health Service in Washington, D.C., with an annual salary of $1,800, considered at the time a royal income. She commenced work at the laboratory, but in 1919 returned to the University of Chicago to complete requirements for her Ph.D. degree.

In her early years at the Hygienic Laboratory she was involved with the ongoing problems of the Laboratory nature of contamination of biological products and her earliest publications reflect this.[1] In the 1920s her publications on anaerobes began to appear. A specimen had been sent to her at the Hygienic Laboratory for identification. It was a culture of an anaerobic organism grown from larvae of the green fly, *Lucilia caesar*. The organism isolated was an atypical anaerobe that was thought to have caused limberneck of chickens. Dr. Bengston confirmed its atypical behavior but classified the organism as *Clostridium botulinum*, a new strain not reacting with type A or type B antitoxin. Further studies with the culture and additional isolations from affected chickens confirmed that the organism was a new strain producing a toxin designated type C.[2] She continued for a time to work on food poisoning from canned food, contributing to the understanding of its causes and mode of prevention.

Research Leads to Standardization

Bengston's research with anaerobes and their toxins included some basic studies which led to the establishment of the official United States and international units for standardizing the antitoxins of the four most common etiological agents of gas gangrene, *C. perfringens, C. oedematiens, C. septicum* and *C. histolyticum*.[3] Some of these studies were accomplished in the mid-1930s (1934–1939) after her work with trachoma was completed.[4] During 1935–1936, Dr. Bengston worked on gas gangrene organisms and prepared the standard for toxins and antitoxins used by the League of Nations Health Committee in Copenhagen, Denmark. This standard was of inestimable value in the prevention and cure of gas gangrene in wounds.

In 1924 she was detailed to Rolla, Missouri, to search for the causative agent of trachoma. She spent seven years there in the United States Public Health Service Trachoma Hospital. During this period she assisted in trachoma surveys and tested every imputed etiologic agent in guinea pigs and other laboratory animals without any success in resolving the question of what caused trachoma infections.

A report by Noguchi of the production in rhesus monkeys of a granular conjunctivitis resembling trachoma as a consequence of injection of a Gram negative organism referred to as *Bacillus granulosis,* which had been obtained from human trachoma infections,[5] set numerous scientists to search for this organism. Noguchi's findings were reported to be confirmed by a group in Colorado and by others at the Rockefeller Institute. However, Bengston noted that many researchers failed to isolate the Noguchi organism from cases of trachoma.[6] She listed 26 authors in search of *B. granulosis* and remarked that there were only a few positive isolations from a large number of cases. Some reported finding a Gram negative organism "somewhat resembling" *B. granulosis.* Other investigators resorted to extreme measures such as self-inoculation with *B. granulosis* obtained from Noguchi and some of them were successful in producing an eye infection, but not trachoma. Nevertheless, Ida Bengston stated, "It must be conceded, however, that the finding of *B. granulosis* in certain sections of the country and perhaps other parts of the world merits its consideration as an etiological factor in trachoma. It's been possible with this organism to produce a granular condition in rhesus monkeys which may correspond to human trachoma and which is easily transmissible from animal to animal. The negative bacteriological findings of many workers remain to be explained."[7]

Bengston next compared the conjunctivitis in monkeys resulting from direct transfer from known human cases by injection of excised tissue ground in sterile saline, with the condition induced by *B. granulosis* injected into monkey conjunctiva. Her results showed a less typical condition from direct transfer than from *B. granulosis* culture injection. Her conclusion was that human experimentation would be necessary to resolve the problem.[8]

It was some time before the trachoma agent (*Chlamydia trachomatis*) was conclusively identified. It was first grown in the yolk sac of chick embryos by Bedson in 1958.[9] At first thought to be a virus, it was later shown by Moulder to be a bacterium.[10]

Rickettsiae: A New Emphasis

Viruses had been among Bengston's suspects as causative agents of trachoma but could not be proven responsible by the techniques then in use.[11] She also considered rickettsiae as possible agents.

Her preliminary studies with rickettsiae in relation to trachoma helped to launch her next and probably most important research contributions. As a member of the typhus unit at the National Institutes of Health (NIH), Bengston was assigned to the study of rickettsiae. The Weil-Felix test using the agglutination of *Proteus vulgaris* strains for detection of antibodies in patients' sera and for differentiation of some of the rickettsial infections, had been in use only a short time when Ida Bengston started work on a complement fixation test to differentiate the rickettsiae. She compared the agents of endemic (mouse) and epidemic (human) typhus, Rocky Mountain spotted fever, tsutsugamushi disease (scrub typhus), and Q fever. After some years of testing she was able to differentiate the various agents by a complement fixation (CF) test using an antigen prepared in the yolk sac of the developing chick embryo. She modified the CF test, adapting it for use in epidemiologic surveys.

Bengston performed some of the early work with tissue culture of typhus rickettsiae (*Rickettsia prowazekii*), which proved useful later in vaccine production during World War II.[12] In 1948, three years after her retirement, she was awarded the U.S. Typhus Commission Medal by Thomas Parran, then surgeon general of the United States.

In 1947 Stanhope Bayne-Jones had inquired of one of Ida Bengston's co-workers just how much of Dr. Bengston's work was her own and what part was an adaptation of the work of others. The co-worker, Sara E. Branham, made some interesting observations in reply to Bayne-Jones. To begin with, she pointed out that Ida Bengston was a very modest person, never inclined to credit herself unduly. Branham noted that Ida Bengston began working with rickettsiae about 1934. She and Rolla Dyer comprised the typhus team; her part of the project was the cultivation of the rickettsiae, which was independent of the other phases of the work. It was undertaken at her own request as she had told Dr. McCoy, director of NIH, that she was tired of establishing standards for tetanus and gas gangrene antitoxins and wanted something challenging.

Bengston grew Rocky Mountain spotted fever rickettsiae on the chick chorio-allantoic membrane for 20 passages without change in virulence. This work she published in 1935.[13] In 1937 she produced a Rocky Mountain spotted fever vaccine from rickettsiae cultivated in guinea pig testicles.[14] She also demonstrated the relationship between Australian and American Q fever.[15] Her publication in February of 1941 on the preparation of vaccines which afforded protection against Q fever in animals was the first publication on the subject.[16] Branham considered Bengston's greatest contribution to be the development of complement-fixation tests for the study of rickettsial diseases. A complement fixation (CF) test for Mexican typhus had been reported in 1936, but it was not a useful test because the antigen was not satisfactory. Ida Bengston and Norman Topping[17] described a specific CF test which differentiated between endemic typhus and Rocky Mountain spotted fever. By 1945 she had demonstrated that a CF test was the most practical means of detecting typhus infection in wild rats.[18] Until that time all testing of rats' sera had been made using the Weil-Felix agglutination reaction.

Most Productive Period

One of the important problems for the bacteriologists in the study of rickettsial diseases was to find a method of growing the organisms free of tissues in quantities sufficient for making serological diagnostic tests. When in 1938 Dr. H. R. Cox of the United States Public Health Service Rocky Mountain Laboratory discovered that the yolk sac tissue of the developing chick embryo provided a suitable medium for prolific growth of rickettsiae, Dr. Bengston was in a position to put this discovery into immediate practical use, and she entered into the most productive period of her career.

During World War II the rickettsial section at NIH was headed by Norman H. Topping. Bengston's CF testing laboratory became a unit within this section. In the war years the volume of routine testing in her laboratory was tremendous, requiring three or four assistants. Bengston was in charge of all the work relating to the CF tests for rickettsiae. In 1941 she published a description of the ether extraction method for preparing rickettsial antigen from the yolk sac of infected eggs.[19] Bengston also supervised the preparation of rickettsial antigens for epidemic and endemic typhus, Rocky Mountain spotted fever, and tsutsugamushi disease. These antigens were used for preparing experimental vaccines, and as antigen in CF tests and mouse neutralization tests. Her laboratory was responsible for filling requests for these antigens from all parts of the United States and from the war areas as well.

A Fruitful Collaboration

In collaboration with Norman Topping and R. G. Henderson she demonstrated that a lethal substance was present in yolk sacs heavily infected with epidemic typhus rickettsiae (*R. prowazekii*) when the material was given by intravenous injection to mice. In a study of 16 strains of endemic typhus using CF tests, Bengston showed that an antigenic homogeneity existed among all strains of epidemic typhus as well as those of endemic typhus, which indicated that it was not necessary to use a number of strains of these organisms in preparation of typhus vaccines. Differentiation between epidemic and endemic typhus organisms (the human and mouse types) could be demonstrated by the antibody titer, higher with homologous antigen than with the heterologous. The results of her experimental work were soon put to use in diagnostic tests as blood sera for typhus testing were received from many foreign nations: Spain, Russia, China, Iran, Bolivia, Colombia, Mexico, San Salvador, Guatemala, Puerto Rico, and Egypt. During her work with typhus she contracted the disease while giving an injection.

In work with tsutsugamushi, or scrub typhus, Bengston developed a diagnostic CF test and showed that there are antigenic differences among strains of scrub typhus in contrast to the homogeneity of epidemic and endemic typhus. This discovery made evident the need for a multivalent antigen prepared with many types of the organism both for diagnostic tests and for vaccines.

The CF test was found more sensitive than the Weil-Felix test for detecting infection in wild rats. Experimental infection with white rats showed that the Weil-Felix test became negative not long after the infection subsided, while positive CF tests could be obtained ten months after infection. The CF test was used in rat control programs as an aid in preventing spread of endemic typhus fever. Much of this experimental work was brought together in 1945 in an NIH *Bulletin.*[20] It included a group of nine papers dealing with typhus fever authored by Norman H. Topping, Ida Bengston, R. G. Henderson, C. C. Shepherd, and M. J. Shear.

A member of a number of scientific organizations, Ida Bengston was a fellow of the American Association for the Advancement of Science, was president of the Washington Branch of the Society of American Bacteriologists in 1943–44, and served as councilor from the branch to the national organization during 1945–46.

One of Ida Bengston's greatest diversions from her heavy work schedule was her farm in the foothills of the Blue Ridge Mountains of Virginia. Endowed with good health and great energy, she would turn from a week of heavy duties to managing a 370-acre farm. With no previous experience of farm life, she nevertheless carried the love of the land from her Swedish ancestors. During the ten years of her ownership, the farm was converted from barren, fallow land to a productive property.

Retiring from the National Institutes of Health in 1946, she lived only six more years, dying at age 71 in 1952. She shared a farewell party with Alice Evans, who retired from the National Institutes of Health at about the same time. It was Alice Evans who prepared Bengston's obituary which appeared in the *Journal of the Washington Academy of Science.*[21] In the obituary prepared by Evans, Dr. Topping is quoted as praising Ida Bengston in these words, "'Dr. Bengston was an indefatigable worker, a true disciple of the scientific method, and loyal to her country, her institution and her colleagues.'"

CHAPTER XI

Alice Catherine Evans

*". . . Renowned for research on undulant
fever; fought for pasteurization of milk."*

Alice Evans was the first woman to be elected president of the Society of American Bacteriologists (now American Society for Microbiology). This recognition accorded her in 1928 was based on her discovery some ten years earlier of the first human case of brucellosis unrelated to contact with goats and her subsequent confirmation of the source of the great majority of infections in milk from infected cows. Her investigations aroused commercial opposition of the dairy industry and arrogant rejection from some scientists who did not deign to accept the findings of a woman without a doctorate degree. It took great perseverance on Evans' part to persuade the scientific community of the validity of her work. In the course of her investigations Alice Evans contracted brucellosis and thereby contributed to the eventual explanation for the apparent scarcity of cases of brucellosis among those exposed to contaminated raw milk. The disease described as typical was an acute brucellosis. It was later proven that many suffered over long periods of time, as did Evans herself, from chronic brucellosis which for many years was attributed to other causes. These dramatic events occurred early in her career so that she had the satisfaction of seeing her discoveries repeatedly confirmed and of experiencing the regression and near disappearance of the disease, first through pasteurization of all milk and vaccination of calves, and later through the near elimination of brucellosis in cattle. In time Evans won acclaim for her scientific contributions.

In 1963, many years after Alice Evans had retired from the National Institutes of Health, Wyndham D. Miles, NIH historian at the time, prevailed upon her to write her memoirs for she had lived through some of the early days of discovery in bacteriology and had been in the midst of controversy.

Alice Catherine Evans was born in Neath, Pennsylvania, January 29, 1881, the only daughter and younger of two children of William Howell and Anne Evans, both of Welsh descent. Her paternal grandfather had settled in Pennsylvania in 1831. Her mother had emigrated from Wales at age 14. Her father was a surveyor, teacher, and a farmer who had fought in the Civil War. Alice obtained her primary education in the district school, then studied in the Susquehanna Institute in Tonawanda, Pennsylvania, where she was one in a class of seven, the last class to graduate from the institute before it closed.

Seeking a Formal Education at Cornell

At the time, it looked as if her formal education had come to an end. She had dreamed of going on to college, but she lacked the means, so she began her career in grade school teaching, one of the few professions then open to women. After four years of teaching, she took advantage of a two-year, tuition-free nature study course at Cornell University College of Agriculture. The course was designed especially for rural school teachers to foster a love of nature in country children. This course opened a new world to her.

During her life at Cornell, the first president of Cornell, Andrew D. White, still lived on campus and could occasionally be seen in flowing cloak strolling along the paths. Burt G. Wilder taught the course in vertebrate zoology which formed part of the nature study curriculum. He was the only member of the original faculty who was teaching during the early years of the class of 1909.

The entomologist John Henry Comstock was another of her teachers about whom Evans relates the following story. "In 1878 John Henry Comstock married Anna Botsford (Cornell '78) and they worked together for more than 50 years. In 1898 she was named Assistant Professor of Nature Study, but trustee opposition to her title was so great that she was reappointed lecturer after the close of the summer school in 1899. Nevertheless, she remains on the record as the first woman to hold professorial rank at Cornell."[1]

Before completing the nature study course, Alice Evans realized that she wanted to continue the study of science. The Cornell College of Agriculture was then accepting out-of-state students tuition free, and, with the help of a Roberts scholarship during her junior and senior years, Evans completed requirements for the B.S. degree in agriculture. Seniors were required to major in some branch of applied science such as horticulture or dairying, or to specialize in bacteriology. It was Alice Evans' choice to major in bacteriology that established the direction she would follow.

During her senior year, Professor Stocking, her teacher of dairying bacteriology, told her that he had been asked by Professor E. G. Hastings of the College of Agriculture at the University of Wisconsin to recommend a graduating student for a scholarship in bacteriology. Alice Evans was asked if she would like to apply. The scholarship had never before been awarded to a woman, but the University of Wisconsin wanted to develop a bacteriology instructor for domestic science students, and Alice Evans was the successful applicant. Professor Hastings became her advisor at the University of Wisconsin and recommended that she spend much of her time on chemistry courses, although she held the scholarship in bacteriology.

Elmer V. McCollum, who taught chemistry of nutrition, was at the time conducting experiments which led to his discovery of vitamin A. Thus Alice Evans and the other three students in the class heard much about "fat-soluble A" and "water-soluble B." The word vitamin had not yet been coined.

At the end of the year 1910, Evans received an M.S. in bacteriology from the University of Wisconsin. Dr. McCollum encouraged her to continue her studies for a Ph.D. on a university fellowship in chemistry, but she decided against it. The financial and physical strain of the past seven years disinclined her to undertake further study at that time. Moreover, in 1910 it was not considered so important to have a Ph.D.; some of the senior faculty at both Cornell University and the University of Wisconsin, and elsewhere, did not have Ph.D.'s.

Entering the Field of Research

In her mind she left the option open to complete the doctorate some day, but now she was ready for a change, so she accepted Professor Hastings' offer of a research position with the Dairy Division of the Department of Agriculture. She began her work on July 1, 1910, there on the university campus. At the time, several state agricultural experiment stations were collaborating with the United States Department of Agriculture in cooperative research while the east wing on the Department of Agriculture building (on Independence Avenue between 12th and 14th Streets, N.W., Washington, D.C.) was being completed. Both the Department of Bacteriology and the Department of Agricultural Chemistry in the College of Agriculture at the University of Wisconsin were involved in agricultural research. Alice Evans started out with the investigation into better methods of cheesemaking, then as now an important industry of Wisconsin. She spent three more years at the university and took one course each year to fill gaps in her education.

When, in 1913, the Dairy Division Laboratories in Washington were ready for occupancy, she set out for the capital city with a stoical demeanor. Contrary to her expectations, the environment of the Bureau of Animal Industry proved to be quite congenial. A number of women scientists were already employed in the Department of Agriculture, some in the Bureau of Chemistry, on work connected with enforcement of the Pure Food and Drug

Act passed in 1906. Several were employed in the Bureau of Plant Industry, where the distinguished plant pathologist, Erwin Smith, was a pioneer in giving opportunities to women. In the Dairy Division of the Bureau of Animal Industry, Alice Evans was the first woman scientist to hold a permanent appointment. She found that her immediate supervisors, B. G. Rawl, chief of the division, and Lore A. Rogers, in charge of research, had a favorable attitude toward women in science.

One of the problems under investigation when Evans joined the Dairy Division in Washington was a search for sources from which bacteria entered dairy products—the thought being that freshly drawn milk was quite healthful if not contaminated. The study required a project director (Rogers), a chemist (William Mansfield Clark), and a bacteriological technician. Evans was assigned to this project as the technician after two of the series of four papers on the subject had already been published.[2] The chemical aspects of these studies led to a field of investigation for which Clark became renowned. Accurate methods for measuring hydrogen ion concentration replaced the titration methods then in use in biological laboratories throughout the world.

In addition to work on this investigation, Evans was given a project of her own: the study of bacteria that occur in milk freshly drawn from the cow's udder.[3] She found the bacterial flora to be varied, with several species commonly present. Her attention focused on the causal organism of contagious abortion, *Bacillus abortus,* as then classified.[4] Warnings of the possibility that this organism might be dangerous to human health had been reported. Her study of the relationship of *B. abortus* to other pathogenic bacteria included the organism causing Malta fever, *Micrococcus melitensis,* as then named. The similarity in habitat of the organisms seemed to her a compelling reason for comparison, despite the suggested unrelatedness of the names. To her amazement, all strains of each type of organism behaved essentially the same in all culture tests then available for differentiating bacteria and in cross-agglutination. She then requested animal inoculations. Since the Division of Bacteriology had no facilities for animal experimentation, the tests were performed in the Division of Pathology of the Bureau of Animal Industry. Pregnant guinea pigs inoculated with *B. abortus* or *M. melitensis* aborted and produced specific antibodies and positive cultures from various organs. Evans then demonstrated that the two organisms could be differentiated by agglutinin-absorption tests.

Her results were presented at the 1917 Annual Meeting of the Society of American Bacteriologists in Washington, D.C. At the time, she commented, "Considering the close relationship between the two organisms and the reported finding of *B. abortus* in cow's milk, it would seem remarkable that we do not have a disease resembling Malta fever in this country. . . . Are we sure that cases of glandular disease or cases of abortion, or possibly disease of the respiratory tract may not sometimes occur among human subjects in this country as a result of drinking raw cow's milk?" According to Evans, the published results[5] were greeted with skepticism on the part of bacteriologists and physicians who brushed them aside with such remarks as, "If the organisms were so closely related, surely some other bacteriologist would have noted it before." Those connected with the dairy industry had other problems at that time, for the Bureau of Animal Industry was carrying on its campaign of tuberculosis eradication in cattle, which was trouble enough for the farmers.

Owing to World War I and the prevailing spirit of patriotism, Evans sought to utilize her efforts in service more closely related to the war effort and to the alleviation of human suffering. She found a position as bacteriologist at the Hygienic Laboratory (now NIH) then located at 25th and E Street, N.W., Washington, D.C., in an old, red brick building housing the entire institution, fewer than 100 people in all. She took up the new post in April 1918 and joined a group of doctors who were striving to improve antiserum used in treatment of epidemic meningitis, one of the dread diseases of World War I, with a fatality rate of more than 50 percent.

The great pandemic of influenza reached Massachusetts in September 1918 and spread to Washington in early October, where, on account of wartime overcrowding, it was very severe. In October 1918, Congress passed a resolution "to enable the Public Health Service to combat 'Spanish influenza' . . . by aiding state and local Boards of Health." As a result, all medical officers of the Hygienic Laboratory were sent into the field or served in Washington. To Evans fell the task of investigating the cause of the epidemic. One of the organisms under suspicion was *Hemophilus influenzae* found frequently in epidemic cases. But she had barely commenced when she herself became ill. When she finally recovered, the war was over. The peak of the epidemic had passed Washington, and the work on meningococci was resumed.

The Controversy Continues

During these early years at the Hygienic Laboratory, the controversy on the significance of *Brucella abortus* in milk continued. After her discovery of the similarity between *B. abortus* and *M. melitensis,* Evans reviewed British and French literature on Malta fever. She learned that, besides the cases readily diagnosed by a significant titer of agglutinins in the blood serum, there were mild cases in which the titer was too low to be considered significant. Because the Maltese objected to the opprobrious use of their homeland in the name Malta fever, the disease had been officially named "undulant fever" at the International Congress of Medicine and Hygiene held in London in 1913. The new name derived from the wavelike character of the fever curve in typical acute cases, but the old name persisted for some time. Evans states, "It is easy to deduce from the name the converse idea that Malta or undulant fever could be ruled out in a case without an undulating fever curve." This was one of the fixed ideas that obstructed the recognition of chronic cases. Another erroneous idea that impeded progress in understanding of undulant fever was the incorrect generic name *Micrococcus* given by Bruce to the organism he reported to be the cause of the disease. It was an understandable error for the early state of bacteriology in 1887 when David Bruce and his wife Mary succeeded in culturing the organism from the spleen of a fatal case of Malta fever. Bruce was knighted for his scientific discoveries and, after his death, Lady Bruce received some recognition when she was made an honorary female fellow of the Royal Microscopical Society, the first woman to be so honored.[6]

Another aspect of the undulant fever problem was the attitude prevalent in the first decade of this century toward milk as a carrier of disease. It had been incriminated in several typhoid outbreaks. Health authorities recognized that cows with tubercular infection might harbor tubercle bacilli in the udder, but Robert Koch had allayed their fears by stating authoritatively (1901) that bovine tuberculosis was not transmissible to man, and it was therefore unnecessary to take precautions to protect humans from bovine tuberculosis. Although human cases of tuberculosis caused by the bovine organism had already been described by Ravenel (in 1900) and by others, Koch's views were widely accepted, and it was many years before overwhelming evidence proved them to be wrong. Evans noted that "The most vocal scientist opposing the idea that brucellae in cow's milk might cause human disease was none other than Theobald Smith, who had been one of the first to warn of this possibility." Smith had been working on brucellosis of cattle for several years before Evans' first significant paper on the subject in 1918. However, in 1919 and again in 1925, he published reports disagreeing with the premise that brucellae in milk might be hazardous to the health of those drinking the milk.[7] Although he recognized brucellae in milk as an indicator of bovine infection, he rejected the human hazard from consumption of such milk.

In 1925, William Welch of Johns Hopkins Medical School entered the controversy. He was then a member of the advisory board of the Hygienic Laboratory. During his visit to the laboratory in the spring of 1925, he checked with the director, Dr. George McCoy, as to Evans' competence and accuracy. Being reassured by McCoy, he then suggested to her that she and Smith resolve their differences. Shortly after, at a meeting of the American Society of Tropical Medicine, Welch complimented her on a paper she had just presented on the geographical distribution of various serological groups of brucellae. He stated, however, that he could not believe that infected cow's milk might be the source of human brucellosis. He then repeated his wish that she would compose her differences with Smith. In her memoirs Evans indicates that, when pressed by the authoritative Welch to "compose her differences" with the authoritative Smith, she made no comment.

Coming to Terms

Later that year, Ludwig Hektoen, director of medical sciences of the National Research Council, held part-time research space in Evans' laboratory. One day he mentioned to her that Theobald Smith had declined to become chairman of the Committee on Infectious Abortion of the National Research Council when he learned that Evans was to become a member of the committee. In his letter to the National Research Council, Smith explained that he was at that time studying cultures of "so-called Malta fever in man," one of which was ascribed by Evans to the cow, and his results so far indicated that Evans' strain and several strains of known bovine origin were not identical. The strain in question, Evans' Baltimore strain, proved to be *Brucella suis.*[8] It had been isolated from a patient in 1922 at Johns Hopkins Hospital and sent to Evans for identification. It was the first strain of *Brucella* of human origin to be identified in this country. Simultaneously, cases of human brucellosis caused by drinking infected cow's milk were being found in southern Rhodesia. When Evans learned from Hektoen that the validity of her work had been questioned in the National Research Council, she wrote to Welch asking him to intercede with Smith noting, "It seems to me that Dr. Smith could not take the point of view that the so-called *B. abortus* is non-pathogenic for man if he knew the evidence that has accumulated in the last few months in South Africa as well as this country." Two days later Evans received a handwritten reply from Dr. Welch saying, "I am very much interested in your letter. I am taking the liberty of sending it to Theobald Smith. I think so highly of the work of both of you that if I can be the means of bringing about a rapport between you and him in this important study I shall be gratified. . . . If it is not too much trouble, can you give me the reference for the South African cases?" She answered the letter by return mail, listing references from recent British and South African medical journals to more than thirty cases of brucellosis in man contracted from infected cows. Welch sent the list to Smith. About a week later, Evans received a letter from Smith mentioning Welch's letter and adding, "On the whole, I think the accuracy of your work does not come into question as far as it has gone. Nor do I think it would suffer if you suspended judgment until the unknown factors responsible for or contributing to the incidence of the human cases have been brought to light."

About six months later, Evans received an invitation to serve as a member of the Committee on Infectious Abortion of the National Research Council, which had been organized under the leadership of Theobald Smith. She accepted and remained a member of the committee for six years "without memorable incident."

That Alice Evans viewed the opposition not only as authoritarian but also as sexist is evident in her remarks about the episode. As she put it, ". . . the nineteenth amendment [giving women the right to vote] was not a part of the constitution of the United States when the controversy began and he [Dr. Smith] was not accustomed to considering a scientific idea proposed by a woman." From 1917 when Evans suggested that milk might be implicated in transmission of brucellosis, the dairymen opposed first the idea and then later the facts. However, by 1930 public health authorities and physicians were beginning to accept the incontrovertible evidence and opposition diminished. A few tragic incidents of dairymen's children, who had never drunk any but certified milk, contracting brucellosis and succumbing to the disease hastened the change of attitude.

Overwhelming Evidence

Dr. Smith continued for some time to raise valid questions about the epidemiology of brucellosis, based on the scarcity of known human infections. But suspicion had been aroused and surveys were underway, Dalrymple-Champneys reported: ". . . by 1929 the floodgates were open and evidence of undulant fever of bovine origin had come from nine European countries and from Palestine and Canada . . . as well as Southern Rhodesia."[9] In Denmark, Kristensen and Holm had reported finding, over a 20-month period, evidence of brucellosis in 500 patients. Simpson and co-workers in 1930 reported finding 375 cases of human brucellosis in Iowa, some (slaughterhouse workers) infected with *B. suis,* others who consumed raw milk but had no other contact with cattle, were infected with *B. abortus.*[10] These reports and others gave evidence beyond a reasonable doubt that raw cow's milk may transmit brucellosis to humans, although the logical question relating to the scarcity of cases in some communities, where cattle were known to be infected and raw milk continued to be drunk, remained unanswered for some time until the evidence for chronic infection was clearly established.[11]

Alice Evans inadvertently provided some of the evidence for chronic brucellosis. Although she had learned from foreign literature that handling brucellae was dangerous work and accordingly took precautions in handling specimens and cultures, she nevertheless contracted the disease, like so many others engaged in research with these organisms. It was not appreciated at that time that brucellae are highly resistant to atomization (aerosols) and that the respiratory tract serves as a ready route of infection. In October 1922 she became ill with brucellosis. *B. melitensis* was shown to be the etiologic agent by positive cultures obtained from the first attack and subsequent episodes in 1923, 1928, 1931. Many years of ill health followed with periods of complete incapacitation alternating with periods of recovery. The last disabling episode occurred in 1943, nearly 23 years after the date of infection. Concomitant with her illness she developed a hypersensitivity to brucellar antigens and was obliged to abandon work with live cultures. Though she thereafter become involved with other research problems,[12] she returned to a study of chronic brucellosis in 1936.

By then acute cases of brucellosis were being reported from all parts of the United States and the problem of chronic disease was emerging. Evans set up and coordinated a project employing field investigations by young physicians in three widely separated cities where a large percentage of milk was still consumed raw, despite knowledge that the herds supplying milk were infected with brucellae. Serological tests were made for evidence of brucellar infection among chronically ill patients in whom satisfactory evidence of specific disease was lacking. In some areas a survey of bovine brucellosis was carried out concurrently as part of the national program of eradication of the disease from cattle. In one locality 23 percent of the cows were found to be infected, and 81 percent of the milk was sold raw.[13]

Results of the survey exposed a total of 22 human cases of probable or proven brucellosis among the 325 cases of chronic illness studied. Five cases were proven by culture; in nine cases the clinical diagnosis was confirmed by positive serology (agglutination test); and in eight, the diagnosis of probable brucellosis rested on clinical evidence alone. None had a history of exposure to brucellae by any means other than ingestion of milk and dairy products. This survey provided the data upon which Evans based her early estimate that the actual number of cases of brucellosis occurring in the United States was at least ten times the number of reported cases. Similar surveys by other investigators in other parts of the country supported Evans' results and explained the discrepancy observed by Theobald Smith between the number of human cases of brucellosis in relation to the number exposed by consuming raw milk from infected cows.

A Chance to Travel

After her election in 1928 as president of the Society of American Bacteriologists, Alice Evans was chosen in 1930 as one of two United States delegates to the First International Congress of Bacteriology, held in Paris, and, in 1936, to the Second Congress in London. In an addendum to her memoirs (National Library of Medicine), Evans left a record of impressions and anecdotes about these congresses and some other trips she made, including a visit to her ancestral home in Wales.

The First International Congress of Bacteriology was held at the Pasteur Institute in Paris. Alice Evans, her friends, Sara Branham, a bacteriologist, and Eloise Cram, a parasitologist, headed for another meeting, left a few weeks early travelling by ocean liner from Montreal, Canada. Evans wrote, "This was the first trip of the season when the Canadian-Pacific used the northern route into the Atlantic. Earlier, the route was south of Newfoundland to avoid the possibility of encountering icebergs. The course was changed too early in 1930," she wrote. Evans relates that in the forenoon of June 29 they were moving slowly on account of a light fog. As they passed through the Strait of Belle Isle, they could see the coast of Labrador with patches of snow and ice. They then entered a field of icebergs and the boat circled south to avoid them. In the afternoon they suddenly sighted an enormous iceberg floating rapidly toward them. The ship was travelling the faster of the two but it took the captain some time to turn the boat and they narrowly avoided a collision. This was a frightening experience for the passengers as it had been only 18 years since the catastrophic encounter of the Titanic.

They landed on the fourth of July at Greenock on the Firth of Clyde in Scotland. After a week of sightseeing in Scotland, the three friends separated, each to visit a place of her special interest. Evans went to France.

In Paris she stayed at Reid Hall, at that time the Paris Center of the American Association of University Women. Located at 4 Rue de Chevreuse, the center was near the Pasteur Institute. Evans arrived in time to enjoy July 14th's Bastille Day celebrations. She mentions the "electric displays" and the dancing in the streets. After the French holiday she spent a few days with a cousin, Mrs. Francis R. Welles, who lived in Bourre on the Cher River in the chateau country. Evans relates that Mr. Welles had been selected in 1880 by Western Electric Company to organize the Bell Telephone Company of Antwerp, he set up headquarters in France. In retirement, the Welleses remained in France. Evans describes their charming home and the grounds, orchards, and vineyards along the river.

She returned to Paris for the conference starting on July 20, 1930. By then Sara Branham had arrived at Reid Hall along with another American bacteriologist, Dr. Rachel Hoffstadt, from the University of Washington in Seattle. Bacteriologists from 29 nations attended the conference. Dr. Alice Evans and Dr. Robert E. Buchanan, of Iowa State University, were the two official American delegates. Only one other woman was serving as an official delegate, Dr. Lydia Rabinowich of Russia, known for her work on tuberculosis.

Evans was well received at the congress and surprised to be greeted as a friend by many bacteriologists whom she had never met. On a bus tour to Louis Pasteur's home in Garches, an Italian member of the congress asked her "in halting English" if "her man" was a bacteriologist. She replied that she was not married, she was herself a bacteriologist and gave him her card. He was delighted to learn who she was for he knew of her work. Her new acquaintance, Dr. Azzo Azzi, editor of an Italian microbiological review journal, became a friend with whom she corresponded for many years.

The most elaborate function of the congress was a formal evening reception. At a small dinner preceding the reception, Alice Evans was one of the guests of Dr. Plotz of the Pasteur Institute. Other guests included Dr. William H. Park and Dr. and Mrs. Bela Schick of New York and Dr. Sara Branham of the National Institutes of Health. Evans was particularly pleased to meet at the reception Professor Olaf Bang of Copenhagen, son of Dr. Bernhart Bang, discoverer of the causal organism of contagious abortion (brucellosis) in cattle.

On the last evening of the congress Evans missed the official banquet in order to attend the Paris opera in the private box of President Doumergue of France, presented to a Dr. Weinberg of the Pasteur Institute for the occasion. Other guests included Dr. Rabinovich, the Russian delegate, and Dr. Ledingham, director of the Lister Institute in London. Evans notes that the box was situated so that the occupants could readily be seen but could not see the performance "to good advantage."

Dr. Jules Bordet, Noble Prize winner and then director of the Pasteur Institute in Brussels, was president of this first congress. Dr. Albert Calmette of the Pasteur Institute in Paris was there to defend, repeatedly, the anti-tuberculosis vaccine, BCG, which he had developed with Dr. Camille Guerin, also of the Paris Institute. The Lubeck tragedies had just occurred that summer (1930) not long before the Congress met. A large number of German babies had died from the injection, by error, of virulent tuberculosis organisms. Dr. Calmette cited statistics of successful inoculation of BCG in many countries, but many at the congress remained fearful, unconvinced. However, Dr. William H. Park spoke favorably of the promising results obtained with BCG in New York City.

The Second International Congress of Bacteriology was held in London in 1936. Evans travelled with Sara Branham but this time they went by freighter. They arrived five days early because Dr. McCoy, director of NIH, had arranged for Evans to confer with two British scientists, Dr. Fred Griffith, on streptococci, and Sir Weldon Dalrymple-Champneys, on brucellosis. (Both of these British scientists were killed during a bombing raid of World War II.) Evans also visited with Dr. John Eyre, who had some three decades earlier been a member of the commission appointed by the Royal Society to investigate the prevalence of "Mediterranean Fever" among the armed forces of the Crown in Malta. David Bruce had chaired that commission which had reported on the incidence of the disease, its association with infected goats, and the discovery of the causal organism, later named for him, *Brucella meletensis.* During the week of the International Congress, Dr. and Mrs. Eyre gave a diner at the Royal Society's Club at which Alice Evans was the guest of honor. Dr. Branham and some other Americans were also present.

Alice Evans was asked to discuss some of the papers presented at the Congress: in the session on brucellae, presided over by Hans Zinsser of Harvard, and in the section on streptococci, chaired by William Scott of Edinburgh, Scotland.

After the congress Evans travelled to Europe by plane, her very first flight. Flying at an altitude of 1,600 feet, the plane offered an excellent view of aerial geography which Evans followed with a map, identifying the coastal features of Holland. In Delft she visited Dr. Albert Jan van Kluyver, who happened at the time to have another American guest, Dr. C. B. Van Niel of Stanford University, who had been one of Kluyver's students. Evans was escorted on a walking tour of Delft by the two native Dutch scientists. They pointed out to her reminders of Antonie von Leeuwenhoek, the seventeenth century naturalist who was born in Delft, who made his microscopes there, and thereby promoted the science of microbiology, among others.

On her visit to Ghent in Belgium, Evans was pleasantly surprised. She had made no advance arrangements beyond her hotel room and she knew no one there. On her arrival she found an invitation from Professor Van de Velde, head of Biochemistry and Bacteriology Departments at the University of Ghent, to visit the university. There she had the pleasure of sitting in Kekulé's chair with the original leather upholstery used by the great organic chemist himself.

In the course of her work at the National Institutes of Health, Evans worked on meningococci with Sara Branham and on the study of clostridial toxins with Ida Bengston. Around 1939 she began investigation of immunity to streptococcal infections.[14] At the time there were some 30 known types of streptococci; when she retired in 1945, 46 types had been characterized and the sulfa drugs and penicillin had been added to the armament against them.

Her retirement coincided with that of Ida Bengston, and they shared honors at the farewell party for them given by their friends and colleagues.

A Lasting Influence

Alice Evans never lost interest in national and world affairs and occasionally spoke out on issues that concerned her.[15] At age 85, when she applied for Medicare, Evans was required to sign a form disclaiming communist affiliation. This she refused to do, declaring it illegal since it denied her constitutional right. She never did sign; the form was processed without her signature. Her interest in young people and minorities was evidenced by a tuition fellowship for Federal City College, in Washington, D.C., which she set up through the auspices of the Washington Branch of the American Association of University Women. Her last years were spent in Goodwin House in Alexandria, Virginia, where on September 5, 1975, she died at age 94, following a stroke.

Some of the honors which Alice Evans received include an honorary M.D. from the Women's Medical College in 1934 (now Medical College of Pennsylvania), D.Sc. from Wilson College in 1936, and D.Sc. from the University of Wisconsin in 1948. She was also made an honorary member of the American Society for Microbiology in 1975.

Alice Evans' independent spirit and uncompromising integrity prevailed throughout her life and helped to establish her among leading scientists. Her science supported her conclusions. Her perseverance and courage in the face of opposition eventually led to changes in public health practice, hastening the pasteurization of all milk, which greatly diminished the incidence of brucellosis in the United States. Evans played a colorful and important role in the period of great discovery in the field of infectious diseases.

University of Chicago Alumni, 1952 ASM meeting. Second row, fifth from left Margaret Pittman, sixth, Sara Branham.

CHAPTER XII

Sara Elizabeth Branham

". . . Battled meningitis for many years;
first to show efficacy of sulfa drugs."

Before sulfa drugs became available, meningitis was one of the dread diseases. Few survived the infection and those who did survive were at risk of severe aftereffects: deafness, blindness, and mental retardation. Meningitis tended to recur in ten-year cycles and, tragically, most often afflicted the young. For many years antisera against the meningococcus which caused the disease were the best treatment and no sure preventive was available. Disastrous meningitis epidemics occurred in army camps and, what was worse, the antiserum prepared during one epidemic was likely to be ineffective against the next wave of infection. One of the pioneers who researched meningitis, studied the variable organisms, and made advances in perfection and standardization of the antimeningococcus antiserum was Dr. Sara Branham. She was also the first to demonstrate that sulfa drugs were effective against the infection and against the dread sequelae as well. These accomplishments were some of her major contributions but by no means the only ones.

Sara Elizabeth Branham was born July 25, 1888, in Oxford, Georgia. In 1904 she graduated from the Palmer Institute in Oxford. She then attended Wesleyan College in Macon, Georgia, where she graduated with an A.B. Degree in biology in 1907. For several years thereafter she taught biology in

Atlanta Girls' School, then in 1917 went to the University of Colorado in Boulder as an assistant in bacteriology. She received a second A.B. degree there in 1919 with majors in zoology and chemistry. The next year she obtained a position as assistant in bacteriology at the University of Chicago while working toward her M.S. degree in bacteriology, which she received in 1920. Continuing her studies there, she was awarded a Ph.D., magna cum laude, in bacteriology in 1923. The summer of 1923 she returned briefly to the University of Colorado, Boulder, as an instructor. That fall she resumed studies at the University of Chicago, as a fellow of the Douglas Smith Foundation for Medical research, and matriculated at the medical school to study for an M.D. degree. She left Chicago in 1927 before completing degree requirements in order to take a position at the University of Rochester with Dr. Stanhope Bayne-Jones. During that year she was offered a position as Bacteriologist at the National Institutes of Health, then known the Hygienic Laboratory of the United States Public Health Service. She eagerly accepted the position and remained at NIH for thirty years until her retirement in 1958. It was at the NIH that her most important research was accomplished. She took a leave of absence in 1932 to complete degree requirements for the M.D. degree, which she received in 1934. In 1945 she married Philip S. Matthews, who unfortunately died four years later. For many years Branham was a professional lecturer in preventive medicine at the George Washington University, Washington, D.C., a position she held until 1952. From 1959 to 1962 she served as visiting biologist, American Institute for Biological Sciences.

First Encounter with Salmonella

While at Chicago, Sara Branham studied with Dr. Edwin O. Jordon, who advised her to "find out about influenza" and, while she made an effort to follow through on this advice, she found it a fruitless exercise. The state of the art in virology was not yet ready for cultivation of viruses. Therefore she soon turned her efforts to a study of *Bacterium enteritidis* now classified with the salmonella group of foodpoisoning organisms. She published reports on the toxicity and antigenic properties of culture filtrates, the soluble antigens, and a specific carbohydrate obtained from these filtrates which reacted with specific antisera. She also published a paper in 1928, co-authored by L. Robey and L. A. Day, which was entitled "A Poison Produced by *B. enteritidis* and *B. aertrycke,* Which Is Active in Mice When Given by Mouth."[1] It was known at the time that these two organisms were the most commonly encountered members of the paratyphoid group causing food poisoning. Mice were used in the experiment with due consideration to the fact, known at the time, that these animals are sometimes carriers of those very organisms. However, a typical paratyphoid infection developed in all test mice and all died. The organisms were isolated from blood and spleen cultures and in some cases from intestinal contents as well. It was demonstrated that nearly half of the mice fed heat-killed broth cultures died but no deaths occurred among mice fed a heat-killed bacterial suspension in saline, evidence that "the poison" was produced in culture.

The Threat of Meningitis

She served on the faculty at the University of Chicago until 1927. That year proved to be a critical one for Sara Branham. She was first appointed associate at the University of Rochester School of Medicine in New York, where she worked with Dr. Stanhope Bayne-Jones—but not for long. She had been in Rochester only a few months when she was called to the Hygienic Laboratory in Washington, D.C. A serious epidemic of cerebrospinal meningitis, which started in China, had reached California. The antiserum which had been used since 1904 was no longer effective against the new strain of *Neisseria meningitidis.* This organism was difficult to work with in the laboratory since it required subculture every second day to retain viability. In 1909 Dr. Louise Pearce of the Rockefeller Institute had been dispatched to France to obtain the typed meningococcus cultures from Dr. C. Dopter,[2] and she brought them back alive by slow boat, transferring the cultures by use of an alcohol burner every second day. The standard antiserum had been prepared from these strains of meningococci.[3] Specific antiserum was the only known therapy during the epidemic years of World War I. With the end of the war the epidemic ended and so did the research. Some laboratories maintained cultures, old stock cultures getting rougher and rougher with each transfer and less specific antigenically, and these were the cultures used to produce antisera. So in 1928 when a severe epidemic started in China, moved to the West Coast, across the United States, and a year later reached Europe, serum therapy appeared to be completely ineffective. It was at this point that Branham was brought into the picture. She too made the slow boat trip to Europe, this time to England, where Drs. M. H. Gordon and E. D. G. Murray had retained their type strains in a dried condition.[4] The organisms were dead but they retained their antigenic specificity. From each type Branham prepared monovalent serum for typing the live organisms that were being sent to her at the Hygienic Laboratory. All of the new strains she collected still had to be transferred every second day.

Knowledge developed very rapidly then. Diversity became evident among meningococcus strains; Gordon and Murray's type I and type III were not separable except by agglutinin absorption. It was demonstrated by others[5] that even the capsular polysaccharide of types I and III were identical. Thereafter these strains were placed in Group I. Branham and co-workers found that more than 95 percent of epidemic strains belonged to Group I. This was also found to be true of strains isolated from subsequent epidemics. Hence this group became known as the epidemic group and was subsequently designated Group A. During epidemics Group A organisms were frequently found in carriers. However, most chronic carriers were found to have Group B organisms. A third group, C, was described later.

During World War I it was believed that when the carrier rate exceeded 20 percent of the population an epidemic occurred. But it was later demonstrated[6] that it was not the number or percentage of carriers in the population but the virulence of the organism they carried which determined the course of events. Branham[7] demonstrated this with experimentally infected animals: guinea pigs and mice.

Differences in virulence between S (smooth) and R (rough) colonies were shown to correlate with antigenic differences. It was further demonstrated that a two-hour agglutination test incubated at 37°C is more specific than the previously used method of incubation at 55°C overnight. Later,[8] capsular swelling by antibody was found to be a quicker method of typing meningococci. This slide test had the additional advantage that it could be used in direct typing of organisms found in cerebral spinal fluid of patients.

Another useful procedure for meningococcus typing, described in 1927 by Noble[9] involved the use of antiserum prepared in chickens. This type of serum provided satisfactory agglutination tests at room temperature, a laboratory procedure especially useful for field tests where water baths were unavailable. Branham compiled and published these methods in 1935.[10]

Until 1940, the titration of therapeutic potency of antimeningococcus serum employed an *in vitro* test, agglutination, or precipitin test which presumed a correlation of antibody titer with protective effect of antiserum. In 1940 Drs. Sara Branham and Margaret Pittman, using the mucin technique[11] to infect mice with as few as ten organisms, worked out a standard method for serum titration based on mouse protection combining it with a preliminary test for halo production on agar plates, an antigen and antibody reaction.[12]

New Discoveries

Following development of the lyophilization process by Flosdorf and coworkers in 1935,[13] it became unnecessary to transfer cultures every second day; and antigenic stability was better maintained in the freeze-dried organisms than in growing cultures.

Monovalent rabbit serum was found superior by Branham to the older and long used multivalent horse serum.[14] This was reported shortly before the discovery of the effectiveness of the sulfa drugs against the meningococcus by Branham and Rosenthal in 1937[15] in mice and, shortly thereafter, in human patients. Sulfadiazine became the drug of choice for treatment of the meningococcus infections. The organisms were later shown to be sensitive to penicillin and some of the broad spectrum antibiotics. But it was found that meningococci quickly acquired resistance to streptomycin and then developed dependence on it.

During World War II there was the usual wartime flare-up of meningitis, but there were means of control by then, sulfa drugs and antisera, and no epidemics occurred. Furthermore, carriers among the armed forces were treated with sulfadiazine and released for military service, unlike during World War I when they had to be quarantined.

Another area which Sara Branham advanced is that of bacterial toxins. Her first publication on the subject dealt with the use of the chick in titration of diphtheria antitoxin, in which she described the use of seven-day-old chicks which succumbed regularly to all diphtheria cultures found to be toxic by rabbit skin test. She noted that approximately one MLD (minimum lethal dose) of toxin for a guinea pig killed a chick within forty-eight hours unless antitoxin had been administered previously. In 1954 she established a weight reference for a mouse test as a more reliable standard than the rather vague age reference used until then[16]

Research on Toxins

Branham worked more extensively with the shiga toxin of *Shigella dysenteriae*. Her first publication on this subject also appeared in 1954.[17] In 1946 she and Karl Habel had described the preparation of an irradiated toxoid from shiga toxin of *Shigella dysenteriae*.[18] Later, in 1954, she explored (with Hottle and Riggs) the variables in irradiating toxin. She discussed the problems of standardizing the dose of ultraviolet light for irradiation of the toxin and the need for a critical end point to avoid destruction of antigenicity, or, on the other hand, a toxic product from inadequate irradiation. The effectiveness of toxoid was tested in mice that were later challenged with unaltered toxin. Safety for humans was tested on six adult volunteers who received two subcutaneous injections of the toxoid given one week apart. Three of the volunteers experienced no discomfort, but the others suffered some elevation of temperature and painfully sore arms at the site of the injection. Branham noted in the publication, however, that the reaction was no more severe than similar reactions which not infrequently followed the injection of typhoid vaccine. It was presumed to be due to endotoxins.

In an earlier publication,[19] Branham discussed the therapeutic value of antiserum against shiga toxin in mice. She reported that antiserum given early enough in the course of infection, no more than eight hours after injection of the organisms, was protective and that it was prophylactic if given from three weeks to eight hours before infection with *S. dysenteriae*. Yet, in general, shiga antitoxin was found to be a poor therapeutic agent in experimental infection since the shiga toxin had such a marked affinity for the nervous system that its effects were not reversed by antitoxin.

Using monkeys *(Maccaca mulatta)* which normally harbor *Shigella paradysenteriae,* Branham tested the infectivity of *S. dysenteriae* in these animals, an infection never reported to occur naturally. Infection was attempted with live cultures introduced by stomach tube and there was no evidence of discomfort or disease among the animals, though organisms were recovered by culture of their excrement. However, intraperitoneal injections of organisms suspended in mucin resulted in the development of neurological symptoms in three of 13 monkeys, one of which died. Larger doses of organisms (20 billion) were found to be lethal for all animals. No clear-cut infection nor characteristic syndrome was produced by either of these routes. Only subcutaneous or intravenous injection of toxin resulted in a characteristic clinical picture with constant pathological findings.[20]

In 1951 Branham reported in the *Bulletin of the World Health Organization*[21] on the use of mice in potency testing of *S. dysenteriae* antitoxin prepared in horses. Somewhat later (1953) she and co-workers demonstrated the immunological reaction in monkeys to toxins injected into isolated intestinal pouches free of bile or gastric or pancreatic juice.[22] She found that shiga toxin was perfectly innocuous when in contact with normal intestinal mucosa of monkeys, although toxin was fatal when given parenterally. The toxin introduced into the isolated pouch produced no evidence of illness but antibodies were developed against the toxin which were protective against an otherwise lethal parenteral injection. She demonstrated that the toxin was detoxified before absorption from the intestinal pouch. However, the study failed to elucidate the role of neurotoxin in pathogenesis of infection. Sara Branham extended her studies on Shigella toxin to consideration of *S. sonnei,* its antigenicity in relation to culture phase.[23] Phase I cultures were found to be remarkably antigenic, inducing an active immunity to the homologous phase but not to other phases of *S. sonnei.* She followed with a study of 100 cultures to determine the incidence of the various phases of *S. sonnei,* 80 cultures from clinical cases of dysentery and 20 cultures from carriers. More than 90 percent of the cultures from cases were found to be phase I while 80 percent of cultures from carriers were phase II. The phase I cultures showed high virulence for mice.

Ever alert to the introduction of new methods or new therapy, Sara Branham tested the effect of cortisone and ACTH on adrenals in experimental diphtheria, shigella, and meningococcus intoxications. Tests in guinea pigs showed no effect of these hormones on the outcome of the experimental infections.[24]

One of Branham's last publications,[25] concerned the three types of *Corynebacterium diphtheriae:* gravis, intermedius, and mitis. Using immunoelectrophoresis, she demonstrated an additional component in the antigen from gravis strain culture filtrates although the toxin was found to be the same from all three strains. Her last publication (in 1960) also dealt with diphtheria antitoxin, the quality of the antitoxin which developed in guinea pigs following injection of diphtheria toxoid in Freund's adjuvant.[26]

Meningitis Expertise Recognized

Sara Branham's expertise was early recognized by inclusion of her work, a chapter on the chemistry of antigens, in *Newer Knowledge of Bacteriology and Immunology.*[27] She contributed to the *Yearbook Supplement* of the *American Journal of Public Health* a chapter on laboratory diagnosis of meningococcus meningitis and identification of the meningococcus in 1935[28] and also in 1936.[29] In 1941 she contributed a similar chapter in *Recommended Procedures and Reagents* of the American Public Health Association, first edition, and in 1945 the second edition.[30] In the third edition she contributed the chapter entitled "The Meningococcus." Her chapter on "Meningitis" in the *Encyclopaedia Britannica*[31] of 1948 covers all forms of meningitis except tuberculous and syphilitic. A similarly broad review of bacterial meningitis appeared in 1963 in *Diagnostic Procedures and Reagents,* fourth edition, of the American Public Health Association.[32]

Sara Branham herself was one of the authors of the tenth edition of *Practical Bacteriology, Hematology and Parasitology,*[33] a standard text for many years.

With E. G. D. Murray, she prepared the section on the genus Neisseria for *Bergey's Manual of Determinative Bacteriology* in 1948,[34] and again in 1957.[35] Dr. Branham prepared the section on reference strains for the serological groups of meningococcus which appeared in the *International Bulletin of Bacterial Nomenclature and Taxonomy.*[36] In this report she referred to the four groups A, B, C, and D and noted that neotype strains had been dried from a frozen state and sealed *in vacuo* and that these were available as reference strains from the American Type Culture Collection, as long as they lasted.

Her contributions to taxonomy were substantial. Her early work, typing strains of meningococci, comparing European and American strains, and studying both carrier strains and epidemic strains from all parts of the United States, well fitted her for the appointment to the International Subcommittee of the Family Neisseriaceae of the International Society of Bacterial Nomenclature, which she served as secretary for several years. She was influential in resolving the differences among the English, American, and French scientists in the development of the classification scheme finally agreed upon in 1954, the A, B, C, and D Group classification.[37]

In addition to the degrees she earned, Sara Branham was awarded an honorary D.Sc. in 1937 from the University of Colorado and was the recipient of a number of honors, among which were the Edward Taylor Ricketts Prize for research in pathology (1924), the Alumni Award for outstanding achievement from Wesleyan College (1950), and the Distinguished Service Award from the University of Chicago Alumnae (1952). She was named Woman of the Year by the American Medical Women's Association in 1959, and she was listed in *Who's Who in America* (first about 1945).

As a member of the Society of American Bacteriologists (now American Society for Microbiology), she served as president of the Washington Branch, 1937–1938 and councilor for several years. She chaired the Laboratory Section of the American Public Health Association 1946–1947 and was a Councilor 1947–1952. She was president of the Tungsten Chapter of Iota Sigma Pi (Women Chemists Association) in 1918–1919 and was elected president of the D.C. Chapter of Sigma Xi for 1953–1955. She was an official delegate to the first and second International Congresses for Microbiology in Paris, 1930, and London, 1936, respectively. She became a trustee of Wesleyan College, 1936–1939, and prepared recorded lectures on "Meningococcus Meningitis" for the United States State Department for distribution to the University of Chunking, China, 1950.

In recognition of Branham's outstanding contributions to knowledge of the Neisseria, the genus Branhamella (catarrhalis) was created in her honor in 1974 for the non-pathogen, formerly designated *Neisseria catarrhalis,* which she had differentiated from the pathogenic neisseria: *N. meningitidis* and *N. gonorrhoeae.*

A Happy Life

Sara Branham proceeded with confidence and freedom derived from a warm and supportive home environment, through her education, early finding an inspiring field in a challenging environment and on into a professional career.[38] She came into the field well prepared, endowed with a brilliant mind, given to diligent endeavor, and the serendipity to recognize the potential of the paths which opened to her. A petite woman of grace and charm with a great zest for life, she augmented her opportunities. Late in life, at age 57, she married Phillip S. Mathews, a retired businessman, and enjoyed a brief (only four years), happy life with him. Her penchant for meticulous detail in research extended to her home and garden which she maintained with equal care. Similarly, her lectures were enlivened with literary references from her classical background in the arts. Her last published lecture was "Defense of Epimetheus Development of Knowledge Concerning the Meningococcus,"[39] in which she suggested that Epimetheus, the one who looked back, "afterthought," was brother to Prometheus, "forethought," whose vision and aggressiveness brought the gift of fire to man. Epimetheus gave a perspective that permitted one to see things that might have been overlooked. Branham stated that if we look back carefully enough, with binoculars as it were, we may begin to have some idea of what went into the building of ancient structures, to appreciate the effort expended with primitive tools, to understand what went wrong with the structures left unfinished, and to complete the work with new tools. She pointed out many instances where a backward look had made possible new advances, such as the testing of the dye prontosil and the development of the sulfa drugs.

Sara Branham died suddenly from a heart attack on November 16, 1962, at age 74. She was buried in the family plot in Oxford, Georgia.

Bernice Eddy and Sarah Stewart, 1971.

CHAPTER XIII

Bernice Elaine Eddy

*". . . Discoveries saved millions from harmful
polio vaccine; career hampered by critics."*

From ancient times the bearer of bad tidings has met with poor reception.
Even to the present day the whistle blower's fate is not a happy one. Dr.
Bernice Eddy's astute observation put her at risk when she reported the
discovery of live virus in animal tests of the so-called "killed virus" poliomyelitis vaccine just before it was to go into commercial production. Er-
rors were corrected, a safe vaccine was produced, but Dr. Eddy was demoted.
Some years later she discovered an unwanted carrier virus (SV40) in tissue
culture used for production of adenovirus vaccine. There was more cause for
concern in this instance for the vaccine had been in use for some time. It took
several years to ascertain that no damage had been done and almost as long a
time for Dr. Eddy's efforts to be appreciated. All these late events in her
career followed an early distinguished performance.

Bernice Elaine Eddy was born in Glendale, West Virginia, in 1903. Her
father, Nathan Eddy, like three of his four brothers, was a physician. When
Bernice was five years old he moved the family to Auburn, a small town not far
from Glendale, where he continued his practice. Bernice attended grade school
in Auburn, but went to high school in Sisterville, living with one of her uncles
there. This country, later considered depressed Appalachia, was pleasant in her

youth. It was an area of farms, woods, lumbering, and rich in oil and gas production. One month before Bernice was to enter college her father died. Her mother, who had been a schoolteacher before her marriage, returned with Bernice, her sister, and two brothers, to her home town, Marietta, Ohio, and took up teaching again. Thus Bernice went to Marietta College, wanting to study medicine but with little exposure to science in high school. She therefore took all the pre-medical courses offered and in 1924 graduated with an A.B. degree in bacteriology.

Not long after graduation, Eddy noticed in the post office an announcement of a Civil Service examination for a bacteriologist in Washington, D.C. Since bacteriology was one of her favorite subjects in college, she consulted her biology professor about applying. He advised her to go to graduate school instead. He had an application at hand for a fellowship at the University of Cincinnati, which he suggested that she apply for. She did fill out the application but continued to plan on going to medical school, for she did not really expect to get the fellowship. When it was awarded to her, she felt surprised and flattered and decided to accept it.

At Cincinnati she worked with Dr. William B. Wherry on studies in immunity. She received an M.S. degree in 1925 and a Ph.D. in 1927 from the University of Cincinnati. Her doctoral thesis concerned pneumococci: a search for protective bacteriophage and enzymatic agents in patients' sputums. She remained at the University as a Harrington-Hogan Fellow in Bacteriology from 1925 to 1929. During 1928–1929 she was also an assistant in pediatrics. The next year, 1929–1930, she was a Davis Teaching Fellow in bacteriology. She also lectured once a week at the Cincinnati College of Pharmacy on economics.

At the end of this academic period, she joined the United States Public Health Service and at her own request was stationed in Carville, Louisiana, to work in the only research leprosarium in the world at the time. Her advisor at Cincinnati, W. B. Wherry, born of missionary parents in India, had acquired a great interest in leprosy, an interest which he transmitted to Bernice Eddy. She remained in Carville for four years, living in a separate compound, segregated from the patients. In time, she became discouraged with the research. The outlook at that time was very poor for a leprosy patient. Some improved and were released, but they always returned. Laboratory research did not seem to offer much promise. While she was there, George McCoy, director of the Hygienic Laboratory in Washington, D.C., visited Carville several times. He encouraged Eddy to come to Washington and sent her an application. Not long after applying for a Civil Service position, she received notice to report to the Biologics Control Division of the National Institutes of Health. She started there in 1937, an associate bacteriologist under the supervision of Walter Harrison.

An Auspicious Beginning

At the National Institutes of Health she immediately became involved in a drive against lobar pneumonia owing to her work with pneumococci at the

University of Cincinnati. A concerted effort was underway to reduce the mortality from pneumococcal infections by treatment of cases with anti-pneumococcal serum. Eddy worked on control of the antisera. Therapeutic antisera for use against many specific types of pneumococci were manufactured by a number of licensed laboratories. Since only homologous antiserum was effective in treatment, typing of the infecting organism was essential. In the Biologics Control Laboratory Eddy helped to work out reproducible tests for potency and specificity of the antisera. These criteria became the minimum requirements for manufacturers. With the advent of antibiotics for treatment of pneumonia Eddy's project was phased out. There had been 32 known types of pneumococci when she started work on the project; there were 75 types at the start of World War II when she was assigned to control of influenza virus vaccines.

Eddy became chief of the influenza virus vaccine testing unit in 1944 and altogether spent 16 years working with influenza vaccine production, standardization, and control. She continued the work after the war when the vaccine became licensed for civilian use. With successive epidemics of influenza the formulas for the vaccines had to be changed to correspond to the prevalent antigenic type(s) of the virus. A new reference standard had to be obtained and standardized each time. For a number of years, Eddy's laboratory was the only one at the National Institutes of Health concerned with the influenza virus, thus diagnostic as well as control work was carried out in her unit.

Introduction to Polio

In 1952, after Eddy learned of Ender's success in growing polioviruses in tissue culture,[1] she became interested and asked to work on polio during the summer when the disease was prevalent and influenza was not. The National Foundation for Infantile Paralysis had a project underway on the use of human gamma globulin for protection against poliomyelitis and Eddy was assigned to work on the standardization of the gamma globulin. She developed a mouse protection test for potency standardization while still head of the Influenza Unit of the Section on Virus Vaccines and Basic Studies. It was following these accomplishments with the gamma globulin and the influenza vaccine that she received the NIH Superior Accomplishment Award in 1953.

The next year Eddy was asked to work on the Salk polio vaccine, the formalin-killed virus vaccine. She was eager to do it. She expected to work out her own methods of testing as she had in the past and was thus somewhat dismayed to find that the National Foundation had set up a protocol for safety testing. This was perhaps the first time the Laboratory of Biologics Control had been told not only what to do but how to do it. The vaccines and the viral control were delayed in arriving so that the deadline for testing was very short. However, Eddy accepted the task and for many weeks she and her staff worked around the clock, seven days a week.

Eighteen monkeys were used to test each lot of vaccine. Twelve rhesus monkeys were injected intracerebrally through a small hole in the skull made by a dental drill, and six cynomologus monkeys were injected intramuscularly. Testing started in January. From time to time some of the monkeys became paralyzed. Eddy had these monkeys photographed and she attempted to recover poliovirus from them. She succeeded in recovering and typing the virus from three of the paralyzed monkeys. Her report to her supervisor on the paralyzed monkeys was not well received. By mid-April the manufacturers had prepared enough vaccine for widespread use; it was approved by a distinguished group of virologists and released for use. In many areas where the vaccine was used there were no untoward effects, but in other areas several cases of paralytic polio developed. There was great consternation among all the people who were sponsoring the vaccine; changes were made in the hierarchy of control in the Department of Health, Education and Welfare from the top echelon to the lowest member on the totem pole, Bernice Eddy. The laboratory was reorganized and became the Division of Biologics Standards (DBS); a completely new team was brought in to work on polio and Eddy was banished from the laboratory.

The Work Continues

Nevertheless, she continued to work with respiratory viruses, including adenoviruses, and in 1956 started collaborating with Dr. Sarah Stewart on research dealing with tumor-inducing virus. This proved to be the most fruitful period of her professional career though a very troubled one.

Her research with Stewart led to the discovery and initial definition of the SE Polyoma Virus, so named for Stewart-Eddy as co-discoverers. One strain of the virus was isolated from a strain of AKR mouse with transplanted leukemia and two strains of the same virus were isolated from the same strain of mice, AKR, with spontaneous leukemia. The virus was passed serially through Swiss mouse tissue cultures inoculated with minced AKR mouse tumor tissue or tissue extract, the supernatant fluid from centrifuged minced tumor tissue. Hamsters injected with 14-day tissue culture cells, or the supernatant from such cultures, developed solid tumors in one to several months. These neoplasms in the hamster were so bizarre that it was not at first certain that only one virus was involved.[2] Yet the viral agent behaved in many ways like typical nononcogenic viruses: it could be propagated in cell culture, it produced lytic changes in cells so that plaques could be demonstrated in tissue culture, it could be assayed by ten-fold infectious virus dilutions, and it caused hemagglutination of erythrocytes. In addition to induction of tumors in the natural host, the mouse, it could produce malignant tumors in rats and hamsters; benign growths in the rabbit.

While this work with Stewart was progressing so fruitfully, Eddy also had other responsibilities at the DBS, one of them being the development and control of adenovirus vaccines intended for use in protection against the common cold and upper respiratory infections. A satisfactory vaccine was produced and licensed for commercial use. In the late 1950s and early 1960s, this vaccine was administered to all army personnel. Around 1959 Eddy turned her attention to spontaneous degeneration which she noted in the monkey kidney cells used as control in preparation of polio virus and adenovirus vaccines.

It had been known for years that monkeys harbor latent viruses. It was Eddy's original intention to test each of the known viruses for oncogenicity, but by 1959 there were more known simian viruses[3] than she had space or time to test. Instead, she obtained control monkey kidney cell cultures that had been used for testing poliovirus vaccines. After further incubation, these cells were frozen with dry ice and then disintegrated by grinding. The supernatant fluid separated from the cell debris was injected into newborn hamsters. Though normal in appearance for 118 days, the hamsters began to show evidence of tumor formation thereafter. Eddy reported this information to her supervisor who showed little interest in her report.

In the autumn of 1960 Eddy was invited to address the New York Cancer Society on induction of tumors in hamsters. Granted official permission to speak, Eddy addressed the society on tumors induced by the polyoma virus and also described tumors induced by the presumed viral agent in monkey kidney cells. Her supervisor angrily reprimanded her for mentioning the discovery publicly and ordered her henceforth to submit for approval anything she was going to say before any outside group. Eddy argued for publication of her work because of the implications, but her work on this virus was not published for another two years.[4] As it turned out the virus was known but its oncogenic potential was not recognized.[5] It had been referred to simply as vacuolating virus. It was the fortieth simian virus in Hull's list of simian viruses,[6] thus it became known as simian virus 40, or SV40.

In May 1961 Eddy wrote a memorandum to the chief of the Laboratory of Control Activities suggesting that since SV40 was known to be exceedingly stable and its effect on the human population was unknown, wouldn't it be advisable to include in the regulation the requirement that the adenovirus vaccine be free of this agent. The same question could have been asked about the polio vaccines but since she had been removed from its control she did not mention that vaccine.[7] Her suggestion was ignored. Only years later did the evidence become convincing that SV40 does not present a great health hazard for humans.[8]

In the Face of Opposition

The demotion of Dr. Eddy continued. She argued with her supervisor to keep her laboratory space and animal facilities but her request was denied. At the same time she was denied permission to attend certain professional meetings and to publish other papers. She was told by her supervisor that control work and basic research were incompatible. She argued that the polyoma virus research was carried out along with a great deal of control work and that both research and control on influenza viruses and adenoviruses had gone on simultaneously. She expressed the wish to continue this interesting combination of activities. But she lost this argument too and was taken off control work entirely.

One of her co-workers, Lawrence Kilham, wrote to an official in the Surgeon General's office seeking help in the matter, stating that "Dr. Eddy's case to many of us represents a somewhat Prussian-like attempt to hinder an outstanding scientist who is making a contribution in an important field of biologics control." This protest was to no avail.

Eddy was demoted from head of a section to head of a small laboratory, and was moved into smaller and smaller quarters with fewer and fewer assistants. In a very small laboratory she worked for a time on the so-called slow viruses, but under conditions hardly conducive to productivity. Her last publications deal with oncogenic viruses. Despite the unfavorable climate, she stuck it out at the Division of Biological Standards until 1973 when she retired at age 70.

She accepted her fate gracefully at the time and became involved with other research and testing. But not all involved with the DBS shakeup took it as calmly. Some written charges were exchanged and a congressional investigation followed sometime later. During the investigation, Senator Abraham Ribicoff, quoting from the allegations of Dr. J. Anthony Morris, said that in 1954 and 1955 "one of the Division's most noted scientists, Dr. Bernice Eddy, discovered that several lots of polio vaccine contained live virus capable of causing the disease itself." He continued, "In spite of Dr. Eddy's finding, which was known to the DBS leadership, the vaccine was released in the spring of 1955 and over 150 individuals associated with its use contracted paralytic polio."[9] It was further recorded that Dr. Eddy was relieved of her duties as polio control officer.

An extensive reply from the secretary of the Department of Health, Education and Welfare and his advisors in the department, at the National Institutes of Health, and the Division of Biological Standards, as well as an *ad hoc* Committee of Experts appointed by the director of the NIH, affirmed that no vaccine known to contain live virus was released for distribution.[10]

Bernice Eddy was married shortly after coming to Washington, D.C., to Dr. Jerald G. Wooley, a physician who, until he contracted tuberculosis, had practiced medicine in South Carolina. After his recovery from the illness, he joined the Public Health Service. He came to NIH and worked in what is now the National Institute of Allergy and Infectious Diseases, notably on choriomeningitis. The Wooleys first lived in Virginia, just across the Potomac from NIH. When the NIH moved from downtown Washington, D.C., to Bethesda, Maryland, the Wooleys built a home on Selkirk Court in Bethesda, where they were rearing their two daughters, Bernice Elaine and Sarah Elizabeth. When Dr. Jerald Wooley died from a heart attack, the children were still young, thus it was fortunate that Bernice Eddy's mother could move in with her to help out for a while.

Eddy remained in the home after the children were grown and had left and after she herself had retired. She often spent time at her farm near Flint

Hill, Virginia, or with her daughters and their families in Hawaii or South Carolina. She also travelled extensively in Asia, South America, England, and elsewhere. This was, in a sense, a continuation of her professional travel during the height of her career when she was frequently a participant at international meetings, often as an invited speaker.

Extensive Publication

Bernice Eddy was very responsive to the need for scientific communication. She prepared carefully detailed papers on her research and control work, publishing nearly 70. Some of her early publications dealt with her attempts to culture the leprosy bacillus. She published six papers on pneumococcus typing, immunological cross-reactions, and taxonomy of the organisms. Although her research on these bacteria was concluded around 1942, she was still called upon for her expertise in the field in 1960 when she again published on the taxonomy, a paper entitled, "Proposal for a Change in the Nomenclature of *Diplococcus Pneumoniae* and a Comparison of the Danish and American Type Designations."[11]

Her publications dealing with the influenza virus and vaccine preparation started to appear in 1947 and continued through 1952. They were principally concerned with standardization tests, e.g., neutralization[12] and antigenic variation of the virus.[13]

There followed a prolific period of publication with Sarah Stewart on the polyoma virus. Their first paper (of a long series) appeared in 1957, entitled "The Induction of Neoplasms with a Substance Released from Mouse Tumors by Tissue Culture."[14] The virus was at first referred to as "mouse tumor agent." In the *Journal of the National Cancer Institute,* the organism was courageously referred to as a tumor inducing virus. Publications followed delineating the properties of the virus, its hemagglutinating and cytopathogenic effects on cells.[15] In the same year a review paper appeared describing the distinctive characteristics known at the time.[16] As information about the polyoma virus accumulated, an abstract of a paper presented at the Canadian Conference appeared in Federation Proceedings.[17] It dealt with the ability of the virus to produce plaques in tissue culture and with the effect of immunization of adult female hamsters on latency of infection in the offspring. Coordinated research between Stewart and Eddy and scientists at the Sloan Kettering Institute for Cancer Research in New York City resulted in the isolation of infectious DNA (deoxyribonucleic acid) from a mouse embryo tissue culture which had been infected with polyoma virus.[18] They found that the infectious DNA was resistant to ribonuclease but inactivated by deoxyribonuclease, while the intact virus was resistant to both enzymes.

Eddy was sole author of a review published in *Advances in Virus Research* entitled "The Polyoma Virus."[19] She prepared the section on "Virus and Cancer" for the 1966 *McGraw-Hill Yearbook of Science and Technology,*[20] and the chapter on "Oncogenic Viruses" in *Basic Medical Virology.*[21] She wrote a section on "Virus Diseases" for the *Encyclopedia of Biochemistry* published in 1967.[22] A comprehensive monograph on "Polyoma Virus" appeared in 1969.[23] In 1970 she prepared a chapter entitled "Infection with Oncogenic Viruses" for *Infectious Agents and Host Reactions.*[24]

Eddy was senior author of eight papers and co-author of one publication about the SV40 virus.[25] "Identification of the Oncogenic Substance in Rhesus Monkey Kidney Cell Cultures as Simian Virus 40"[26] was one of her most important papers. In 1966 she reported that repeated large doses of either adenovirus type 12 or SV40, injected into hamsters some time after an initial infecting dose of homologous virus but before tumors appeared, resulted in inhibition of tumor development.[27]

Despite the low level of research activity that she was reduced to during her last years at DBS, Eddy continued to publish. The year before her retirement, four papers appeared: one on viral infectivity and oncogenicity,[28] another on problems encountered in the detection of the oncogenic potential of viruses in cell culture.[29] The last two papers dealt with the possible therapeutic effect of clam extracts on cancer cells in culture.[30]

Professional Associations

Over the years, Bernice Eddy was active in a number of scientific organizations. She was a fellow of the American Association for the Advancement of Science; she served as secretary-treasurer, vice president, and president of the Washington Branch of the American Society for Microbiology (ASM). She was a member of the Board of Managers and vice president of the Washington Academy of Science and a member of the Board of Directors of the American Association for Cancer Research. She was an editor and contributor to the Diplomatic Forum of the American Board of Microbiology, a member of the Board of Governors and secretary-treasurer of the American Academy of Microbiology. She also served on the Committee on the Status of Women Microbiologists of ASM. She was elected to Sigma Delta Epsilon (a graduate women in science honorary society) in 1950, and in 1967 she was elected to honorary membership in the society.

She was a frequent guest speaker at professional meetings in the United States as well as foreign countries. In 1953, when she received the NIH Superior Accomplishment Award for work on poliomyelitis gamma globulin, the statement read in part, ". . . for the valuable and outstanding part she played in recent development related to the use of poliomyelitis immune globulin, frequently called, 'gamma globulin' . . . and to the anticipated completion of promising work on poliomyelitis vaccine. . . ." In 1967 she received a Superior Service Award from the Department of Health, Education and Welfare, and in 1973, at the time of her retirement, the DHEW secretary's Special Citation. She also received the Emeritus Scientist Award in 1975 from the D.C. Section of the Society for Experimental Biology and Medicine and the NIH Director's Award in 1977.

Bernice Eddy was a broadly based scientist who pioneered a critical area of microbiology and public health, the development of standards for antisera and vaccines and the establishment of criteria for evaluation of biologic products. A woman of independent judgment, she chose to work on one of the most intractable problems among infectious diseases, leprosy, a scourge of antiquity. Also, tenacious under siege, she maintained a steady course and suffered harassment with remarkably good grace.

Sarah Stewart receiving Federal Women's Award from President Lyndon Johnson, 1965.

CHAPTER XIV

Sarah Elizabeth Stewart

*". . . First female graduate of Georgetown
University Medical School; pioneer in the
study of virus in cancer."*

Sarah Stewart lived through a period of great hope for a solution to cancer, since during her most active years evidence was accumulating that many of the malignancies of animals were of viral etiology. Dr. Stewart herself promoted this climate of rising expectations by her discovery, with Dr. Bernice Eddy, of the polyoma virus and her subsequent exploration of human lymphomas and other malignancies. She was internationally acclaimed for her many contributions to the field of viral oncology, a field which she pioneered with great determination. She developed an interest in viral oncology when it was an unpopular concept and she persevered despite early rejections of her proposals. The Microbiology Laboratory of the National Institutes of Health, where she worked in the late 1930s was not interested in cancer and the National Cancer Institute was not interested in viruses. She responded to the challenge by the addition of another doctorate degree, an M.D. from Georgetown University, where she was the first woman to receive a medical degree from that institution. On her return to NIH in the 1950s, armed with a medical degree, she resumed her crusade and launched the research that won her renown.

Sarah Elizabeth Stewart was born August 16, 1906, in Tecalitlan, Mexico, where her father, George Stewart, a chemical mining engineer, owned gold and silver mines. Her mother, Maria Andrade Stewart, gave the children American names—Laura, Arthur, Sarah, and Helen—which easily translated into Spanish while the family lived in Mexico. Their plan was eventually to settle in the United States, but a nearby bandit uprising forced their departure sooner than intended. Sarah was five years old when the family, abandoning their home and most of its contents, fled to Mazatlan, where they were rescued by an American warship. Arriving in San Francisco, they travelled to Oregon, where Mr. Stewart owned property in Cottage Grove. The children had been taught English in Mexico, learning from their father and from records played on an Edison phonograph. Sarah had started school in Mexico and entered second grade in Cottage Grove in 1912. However, her father's health deteriorated in Oregon and the family moved to the drier climate of New Mexico, near Las Cruces, where Sarah completed high school. She remained in New Mexico for college, graduating from New Mexico State (1927) with two bachelor's degrees, one in home economics and the other in general science.

The Early Years

After graduating from college, she taught school in the Tatum, New Mexico, high school. She soon realized that teaching was not for her and applied for fellowships to graduate school. She received offers from Michigan State University and the University of Massachusetts in Amherst, and chose the latter. There she received an M.S. degree in 1930 with a thesis on botulism.

She then returned west to be near her family, taking a position as assistant bacteriologist at the Colorado Experimental Station, a position she retained for three years. In 1933 she took up graduate studies at the University of Colorado School of Medicine in Denver, working toward a Ph.D. degree. In 1935 she visited Washington, D.C., and while there applied for a position at the National Institutes of Health (NIH). There was no position open at the time, but Dr. Ida Bengston agreed to accept Sarah Stewart as her assistant in research on botulism and other anaerobic pathogens. A position became open for Sarah Stewart the following year.

Dr. Bengston had devoted many years to research on anaerobic bacteriology and by 1936 had become interested in virology. Her work with anaerobes was turned over to Sarah Stewart when Dr. Bengston left the Washington area to engage in a study of trachoma in the state of Missouri. During the next several years Sarah Stewart published seven papers on anaerobes. All dealt with standardization of toxins and antitoxins of the gas gangrene producers, *Clostridium perfringens,* and related species and with procedures for immunization. This period at the National Institutes of Health was interrupted by Sarah's leaving on assignment to the University of Chicago, where she completed her Ph.D. requirements in 1939. On her return she continued research on anaerobes in an Office of Strategic Research and Development

(OSRD) project until 1944. During this time her interest in virology, notably viral oncology, developed to the point that she sought support at NIH for research that would test some of her own ideas and that would extend the work of others on animal tumors of proven viral etiology. It was then that she was rebuffed both by the chief of the Laboratory of Microbiology at NIH and by the director of the National Cancer Institute (NCI), who told her that she was not qualified for that type of research.

In 1944 Dr. Stewart became an instructor in bacteriology at Georgetown University School of Medicine. She was allowed to take courses in the medical school and in 1949 was awarded an M.D. degree. She interned at the United States Public Health Service Hospital on Staten Island, New York. In 1951 she returned to work at NCI as an officer in the Commissioned Corps of the United States Public Health Service (USPHS), where she later became a medical director.

A Viral Source of Cancer?

There was considerable opposition at the time to the idea of viral etiology of cancer. However, Stewart launched her research in this field against the mainstream of cancer research at the time. Her first efforts were directed toward confirming that the Gross leukemia of mice was truly of viral etiology. Her first publication on viral oncology concerned this work: "Leukemia in Mice Produced by a Filterable Agent Present in AKR Leukemic Tissues with Notes on a Sarcoma Produced by the Same Agent."[1]

She and her co-workers had found the research quite exciting but the information did not elicit much interest in the scientific community until several full-length papers were published giving details of the experiments.[2]

Live virus research was not permitted in the Baltimore Clinical Center laboratories where Dr. Stewart was stationed, so she requested permission of Dr. Victor H. Haas, director of the National Microbiological Institute, to carry on her research in the Biologics Control Laboratory, which was then part of the Microbiological Institute. He agreed to the arrangement. Stewart had several times attempted unsuccessfully to fulfill Koch's postulates with the tumor producing agent which she maintained in x-ray irradiated mice. It became obvious to her that a tissue culture laboratory was needed for multiplication of the tumor producing agent. Dr. Bernice Eddy of the Biologics Control Laboratory agreed to work with Sarah Stewart on the problem.

Thus it was that they worked out the characteristics and potentiality of this agent which was not referred to as a virus until 1959. Their paper, published in 1958, defined the "tumor agent carried in tissue culture" as separate and distinct from the Gross leukemia agent.[3] The following year the "agent" was boldly referred to as SE polyoma virus, so named for Stewart and Eddy and to distinguish the virus from a prior named polyoma virus.[4] A series of papers followed. It was discovered early on that the tumor virus behaved in tissue culture much like any of the classical viruses. In the other tumors of animal viral etiology, such as Rous Sarcoma (in the chicken), virus could not be recovered in tissue culture. Thus the success of Stewart and Eddy in cultivating the virus in embryonic mouse cell tissue cultures and increasing the yield of the virus for further study was a considerable advance, making possible exact titration of the virus, electron microscopic studies, and many other experiments.

Besides demonstrating that the polyoma virus can replicate in tissue culture, that it produces a wide variety of neoplasms in mice, and also causes tumors in hamsters, Dr. Stewart and her collaborators demonstrated over the next few years that the virus causes both cell necrosis and cell proliferation in tissue culture, that it is highly antigenic, and leads to formation of specific antibodies in infected animals whether they develop tumors or not. Uninjected animals developed antibodies but no tumors from contact with their experimentally infected litter mates, mice infected by parenteral injection also developed antibodies but, despite that, they developed tumors, and the animals becoming infected by a natural contact route remained free of overt infection. Since polyoma virus can be plaqued, i.e., causes visible cell necrosis in culture, it could be demonstrated that only one virus was involved in production of the bizarre range of tumors. This was further confirmed by specific hemagglutination, the production of a hemagglutinin also made possible the titration of virus and the titration of antibody by determination of hemagglutination inhibition.[5]

Research Gains Momentum

Stewart's research was reported in the *NIH Record*,[6] and in the lay press. *Time* magazine quoted the director of NCI, Dr. John R. Heller, as exclaiming that "the hottest thing in cancer is research on viruses as possible causes."[7] Drs. Stewart and Eddy's work with Gross leukemia virus was mentioned and it was noted that they did not get what they were looking for, they got something better, the polyoma virus. Stewart described a polyoma virus vaccine "that protects a big majority of normally susceptible animals against the polyoma virus' effects." But it was rightly pointed out that the real problem remained: applying these findings to man.

Dr. Stewart and her co-workers also worked on the Epstein-Barr virus, which causes Burkitt lymphoma. She described brain lesions in experimental animals produced with an "agent" from Burkitt tumor cultures.[8] She also described the herpes-like virus recovered from the SL_1 line mice.[9] Between 1967 and 1969 she and her co-workers published five papers defining the herpes virus of Burkitt lymphoma.

After her retirement from government service in 1970, Sarah Stewart continued her research as a professor of pathology at Georgetown University. Her research emphasis there was an extension of work started at the National Cancer Institute. Beginning in 1965 she published a series of papers dealing with Burkitt Lymphoma: tissue culture, cytogenic studies,[10] and methods of culture of this herpes-type virus and antigenic identity of the three viral lines isolated.[11]

During this same time, Stewart was investigating human tumors searching for viruses. She reported isolation of several viruses from the specimens studied. In June 1963 she presented a paper at the Symposium on Mammalian Leukemia Viruses, held at the Accademia Nazionale dei Lincei, Rome, Italy, where she had spent several months on sabbatical. In her discussion of viruses in cultures of human leukemia cells, she noted that there had been several reports of presumptive viral activity when fluids or filtrates of human tissues or tissue culture of such specimens were tested, but she pointed out the impossibility of identifying a virus recovered from mice inoculated with materials derived from human materials. It was impossible at that time to know whether a virus obtained from the inoculated mice was of human or murine origin, there being no methods for identifying, differentiating, and classifying the leukemia viruses. She suggested that it might be possible by selective and repeated passage to adapt to heterologous hosts the oncogenic viruses which form at the cell membrane and incorporate host cellular protein in forming their outer coat. It appeared to her possible that on repeated passage, the virus membrane might become more and more like that of the host cell and thus become adapted to it. Reporting on her own work, she stated that lymphomas and proliferative lung lesions had been produced in thymectomized neonatal hamsters inoculated with supernatant fluids from cultured specimens obtained from human leukemia patients. Nevertheless, she observed that the results did not give a definitive answer, a latent hamster virus might have been activated. In 1967 she reported the isolation of a myxo-type virus from two human sarcomas.[12]

Sarah Stewart was well aware of the problems encountered in oncogenic virus research with human tissue.[13] From animal studies it was evident that DNA viruses were frequently not recoverable from the tumors which they induced but that "footprints" sometimes remained which were demonstrable by immunological procedures. Many RNA tumor viruses were found to be recoverable from the natural host, such as Rous sarcoma virus from the chicken. To adapt these viruses to another host cell in tissue culture, such as hamster cells, it was necessary to grow them in the presence of cells from the natural host, in this case the chicken. Murine sarcoma virus seemed to need a helper virus as well as mouse cells to mature in hamster cell cultures. Stewart surmised that it might be possible by such techniques to adapt human oncogenic viruses to other hosts if a helper virus could be found.

From Hamsters to Humans?

She and co-workers were successful in infecting hamster brain cells in suspension culture when grown in contact with human tumor cells carrying the virus. She noted that by analogy one could expect that at least some human tumors are virus induced since the viral etiology of many animal tumors was definitely established. Stewart established a continuous cell line in culture, designated SS_5, from a lymph node biopsy of a patient with Hodgkins disease.[14] Chromosome studies were carried out with cells from the patient's bone marrow and from the lymph node biopsy before culture and after four months in continuous tissue culture. No evidence of abnormality was found. However, two types of virus-like particles were found in electron micrographs of the tissue culture cells, one a herpes-type virus, the other of different morphology. The herpes virus was separated out in monolayer cell culture (W138), where it did not replicate. The other virus caused cellular changes in the W138 cells and after some 20 passages, abundant virus became evident as extracellular particles. When the virus was introduced into human lymphocyte suspension culture, massive virus budding from the cell membrane became evident. Immunologically the virus, a paramyxovirus, was similar to the simian virus, SV5. In discussion of her findings, Dr. Stewart noted the possibility of the virus being a contaminant, but the negative control W138 cultures made this unlikely. Since various investigators had isolated viruses similar to SV5 from human tissue, she believed that the virus might well be from the original specimen obtained from the Hodgkins disease patient.

In her published work[15] on the virus obtained from human leukemia tissue, she noted that it was not possible with viruses from human tumors to fulfill Koch's postulates; even though the virus could be grown in tissue culture, it could not be injected into humans as a test of the virus's capacity to produce leukemia in humans. It simply was not an ethical consideration. She had obtained proliferative foci in some tissue cultures and injected the material into thymectomized hamsters and mice, some of which did develop tumors. But this result could not be considered a definitive answer.

In 1968 she reported[16] that a virus recovered from a freshly established Burkitt lymphoma culture, known to carry a herpes-type virus, had been serially passaged in hamsters by intracerebral inoculation through 60 passages. She found that similar, long-term tissue cultures initiated from the same lymphoma specimen were not infective by intracerebral inoculation of hamsters. However, when cells from such cultures were grown in contact with minced hamster brain in suspension shaker cultures and cells from these cultures were inoculated into newborn thymectomized hamsters, it was possible to demonstrate infectivity. Cultures of hamster brain alone injected into thymectomized litter mates were negative. Stewart also reported the establishment of virus in hamsters from three different lymphoma lines passaged in weanling hamsters with cells from brain extract from infected animals. All three lines produced the same syndrome in the central nervous system. By *in vivo* neutralization tests, it was shown that all three were antigenically identical. Then a human lymphoblast suspension culture was infected with hamster-brain passage virus in its sixtieth passage in hamsters and the infecting virus was shown to be morphologically and antigenically identical to the herpes-type virus of Burkitt lymphoma. Control cultures of human lymphoblasts were shown to be virus free.

A Breakthrough

Sarah Stewart's last published work dealt with a virus isolated from a human sarcoma. It was first reported in the *Journal of the National Cancer Institute*,[17] later in *Science*,[18] as a C-type virus budding from the cell membrane in tissue culture. It was further characterized in a subsequent publication[19] in which she observed that there was unquestionable evidence that oncornaviruses of the C-type, which by definition bud only from the plasma membrane and in which the mature particles have a centrally located nucleoid, are the agents of avian, murine, feline, and hamster lymphomas and sarcomas. It appeared to her only reasonable to believe that C-type viruses might also play a role in human neoplasia. She also pointed out that there had been several earlier reports by others of finding what appeared to be true C-type viruses in tissues derived from human tumors. In three cases short-term tissue cultures had been established.

Referring to her own research, she described the virus (isolated from a rhabdomyosarcoma from a female patient) which she had established in tissue culture where its development could be observed. It was found to be somewhat unusual in development, first becoming evident in electron micrographs as a doughnut-shaped body within the cisternae of the endoplasmic reticulum. A similar virus had been seen in tissue sections from the original sarcoma. In tissue culture the virus was soon "lost"; it could not be passaged from tissue culture nor found in electron micrographs. However, treatment of the tissue culture with 5-iododeoxyuridine, followed by treatment with dimethylsulfoxide (5-IdU/DMSO), resulted in production of mature virus from culture, 17 months after the culture was initiated. The development of this virus could then be observed and it too was found to be somewhat unusual. In electron micrographs the virus was first seen as a doughnut within the cisternae of the endoplasmic reticulum. It later developed a nucleoid as a mature virus which was released from the cell by budding from the cell membrane. The 5-IdU/DMSO treatment was applied to tissue cultures of murine plasma cell virus which seldom matured past the doughnut body. Following such treatment, abundant mature murine virus was produced in tissue culture. Stewart then applied the technique to another tissue culture obtained from a male adenocarcinoma of the lung. Following treatment (5-IdU/DMSO), two types of viruses were produced. Chromosome analysis showed the cells to be human male in the cultured adenocarcinoma and human female in the cultures from the sarcoma. In the sarcoma-derived tissue culture, the cells were transformed after about two months, growing out as fibroblasts. The virus was shown to have the mammalian group-specific antigen (gs-3) that reacts with antibody against gs-3 antigen of murine leukemia; the virus, however, did not contain gs-1 antigen of mouse, cat, rat or hamster virus, which suggested the possibility of the virus being of human origin.

This last paper of Sarah Stewart's was presented by one of the co-authors, George Kasnic, Jr.; Dr. Stewart had become too ill with cancer to present the report. She moved to Florida with her mother, who had for many years lived and travelled with her, to be near her sisters, her brother having died some years before from cancer. Sarah Stewart died at age 70 in New Smyrna Beach, Florida, on November 27, 1976.

Sarah Stewart's research on polyoma virus won almost immediate acclaim. She was invited to speak here and abroad. In 1962 she was awarded an honorary doctor of laws degree by her alma mater, New Mexico State University. In the following year she was awarded the Lenghi Prize, presented to her in Rome, by the president of Italy, Antonio Segni, on behalf of the National Academy of Lincei of Rome. The award came at the end of the six months' sabbatical with D. Tavari at the National Academy. The prize, two million lire (then about $3,000) was given biennially to an investigator who had made important scientific contributions in the field of virology. Dr. Stewart, internationally recognized for her relationship to cancer viruses, won recognition for her research on the polyoma virus which she (and Dr. Eddy) isolated and characterized.

The following year, 1964, Stewart received the Research Award from the James Ewing Society. In the same year the Philadelphia Variety Club selected Sarah Stewart to receive the Heart Award, which is bestowed each year on one who is deemed to have served the welfare of mankind most notably. Dr. Stewart, medical director in the Commissioned Corps of the USPHS, was honored for "research studies of the viral etiology of neoplasms." She was also selected by Georgetown University for its "Medical Men of Georgetown" honor roll in 1964. In 1965 she was elected to Alpha Omega Alpha, an honorary medical fraternity. That year she also received the Federal Woman's Award from President Lyndon Johnson. "Had she been any less the brilliant, innovative, original, industrious, dedicated and resolute pioneer, her career would never have gotten off the ground, never have gotten started."[20]

Hope for the Future

Sarah Stewart lived through a period of great hope and expectation. Her success with the polyoma virus contributed to a belief that a breakthrough on human cancer was imminent. Her research stimulated the belief that all human malignancies would be found to have a viral etiology and thus be more susceptible to prevention and treatment. She continued for as long as she was able to search for such agents in human cancer tissue, until she succumbed to the disease. Sarah Stewart was celebrated during her lifetime in interviews and photographs in newspapers and magazines. All praised her research discoveries.

To Sarah Stewart, research was never lonely. It was exciting, exhilarating. Her dedication to research, to pursuit of a specific goal, led to new concepts and set the course for much research which followed. She also loved music and nature. She built a cottage in Drumpoint, Maryland, along the Chesapeake Bay, where she could be close to nature.

She was fortunate in many ways. Her work with oncogenic viruses of animals introduced a new host parasite system for study but her success did not come by accident. She had suffered rejection time and again during the five years or more when she tried to interest several laboratory directors in her proposals for oncogenic virus research. The fortuitous arrangement made to work in Dr. Bernice Eddy's laboratory happened at a most auspicious time, just after Gross had described a new virus causing mouse leukemia.[21] Their simple confirmatory test yielded the SE polyoma virus and all the fruitful research which followed.

Highly motivated to self improvement, Sarah Stewart developed her own career, promoted her own opportunities, and attained a large measure of success. With abundant reason for satisfaction in her accomplishments, she never rested on her laurels but continued her research almost to the end of her life.

CHAPTER XV

Margaret Pittman

*". . . Crusader in whooping cough vaccine
production; in the forefront to standardize
vaccines worldwide."*

A certain risk was acceptable in the first vaccines. The chance of being
saved from certain death portended by rabies or from the permanent disfig-
urement of smallpox was worth taking a risk. Disturbing as the rare misfor-
tunes from the vaccine might be, the probability for the victim was much
worse without the vaccine. The first consideration was specificity and effectiveness, that a vaccine be protective against the target disease. Avoidance of
toxicity was always a requirement, but idiosyncrasies of the individual recipients made it difficult. Dr. Margaret Pittman in the Bureau of Biologics of the
National Institutes of Health (later a division of the Food and Drug Administration) was for most of her research career involved in production, testing,
and standardization for Vaccines to prevent typhoid, cholera, and pertussis
(whooping cough). As emphasis shifted from efficacy to the elimination of all
toxicity in vaccines, Dr. Pittman was at the forefront in these investigations
both at home and abroad.

An Early Interest in Medicine

Margaret Pittman was born in 1901 in Prairie Grove, Arkansas, into a family of
considerable talent and achievement. One of her more illustrious antecedents

was Cyrus Hall McCormick, the inventor of the reaper. Her father, James Pittman, was a physician whose family had lived in the vicinity of Prairie Grove since before the Civil War. He obtained his medical training in St. Louis, then moved with his bride, Virginia Alice (Jennie) McCormick, to McAllen, Oklahoma, in 1898. Because he contracted malaria there, he and his wife returned after a year to Prairie Grove, where he set up practice in the town with three other physicians, one, Dr. E. G. McCormick, his wife's brother. Around 1908 the family moved to Cincinnati, Arkansas, a former Indian trading center, 16 miles from Prairie Grove. His practice was typical of the horse and buggy country doctor; calls were made day or night without thought of payment, which was often in-kind. Young Margaret and her sister Helen, a year older, assisted in administering anesthesia to patients with fractured bones.

Dr. and Mrs. Pittman were leaders in the church and cultural activities of the community which had one store, a blacksmith shop, a barber shop, a post office, and a two-room rural school (four grades per room). Dr. James Pittman died young as a consequence of infection following an appendectomy. On his deathbed he requested that the daughters (then 15–20 years of age) be sent to Hendrix College, a Methodist institution in Conway, Arkansas. The University of Arkansas in Fayetteville was closer, but Dr. Pittman had attended the university and considered its moral standards not high enough for his children. His death left his wife and three children in very modest circumstances. Being resourceful, determined, and industrious, Mrs. Pittman managed to support the children and to see them all graduate from college. Margaret Pittman remembers this period of her life as a busy, pleasant time. Though the family had very limited financial resources, she never felt deprived. She had completed high school in three years in Prairie Grove, while living with her grandparents. Then she spent two years at an academy in nearby Silasm Springs, before going to Hendrix College, where boys outnumbered girls ten to one. She majored in mathematics and biology at Hendrix and won the mathematics medal. She graduated *magna cum laude* in 1923. During their college years, the children returned home for the summer (a journey of 300 miles that required two days in a cross-front Ford). They helped their mother raise and can vegetables and fruit. In the fall two barrels of canned food along with many pounds of dried navy beans were shipped to Conway for their use.

Margaret's sister Helen taught school for a few years before taking up a career in nursing. After a number of years as a public health nurse in St. Louis and Houston, she was appointed chairman of the Department of Nursing at Sacred Heart Dominican College in Houston, Texas, where she served until she retired at age 75. Margaret's brother James became a physician and surgeon. He served as chief of the surgical staff of Herman Hospital, Texas Medical Center, Houston, for many years before retiring at age 65.

After graduation from Hendrix College, Margaret Pittman taught science, Spanish, and other subjects at the Girls' Academy of Galloway College in Searcy, Arkansas. Starting as an instructor at a salary of $900 a year, she became principal of the academy in her second year there. Her salary as principal was $1,200 a year. From these two years of teaching Margaret saved $600 to attend the University of Chicago to obtain a master's degree in bacteriology, preparatory to medical laboratory work. This was second best to a medical degree, which was not feasible for financial reasons. At that time (1925), bacteriology was still a young field and so few courses were taught that it was possible to complete work for the M.S. degree in 12 months. During that year (1925–1926) Margaret augmented her savings with babysitting. Her mentor, Dr. I. S. Falk, encouraged her to continue studying for her doctorate and, since she was offered a fellowship that provided $75 per month, she was able to do so. From 1926 to 1928 she held a research fellowship from the Influenza Commission of the Metropolitan Life Insurance Company. At this time the etiology of influenza had not yet been determined.

The Beginning of a Research Career

In the fall of 1928, Dr. Rufus Cole of the Rockefeller Institute, in his search for an assistant, wrote to Dr. C. P. Miller at the University of Chicago asking for a recommendation. Dr. Miller recommended Margaret Pittman. Although she had not completed the writing of her Ph.D. dissertation, she left Chicago to work with Rufus Cole at the hospital of the Rockefeller Institute for Medical Research as a research scientist. She completed the writing of her dissertation at night while working at the institute. During the summer vacation of 1929 she returned to the University of Chicago, took her final examinations, and received the Ph.D. degree.

Her thesis research had dealt with pathogenesis of pneumococcus pneumonia, and her first two publications, with I. S. Falk, were on this subject. The first dealt with virulence of the organism,[1] the second with pathology of pneumococcus infections in mice.[2]

At the Rockefeller Institute she was assigned the project, "Does *Hemophilus influenzae* cause influenza?," one of the perplexing problems of the time. While searching for the best approach to the problem, she also studied the bactericidal activity of normal animal serum. In order to facilitate counting of the Hemophilus colonies, she modified the culture medium (Levinthal's chocolate agar) by filtration, making it transparent. In her first test with this new medium, she detected two types of colonies, one type so large she questioned whether it was a contaminant or whether there might be two colonial forms of *H. influenzae*. The latter proved to be the case, and engendered much excitement, for this was the first time that a strain of *H. influenzae* had been shown to be encapsulated, 35 years after Pfeiffer had isolated the organism during the pandemic of 1898. The strains associated with meningitis were found to be encapsulated, as were the organisms of serological type *b*. This offered hope that the type-specific antiserum might be effective in treating *H. influenzae* meningitis, which to that time was 99 percent fatal. With the assistance of a horse named Browny, which she herself inoculated, Pittman obtained blood which was then processed for antiserum.

Infants and young children with *H. influenzae* meningitis treated with the antiserum showed marked improvement initially, but most of them relapsed and died. This work became the basis for the preparation and use of a much more effective rabbit serum prepared sometime later by Hattie Alexander. Pittman noted in her published paper[3] that the antiserum sterilized the spinal fluid but did not eliminate the disease. Earlier, she had collected blood for culture from patients in the hospital and had isolated and serologically differentiated six distinct types of *H. influenzae* designated *a* through *f*. This research, published in 1931,[4] elicited worldwide attention and gained Margaret Pittman an international reputation before she was 30 years old.

Her service at Rockefeller Institute ended in 1934. At that time her salary was $2,500 per year. The Depression gripped the country and retrenchment was the order of the day. Taking a salary cut, she accepted a position at the New York State Department of Health Laboratories, where she prepared biologics and engaged in laboratory diagnoses for a year and a half. In 1936 she entered federal service at the National Institutes of Health as a P3 (equivalent to a modern day GS9), at the fine salary of $3,200 a year. It was her good fortune that President Roosevelt in that year started Social Security, producing one of the first great expansions of the government.

The Years at NIH

At the National Institutes of Health (NIH), then located at 23rd Street, N.W., in Washington, D.C., Pittman first worked with Sara E. Branham, one of her teachers at the University of Chicago, on a potency assay of antimeningococcus serum, developing standards for the serum. With the use of Petroff's observation that halos developed on serum plates, Pittman found that the precipitin reaction around colonies on immune serum agar plates was directly correlated with the potency assay of each lot of antiserum as shown by a mouse protection test. Although this work was published, it was forgotten after the introduction of sulfonamides and antibiotics. Later the phenomenon was described by Orjan Ouchterlony.[5]

From vitro tests, Branham and Pittman proceeded to mouse protection tests with titered antimeningococcus serum. With this test they introduced the first statistical method, the Reed Münch test, into biologics testing. Pittman found her mathematical background to be good training for evaluation of statistical methods which soon came into general use and now serve as a foundation for biologics testing. The results of the mouse protection test were published with Branham and others in 1938.[6] Later reports appeared in 1940, 1941, and 1943.[7]

When in 1941 NIH moved from Washington, D.C., to its current site in Bethesda, Maryland, Margaret Pittman acquired her own research laboratory and started to take up her research on *H. influenzae* once more. However, World War II intervened and she was soon caught up in emergency problems of the times: the problems of contamination and pyrogenicity of blood and blood products, identification of the bacteria and determination of their relation to pyrogenicity, as well as collaboration in the development of standards for pyrogen testing.

Up to this time chills and fever were not an uncommon sequel to serum therapy in patients. Sterility tests of biologics were incubated only at 37°C. In studying this problem, Pittman, with cooperation of manufacturers of culture media, investigated the thioglycolate medium then in use. She found that the methylene blue oxidation-reduction indicator in the medium inhibited growth of some organisms found as contaminants in blood and blood products. The formula for the medium was revised by substitution of reasurin as the indicator and by addition of cystine to better support growth of anaerobes.[8]

In 1945 her publication (with T. F. Probey) on "The Pyrogenicity of Bacterial Contaminants Found in Biologic Products" appeared.[9] Later she published results of a study of bacteria implicated in transfusion reactions and of bacteria isolated from blood products, serum, and albumin.[10] At that time at least 11 fatal transfusion reactions had been recorded in the literature, in addition to many severe reactions caused by bacteria. During World War II Pittman received many cultures of bacteria isolated at some stage of processing plasma and albumin. Altogether she studied 98 cultures obtained from blood and blood products and 11 from vaccines and antigens. She identified a variety of bacteria from the plasma and albumin, micrococci predominating. From the vaccines and antigens she found only spore formers and Gram negative rods. But the organisms cultured from blood and serum, all of which had induced transfusion reactions, were all Gram negative rods, either coli-aerogenes group or pseudomonads. Many of these Gram negative organisms failed to grow at 37°C but grew luxuriantly at temperatures ranging from 2.5°C to 10°C. Changes in the test medium and reduction of the incubation temperature were recommended, but the changes were slow in being adopted.

A Focus on Pertussis

During this same period Pittman was asked to work on a pertussis vaccine. Beginning in 1944 emphasis was placed on the development of a standard of potency for a pertussis vaccine. Early advancement of the assay was due to the finding by Dr. John F. Norton of Upjohn Company, a former professor of Pittman's at the University of Chicago, that mice could be infected intracerebrally with *Bordetella pertussis* and that they could be protected by pertussis vaccine. Pittman and Pearl Kendrick, a pioneer in the development of effective pertussis vaccine, were notified. The two laboratories, at NIH and the Michigan State Laboratory, kept in contact during the development of standards for the vaccine, and by 1949 the United States standards for pertussis vaccine went into effect.

In the meantime Pittman found that the Reed Münch method for calculating the 50 percent preventive endpoint of a vaccine was not satisfactory. The Wilson-Worcester method, comparable to the probit statistical method was found preferable.[11] Although limited to specific application, the method continues to have worldwide use where computers are not available.

As the potency of the vaccine improved during the period of development of standards, physicians' confidence in the vaccine increased and more and more children were vaccinated. During the period 1945 to 1954 there was a ten-fold drop in mortality from whooping cough (pertussis) in the United States.[12] However, the safety of the vaccine did not present as bright a picture as did its potency in protection against pertussis. During the 1950s and 1960s further requirements were developed for greater safety of the vaccine, e.g., the mouse weight gain test.[13] Late neurological sequelae to the vaccine were found to be of the same nature as those which sometimes followed the disease itself but the benefit-to-risk ratio of the vaccine enormously favored it.[14] Pittman estimated that had the 1940–1944 pertussis rate of 84.7 deaths per 10,000 under one year of age continued, there would be more than 3,000 deaths annually and several hundred children left mentally retarded or incompetent.[15] She estimated the incidence of fatal encephalopathy following pertussis vaccine at one in five to ten million injections.[16]

Work on Cholera

Margaret Pittman was also involved with the Cholera Research Laboratory in Dacca, East Pakistan (Bangladesh). This was a Southeast Asia Treaty Organization (SEATO) project headed by Joseph E. Smadel, then an associate director of NIH. He was the principal organizer and leader until his death in the mid 1960s. Pittman and her colleague, John C. Feeley, were associated with the project from the design of the laboratories and the selection of the first equipment. After Smadel's death, Pittman served as NIH project director of the Cholera Research Laboratory for about five years. Her special interest in the cholera studies was the relation of laboratory potency assay to efficacy of the vaccine. Eventually it was shown that the mouse potency assay of the cholera vaccine was directly related to the effectiveness of the vaccine in field trials.[17]

Pittman served as consultant to the World Health Organization (WHO) in the formulation of the proposed requirement for cholera vaccine. After retirement she again served as a consultant to WHO in Cairo, Egypt, and Madrid, spending three months in each place during 1971–1972.

Pittman's research on neonatal tetanus immunization in New Guinea was an extension of Schofield's work demonstrating that immunization of pregnant women in New Guinea with three doses of tetanus toxoid protected newborns in rural areas where they were delivered unaided and often left for some time on the bare ground. Pittman and her collaborators, Carolyn Hardegree, M. F. Barile and Frank Schofield, worked out the standards for an adjuvant toxoid which was effective in a single injection.[18]

During the 1960s WHO conducted field trials of typhoid vaccine. Pittman was invited to participate in the comparative laboratory assays of the vaccines. Twenty-one laboratories participated in the study. This provided an opportunity for her to evaluate the U.S. reference typhoid vaccine along with the field trial vaccine.[19] This study led to the establishment of the United States standards for typhoid fever vaccine and to the collaborative investigations by Pittman and her colleagues of the importance of the Vi antigen in human immunity. It had been known since 1934 that the presence of the Vi antigen correlated with the virulence of the typhoid organism *(Salmonella typhi),*[20] but the role of the Vi antigen in producing immunity against typhoid and its influence on assay of vaccine potency in laboratory animals was not well delineated. Pittman, along with her colleagues Wong and Feeley, determined, using a Vi degrading-enzyme isolated from *Bacillus sphaericus,* that the protective activity of typhoid vaccine for mice was due to a combination of Vi antigen and other factors and the Vi antigen was a major factor in protection of animals vaccinated intraperitoneally, other routes being less critical.[21]

A Continuing Commitment to Pertussis

Despite these diversions into other fields, Pittman steadfastly pursued her research on pertussis. The report that pertussis vaccine uniquely sensitized mice to histamine[22] was of particular interest to Pittman as possibly being related to the cause of vaccine reactions and the severity of whooping cough. Among her early studies of the phenomenon, Pittman noted that the alum adjuvant influenced toxicity and the strain of mouse used for testing was also critical. She pointed out that there was no information on the correlation of laboratory assay results with untoward reactions in children. During the early 1950s she reported at the VI Congresso di Microbiologia, in Rome on the unreliability of standards based solely on the number of organisms or on turbidity of the vaccine.[23] She cautioned against the use of extremely high numbers of organisms (ten times ten to the tenth power or more) with high potency because of marked reactions in the recipients. The United States standard, by setting an upper limit of potency units and number of organisms as well as the total human immunizing dose (three single doses), had lessened the toxicity hazard. Pittman found that with living *B. pertussis* organisms, the maximum sensitization in mice was reached in ten to 15 days and persisted for several weeks after the bacteria could no longer be recovered from the lungs. She pointed out the parallelism between the course of sensitization in mice infected by the respiratory route and the time of onset and duration of paroxysmal coughing in the child suffering from pertussis.[24]

Maria G. Stronk, an American Association of University Women fellow from Holland working in Pittman's laboratory, also observed that the histamine sensitivity in mice resulting from an injection of pertussis vaccine was associated with hypoglycemia. Pittman and others had shown earlier that the genetic makeup of the mice significantly influences the capacity to be sensitized to histamine by pertussis vaccine. It was found that this phenomenon is related to the immune response of the host and is not limited to pertussis vaccine but can also be elicited by tetanus toxoid. Hence, a study was initiated with Manclark and others to selectively breed a "standard" mouse from the NIH-BS strain which Pittman had used since 1943 in her studies for the control tests for pertussis vaccine. The resultant strains (HSFS/N and HSFR/N) proved to be genetically more uniform with predictable characteristics, easily immunized, and showing low variability in response to pertussis vaccine.[25]

Taxonomy of the organisms she was working with always interested Pittman. Some of her early work with *H. influenzae* was concerned with differentiation of strains and with identification of *H. aegyptius.* She contributed the section on Hemophilus in *Bergey's Manual of Determinitive Bacteriology* for the fifth (1939) and sixth (1948) editions. By the time the seventh edition was published (1957), the whooping cough agent had been placed in a new genus, Bordetella. Thus for the seventh and eighth (1978) editions of the *Manual,* Pittman contributed the sections on both Bordetella and Hemophilus. She contributed to chapter 14, on whooping cough and chapter 15, on hemophilus infections in *Diagnostic Procedures and Reagents* (fourth edition).[26] She also contributed a chapter on "Bordetella Pertussis" to Mudd's *Infectious Agents and Host Reactions.*[27] She has a paper on pertussis vaccine testing in the *Proceedings of the Round Table Conference on Pertussis,* Bilthoven, Holland, 1969.[28]

Professional Honors

During these very active years, Margaret Pittman served several professional societies in a number of capacities: American Academy of Microbiology, Board of Governors, 1963–1969; American Society of Microbiology, councilor, 1955–1956 and 1958–1960 and president, Washington Branch, 1949–1950. She is a diplomate of the American Board of Microbiology, and in 1976, was made an honorary member of the Society. She has served on a number of committees of the Washington Academy of Science and become their first woman president in 1955. As president of the academy she was instrumental in establishing the Washington Joint Board on Science Education, which brings together area scientific and engineering groups for the promotion of science talent and education.

Pittman has served as a delegate to international congresses and as a member of a number of special boards and commissions. In 1950 she was a delegate to the Fifth International Microbiology Congress in Rio de Janeiro, she participated in the conference on whooping cough at the International Children's Center in Paris in 1957, and she was a member of two WHO study groups, both held in Geneva, Switzerland, for the formulation of International Recommended Requirements for Biological Substances: cholera and yellow fever vaccine in 1958 and sterility in 1959. She also served WHO as consultant at the Biological Standardization Conference on Pertussis Vaccine in 1962, also in Geneva. Pittman participated in the Conference on Whooping Cough held in Prague in 1962 and a similar conference in Utrecht in 1969. In 1962, she was made a member of the NIH Cholera Advisory Committee and in the same year a member of the Panel of Expert Consultants to the Technical Committee for Pakistan-SEATO Cholera Research Laboratory, Dacca. She organized and participated in the Pertussis Vaccine Symposium sponsored by NIH's Division of Biological Standards (DBS) in 1963. She served on the Armed Forces Epidemiological Board, Commission on Immunization, as an associate member from 1967 to 1972 and was a member of the United States Pharmacopoeia Advisory Panel on Sterility Tests and Standardization Procedures (1967–1970) and on Biological Indicators (1970–1973). During the same period, 1967–1970, she was a guest lecturer at Howard University College of Medicine in Washington, D.C.

After her retirement in January 1971, Margaret Pittman remained, by invitation, a guest worker in DBS, later Bureau of Biologics of the Food and Drug Administration. Freedom from administrative responsibilities opened opportunities for her to serve as consultant to the Board of Directors of Connaught Laboratories, Ltd., Toronto, Canada; and from December 1974 to March 1975, she was a consultant to the State Institute for Serum and Vaccine, Razi, Teheran, Iran. She extended her bibliography from 72 publications at the time of retirement by more than 20 papers. Some were on backlog data, others developed during visits to foreign countries. Probably the most important papers are those that deal with the hypothesis that pertussis toxin (a "true exotoxin, the histamine sensitizing factor") is the cause of the harmful effects and prolonged immunity of whooping cough[29] and the paper dealing with the pathophysiological reactions of the mouse infected with *B. pertussis* by the intranasal route.[30]

These two papers were the culmination of her work at the University of Glasgow, Scotland, where she was a visiting scientist and consultant. The research work was carried out in collaboration with Professor A. C. Wardlaw, chairman, Department of Microbiology; five graduate students; and Brian L. Furman, pharmacologist at the University of Strathclyde, Glasgow.

A profusion of honors has been bestowed upon Margaret Pittman, not the least of which is the Federal Woman's Award, which she received in 1970. However, the honors started early with the Hogan Mathematical Medal in 1922 at Hendrix College. As a graduate student she was elected to Sigma Xi, a graduate student equivalent of Phi Beta Kappa. Hendrix College, her alma mater, awarded her an honorary LL.D. in 1954. She has been listed in *American Men (and Women) of Science* since 1936 and was first listed in *Who's Who* in 1960. In 1963 she received a Superior Service Award from the Department of Health, Education and Welfare (DHEW) for ". . . notable contributions to the understanding of the relationship between the effectiveness of bacterial vaccines in man and their potency as determined by laboratory tests." The distinguished Service Award from DHEW was presented to her in 1967 for ". . . pioneering contributions to standardization and testing of vaccines against infectious disease which have enhanced preventive medicine and reflected credit on the Federal Service."

The Federal Woman's Award cites ". . . her unique achievements in the development of safe and effective vaccines and other immunizing agents of bacterial origin." It further states, "In her 34 years with the National Institutes of Health she has distinguished herself by her significant contributions to the standardization of vaccines for whooping cough, cholera, typhoid, and other human illnesses, as well as allergies. As Chief of the Laboratory of Bacterial Products, her ability to identify problems, stimulate research and evaluate results have made her an unusually effective leader and her extensive collaboration with national and international organizations in research and in the establishment of international standards have been of immeasurable benefit to the health of the people of the United States and of other countries."

In 1973 Pittman received the Professional Achievement Award from the University of Chicago Alumni Association; she was made honorary member of Sigma Delta Epsilon, Graduate Women in Science, in 1974, and honorary member of the American Society for Microbiology in 1976.

A Varied Life

These well deserved tributes speak to only one side of Margaret Pittman, the professional side. She is a great devotee of horticulture and a travel enthusiast. She had ample opportunity in official capacity to see the world and some of these trips were extended for pleasure, for example: from an official visit to Stockholm, she took the opportunity to visit the North Cape. In the interest of cholera she visited Bangkok, Taiwan, Calcutta, Bombay, and the Philippines. After attending the International Microbiological Congress in Rio de Janeiro (1950), she visited most of the countries of South America. Following professional visits to Iran, she made side trips to Teheran, Isfahan, and Shiraz, memorable for the rugs she acquired. In a later trip she travelled to the Abadan area and sites of the Elamite civilization, including Susa (Sushan), then under excavation.

Margaret Pittman has long been active in the Mount Vernon United Methodist Church of Washington, D.C., working with its welfare group, among others, and while chairman of the church finance committee formulated successful plans for paying off a $200,000 debt. She has been a member of the Board of Trustees of this church and chaired the Pastor Parish Relations Committee. She is also a member of the Board of Directors of the Downtown Geriatrics Day Care Center.

She admits to no discrimination as a woman and her career pattern supports that assertion. She is impatient with women who expect too much too soon with too little preparation. She herself never asked for a promotion. She was, she says, fortunate in being at the right place at the right time and she credits Dr. Roderick Murray, the first director of the Division of Biologics Standards at NIH, for many of her opportunities. This division was created by an Act of Congress after the poliomyelitis vaccine catastrophe which made evident the deficiency in support for the control of biologics. Murray persuaded Margaret Pittman to take over as chief of the Laboratory of Bacterial

Products at DBS. At the time she was little inclined to diminish her research for administrative duties; however, it opened new vistas for her and won her many honors.

Margaret Pittman praises her staff for their high *esprit de corps* and their outstanding research contributions to the standardization of bacterial and allergenic products. She has been an ideal and a great model for many young people whom she has assisted and guided. A woman of great heart, she has friends around the world.

Westcoast, Midlands, and Elsewhere

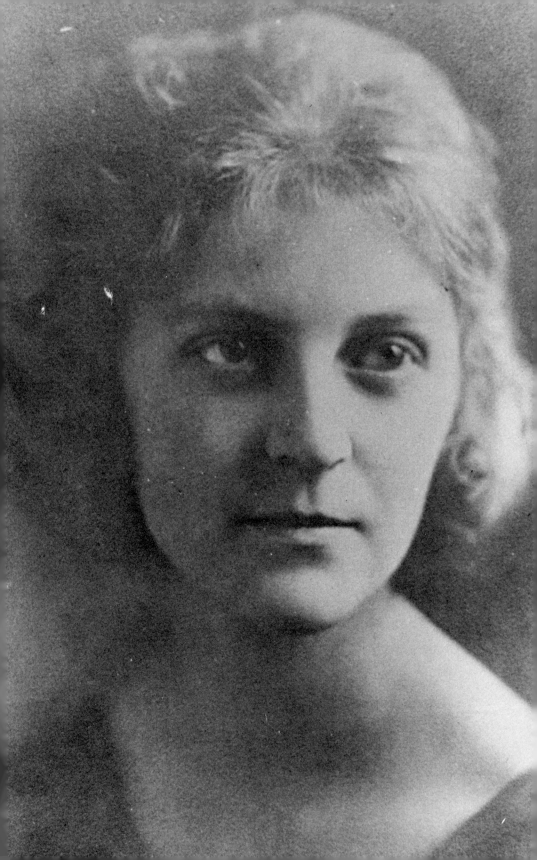

CHAPTER XVI

Bernice Ulah Eddie

". . . Masterly research in arthropod-borne diseases; direction of decades of work by a number of women scientists at Hooper Laboratory."

Man's best friends can sometimes become his worst enemies. The friendly family dog with rabies will at least show suspicious behavior. Not all pets do. Parakeets, one-time favorites among bird fanciers, can carry psittacosis yet show no symptoms. The disease is readily transmissible to humans and resulted in a problem of considerable significance at one time. Dr. Bernice Eddie, at the George Williams Hooper Foundation in San Francisco, California, investigated this disease and many others common to man and animals. She helped to establish that the dread disease plague was carried by wild rodents in California, as well as by squirrels. Her studies extended to wild seals, canary birds, and arthropods, all in working out the transmission cycle from animals to humans.

    Bernice Ulah Eddie was born in 1903 at San Francisco and brought up near Nevada City, California, where her father, Hamilton Eddie was a mining engineer. He had come there from Scotland. Her mother, Louise Marcelin, of French extraction, was educated in Paris. After Mr. Eddie's death following a mine accident, the family moved to San Francisco. Bernice and her older sister, Marceline, had learned about nature from their father and acquired a love of culture, music, and the arts from their mother. Bernice attended Lowell High School in San Francisco and after graduation continued her education at the University of California in Berkeley, traveling each way by ferry from San Francisco. In 1922 she received a B.A. degree and in 1923 a master of public health degree. Many years later, 1941–1942, Eddie interrupted her career to take a doctor of public health degree with Dr. Thomas Francis, director of the Virus Laboratory at the University of Michigan.

After receiving the masters' degree, Eddie worked in the bacteriology laboratory of the Department of Public Health in Santa Barbara, California, until 1926, when she came to the Department of Bacteriology at the San Francisco Medical Center. In 1930 she joined the staff of the Hooper Foundation for Medical Research. During the next 14 years, Eddie held increasingly more responsible positions at Hooper, becoming an instructor in research medicine in 1937, a position she still held when she left to study for her doctorate. After receiving her degree, she returned to Hooper Laboratory, where in 1945 she was named lecturer in public health at the University of California in Berkeley, in addition to her laboratory responsibilities. The following year she was made assistant professor of research medicine, as well as assistant director of the Hooper Foundation Laboratory, a position she retained to the end of her career. In 1948 she became associate professor of research medicine and, in 1964, professor of experimental pathology. During 1967 she served as acting director of the Hooper Foundation. She continued her scientific career working with K. F. Meyer until his retirement in 1954. Since Meyer continued in active emeritus status for nearly 20 years, Eddie truly worked with him until the end of her life in June 1969.

The Start of a Mentorship

She learned a great deal from K. F. Meyer, who gave her increasing responsibility. During the long periods when he was away from the laboratory, it was Eddie who supervised the graduate students, carried on the research, and devised diagnostic tests in all sorts of problem areas which came to the Hooper Laboratory from all parts of California and beyond. Meyer was demanding but respectful of Eddie, sometimes addressing her as "most venerable lady." Her devotion to her work exceeded his demands. She was notorious for the long hours she spent in the laboratory. In time she became a close friend of K. F. Meyer's family.

Eddie was not an absolutist. She tended to see both sides of questions and to compromise. Consequently, she sometimes appeared indecisive. With regard to research, she was firm and decisive once she knew what she wanted to do. She was very loyal to Meyer, yet always a very private person.

Her research interests were broad but principally related to virology. Much of her early work concerned psittacosis (later ornithosis) to which she made some of her most important contributions. In 1933 Meyer and Eddie began a series of reports on psittacosis in birds and man. There had been epidemics of the disease in South America and Europe with high fatality rates. This caused concern among public health officials and led to the epidemiologic surveys and research that were to engage Eddie for many years. With quarantine against South American psittacine birds, efforts were made to replace these avian pets with Australian birds, the so-called shell parakeets, but it was soon found that these birds also were infected.[1]

Though there had been no evidence of human infections associated with the Australian parakeets, they were not considered a safe replacement. It appeared that the unhappy conditions of transit not infrequently incited a full-blown infection in birds apparently healthy in their native habitat. A survey of other birds and some animals demonstrated that several of them carried the infecting organism, either in a latent form or as an active infection. These included canaries, butterfly finches, conures, sparrows, and some mice. These findings were published in a series of articles in the Proceedings of the Society for Experimental Biology and Medicine for 1933. A description of cytological studies of the virus in the sparrow was published in 1935,[2] and a report of the successful ultrafiltration of the virus in 1937.[3] Articles were also published to inform public health officials and medical practitioners about control and diagnosis of psittacosis.[4] Eddie was successful in developing a complement fixation test for diagnosis of latent avian psittacosis using tissue-culture antigens, work that was published in 1939.[5]

When in 1941–1942 Eddie went to Michigan to obtain her doctorate with Francis, she worked on the psittacosis problem for her thesis research, publishing with Francis the results of a survey of game birds of Michigan.[6] This survey revealed infection in pigeons, turkeys, and chickens, but not among the wild fowl tested. After her return to Hooper Laboratory she continued the search for vectors and implicated canaries, finches, and ducks as susceptible to infection. Sylvatic infection was also revealed in Pinon mice, opossums, muskrats, and woodrats. Some years later Eddie found psittacosis organisms in fur seals. She also isolated the organisms from some ectoparasites, turkey mites, and chicken lice.[7]

The Search for a Cure

A vaccine was developed to protect individuals at high risk such as laboratory personnel.[8] Vaccinated birds appeared to be immune to challenge with large doses of psittacosis organisms, but, on autopsy, their cultured tissues were found to contain live organisms. Efforts were then made to cure the infected birds. Penicillin and aureomycin were first among antibiotics to be tried in experimental infections. These antibiotics had been successfully used in treatment of human cases, but in parakeets, which were carriers of the organisms, the intracellular organisms were not reached; the infection was not cleared.[9] With the advent of the tetracyclines the disease became less menacing. Infections in birds could be pretty well controlled[10] and human infections, if they occurred, could be abated and successfully treated.

When it became evident that the disease was not limited to psittacine birds, the name ornithosis was proposed for the syndrome. The etiologic agent also underwent a series of name changes as it became better characterized, from psittacosis virus to Miyagawanella, a genus name that Meyer and Eddie protested as being historically inappropriate, to Bedsonia and later to Chlamydia. Careful studies of the organism on embryonated egg culture and tissue culture were described by Eddie, as were techniques for isolation, mouse passage, egg inoculation, identification, and diagnosis of the infection by means of complement fixation tests, neutralization tests, and plaque assay in tissue culture. The immunity produced in animals following vaccination and following tetracycline treatment was described in a series of reports which continued to the end of Eddie's life, some work being published posthumously. Review articles concerning psittacosis (ornithosis) were published in public health journals[11] and handbooks[12] and for the lay public in *All Pets Magazine* of November 1954.[13]

Broadening the Scope of Research

Eddie also contributed to the undulant fever investigations underway at Hooper when she arrived there. Studies on contagious abortion in cattle had begun in the early years. Mention was made in 1917 of the presence of characteristic organisms in certified milk and the potential hazard they posed.[14] In 1920 the publication by Meyer and Shaw appeared establishing a new genus, *Brucella* (honoring David Bruce, the discoverer), for the organisms causing the bovine (*Brucella abortus*) and caprine (*B. meletensis*) contagious abortion.[15] Eddie contributed to the 1929 report of successful infection of monkeys (*Macaccus rhesus* and *M. cynomolgi*) by the cutaneous route but not by feeding, although agglutinins could be demonstrated in blood serum following contact with the organisms by either route. It was also noted that old laboratory strains of brucella proved to be of low virulence.[16] In a succeeding paper the bacteriology of the brucella group was described and comparisons were made among cultures from humans and from animals of different geographic regions. The picture was anything but clear, however; uncertainty was expressed as to the mode of human infection.[17] In 1934 the opsono-phagocytic test was described as an aid to identification of latent brucella infections which were not necessarily revealed by serologic test or by skin testing.[18] In the following year a publication appeared dealing with the problem of caprine brucella infections in the United States.[19] This investigation had followed a specific request from goatherders in the western states, several of whom had been infected. Several goats from more than one herd had been transported to Hooper Laboratory, where they were tested for serum antibodies; milk from lactating animals was cultured, and tissues from animals that died or were sacrificed were tested by culture and by guinea pig inoculation. Most goats appeared to be healthy but cultures from the udder and some other tissues were positive. Antibodies were demonstrated in low titer in only a small number of animals. The disease was considered selflimiting in goats; veterinarians handling afterbirth were most severely infected. Many who drank the goats' milk showed no evidence of infection; no tests for antibody were made. Belle

Stewart, Eddie, and others described an improved technique for culture of brucella from blood by use of a large volume of blood held several days in the refrigerator to allow release of the organisms from the white cells before culture.[20] Dr. Lyle Veazie, who later became a professor of microbiology at the University of Oregon School of Medicine, also worked on the brucellosis research at Hooper.

Laboratory acquired brucellosis soon became a recognized problem. A questionnaire sent out from Hooper Laboratory to 98 United States laboratories revealed 74 recognized cases, 11 of them at Hooper.[21] Eddie's last publication on brucellosis, in 1949, discussed differential diagnosis between brucellosis and the rickettsial infection, Q fever.[22] The patient's history was the same: contact with milk or meat producing animals, similar symptoms. Emphasis was placed on a rising antibody titer to identify current illness since sensitivity to both organisms was probable.

Confronting Botulism

Eddie also participated in the research on botulism, a continuing interest at Hooper Laboratories following a serious outbreak in 1920 of this often fatal condition acquired from improperly canned food. The California and National Canners Association both sought help with the problem. In 1950 Eddie published with Meyer a survey report, "Fifty Years of Botulism in U.S. and Canada." This report, compiled at the request of the Cannery Inspection Board of the California State Department of Health, was updated and extended in 1964 to cover the years 1899 to 1964.[23] Outbreaks of botulism were still occurring in 1963 (53 cases), some from defective seams in cans of fish. Two deaths had resulted in 1960 from ingestion of smoked whitefish packed in plastic bags. The authors point out that great public indignation and, often, sensational publicity followed reports of human deaths from commercially canned products (12 deaths between 1960 and 1963), yet 42 deaths caused by home canned food products led to no action to prevent any such future fatalities. The report amply confirmed that under-sterilization and inadequate curing had been the prime causes of botulism. In more than 75 percent of the outbreaks (651 outbreaks between 1899 and 1963), the products had been "homemade." The admonition followed ". . . all canning and preserving instructions should be supplemented by the rule that home-canned and home-processed food under no circumstances be eaten or even tasted before they have been boiled." The report also provided evidence of the widespread distribution of botulism outbreaks, e.g., in 1955, seventy-one cases with forty-three deaths occurred in 12 states, all due to home-canned products. Better diagnosis and early treatment with antitoxin eventually led to lower mortality rates.

Gunnison's Contributions

Janet Gunnison's more basic research on the toxin producing organism, *Clostridium botulinum,* preceded Bernice Eddie's epidemiological surveys in this field. Gunnison had come to Hooper Laboratory on a Claypole Fellowship to work for her master's degree, which she received in 1926 under Paula Schoenholz, who had done much of the early serological studies on *C. botulinum*. Born in San Francisco in 1904, Gunnison graduated from the University of California, Berkeley, with an A.B. degree in 1925. With K. F. Meyer, she described type D botulinum toxin[24] obtained from a specimen submitted to the laboratory from South Africa. She tested it along with types B and C toxins in monkeys and showed that the animals were very sensitive to type B toxin, confirming earlier work, and little affected by C and D toxins given by mouth. She was also the first to describe type E toxin. This she isolated from a culture received from the Ukraine[25] establishing the MLD for guinea pigs and other laboratory animals by feeding and by injection. Type E botulinum toxin was found, like type B toxin, to be fatal to macaque monkeys by mouth, and was therefore presumed to be similarly capable of producing human intoxications, which proved to be the case. After moving to the Department of Bacteriology in the UCSF Medical School in 1931, she continued to work with clostridial toxins for several years, at the same time diversifying her research to include other bacteria of medical importance. She was co-author (with Max Marshall and others) of the text "Applied Medical Bacteriology."[26] During the 1950s she became much involved in the investigation of antibiotic synergism and antagonism then under study in the department by E. Jawetz and V. R. Coleman.[27] For many years she taught medical microbiology and, at the time of her retirement in 1965, was an associate professor of microbiology.

Leptospirosis also engaged Bernice Eddie's interest. With Belle Anderson-Stewart and Meyer, she described canine, murine, and human leptospirosis and the difficulties of differential diagnosis between *Leptospira canicola* and *L. icterohemorrhagia*.[28] The next two of her publications dealt with the epidemiology of leptospirosis in humans. Eddie occasionally became involved with reports on general virology, e.g., human pneumonitis viruses and their classification, but other professionals were recruited for large problems such as poliomyelitis research.

Beatrice Howitt was recruited for this purpose from the Connaught Laboratories in Toronto. A Californian born in San Francisco in 1891, she had received baccalaureate and master's degrees from the University of California in Berkeley. Largely self-taught, she had been in charge of the Stanford University Hospital laboratory during World War I until the men returned. It was the resulting demotion which spurred her to attend the university and get a degree. At Hooper Laboratory she studied poliomyelitis in monkeys and reported on the successful use of convalescent serum for therapy of polio.[29] Her contributions to the study of Equine Encephalomyelitis were more extensive.

"Black Death"

The investigation of plague was a large project undertaken at Hooper Foundation Laboratory as a consequence of occasional human cases in San Francisco, a port city offering the ideal ecology for spread of the infection: the entrance of ships from endemic plague areas and the inevitable presence of rats with fleas. Plague, that dread disease, the "Black Death" that throughout recorded history had swept in great pandemics over the world, killing millions, first was reported in California around 1900. More than 120 cases of plague with 113 deaths were reported between 1900 and 1904. This early epidemic led to the broadening of the powers of the California State Board of Health to control disease.[30] In 1923, plague struck Los Angeles, the last such epidemic in the state. However, sporadic cases continued to occur. Animal reservoirs of the disease were discovered in ground squirrels and other rodents and in their fleas. K. F. Meyer had worked with George McCoy of the United Stated Public Health Service on investigations of the role of wild and commensal rats in plague transmission in an attempt to explain explosive epizootics which occurred among rats. It was at this stage of the investigations that Bernice Eddie became involved with the study of sylvatic plague and its persistence in wild rodents.[31]

Later, during World War II, when Hooper Laboratory geared up for vaccine production, others were brought in on the study with its "mouse town," where normal mice were exposed to infected mice and their fleas to test the protection afforded by the test vaccines. Eventually a crystalline protein antigen from *Pasteurella pestis*, the etiologic agent of plague, was found to protect mice. American servicemen were also protected in endemic plague areas.[32] Among those recruited from within Hooper Laboratory from other projects were Adeline Larson and Lucile Foster. Foster came to Hooper after graduation from Berkeley to take a course with Meyer. She was offered a temporary position as a laboratory assistant—and spent the rest of her professional career at Hooper. She moved from project to project at first, but after 1942, worked directly with Meyer.

The Work of Dozier and Heller

Only two women succeeded in obtaining a Ph.D. degree with K. F. Meyer, both during the 1920s: Carrie Castle Dozier, who soon left to teach at Mills College, and Hilda Hemple Heller, a woman of great spirit who had an adventurous career. Born in 1891 in Ann Arbor, Michigan, Heller obtained an A.B. degree from Stanford University in 1913, an M.S. at University of Michigan in 1915, and then spent 1915–1916 at the State Serum Institute in Copenhagen and 1916 at the Lister Institute in London. The year 1917–1918 she spent at the Pasteur Institute studying gas gangrene clostridia of such deadly import in the war wounds of World War I. On returning to California in 1918, Heller studied with Meyer, obtaining her doctorate in 1920.[33] She remained for several years at Hooper, but after her marriage to the director of the San Francisco Zoo, she became more interested in collecting exotic animals than in bacteriology.

Meyer did not encourage Bernice Eddie to get a doctorate. It was her mother who encouraged her and accompanied her to Ann Arbor. Her mother lived with her for many years in her five-room apartment near the University of California Medical School and the Hooper Laboratory. Located on a hill overlooking San Francisco, the apartment was beautifully furnished with oriental rugs and French furniture. Eddie kept birds and other pets. Each season she attended musical concerts and theater productions. She was an opera buff and on appropriate occasions would attend the opening of the opera, with friends, in gala attire.

Her travels were extensive and worldwide. Travelogues from some of her trips with her friend, Dr. Hulda Thelander, pediatrician to the Meyer family, record her impressions of some of the last journeys she was able to make: in 1962 Eddie and Thelander attended the World Medical Congress in New Delhi, India, traveling around the world in 60 days. First visiting Egypt and the antiquities of the Nile, they saw Abu Simbel, the temples built by Ramses II for himself and his favorite wife, Nefertiti, before the intrusion of the Aswan Dam. They made professional visits in Asia, to the Pasteur Institute, where anti-venom was produced for treatment of the nearly 1,000 individuals bitten each year by cobras, kraits, and other venomous snakes, according to Thelander's diary. In Kuala Lampur they visited the International Center for Medical Research and Training (ICMRT), which was supported in part by the Hooper Foundation. Eddie was greeted and entertained there by many friends from the Hooper Laboratory. The travelers returned by the western route through Hawaii completing the circumnavigation.

Travels

There are diaries from both Thelander and Eddie from their Australian trip of 1964. A visit to the South Pacific with the "Medical Jet Set," as they referred to it, is described. They had signed up for a continuing medical education tour, arranged by the University of California, Los Angeles, of major medical centers in Australia, New Zealand, and Tahiti. Thelander's account is full of medical details and observations. Eddie's has more about native animals and plants. She noted the beauty of flowering trees; it was spring there as they drove through the "rolling hills covered with green carpet and speckled with sheep." She also wrote that the kangaroos are friendly and would follow you like a dog, but that the koala bears just "stole her heart." She included in her diary bits of history of New Zealand and of the social customs, most notably, the "finger food" in Tahiti, which disturbed her sense of propriety and public health standards.

The last trip recorded, in 1966, was to Africa. In Johannesburg, South Africa, they donned miners' garb with headlamps and descended into a gold mine 3,000 feet below ground. They rode the miners' car underground to the end of the line, then walked through the long corridors of the mine. Following this, they flew to Nairobi for a two-week safari, motoring to the Serengeti plains and stopping to see the Olduvai Gorge. Day after day they hunted animals with a camera. On their return to Nairobi, they attended church, as was their custom; Eddie was a faithful member of All Saints Cathedral in San

Francisco. After a short stay at the famous Treetops Hotel, they flew to Entebbe, Uganda, motored to Murchison Falls on the Nile, and at Lake Manyara saw Mt. Kilamanjaro in full splendor.

Bernice Eddie and the many other excellent women scientists at Hooper Laboratory through the years were key personnel, from the faithful support workers who made possible the meticulous, laborious tests, animal experimentation, chemical analyses, and cultures of bacteria and viruses, to the innovative scientists whose ideas were interwoven into the Hooper publications and consultant advice.

Dr. Eddie's close contact with K. F. Meyer, and the teaching responsibilities that increasingly fell upon her shoulders, brought her into prominence at the University of California Medical Center in San Francisco and within the scientific community. Many outside requests and research problems were referred directly to her. In her areas of expertise, psittacosis and arthropod transmission of disease, she was frequently called upon for consultation.

She lived her research, was always very personally involved. She led a full and rewarding life, continuing her work even in failing health up to the last week of her life in June of 1969. Recognition of her value to the university was made in appointments to university committees and, after her death, in a fellowship in her name, established at the medical center. The *Hooper Newsvector* of July 1969 noted that her meticulous scientific work and her high professional competence were well known. A pioneer in the study of psittacosis, she lived with an intense devotion to her work and compassion toward others, a rare altruism that heartened all who came in contact with her.

CHAPTER XVII

Elizabeth McCoy

*". . . One of the foremost women in the history of
bacteriology inspired scores of students to enter
the field."*

D r. Elizabeth McCoy achieved emeritus status at the University of Wisconsin-
Madison in 1973, yet she could be found in her laboratory busily engaged in
research and writing almost to her dying day in the Department of Bacteriology, where she was a distinguished educator for more than forty years. An
unassuming person, she was vigorous in pursuit of research and promotion of
education for students of microbiology and she quietly won renown for her
many accomplishments.

During her later years, Elizabeth McCoy resided on the property first
owned by her grandparents, who came to Wisconsin as pioneer settlers. Her
maternal forebears were early immigrants to a settlement on Long Island.
According to family records going back to 1632, they were Quakers who had a
part in the split of the Friends church community. Her great, great-grandfather
was Elias Hicks—the splitter. Her grandmother, Rachel Hicks Willits, had the
Elias Hicks' diary, which tells of the split of the Hicksites from the orthodox
Quakers. This diary was handed down to Elizabeth McCoy.

Quaker Roots

Her grandfather William Williamson, also a Quaker, married Rachel Hicks Willits. In 1890 they moved to Wisconsin, settling within three or four miles of the McCoy family, who settled in Wisconsin during the same decade. The McCoys were of Scottish descent; both grandparents were born in Scotland and came to the United States by way of Canada. Elizabeth's parents were Esther Williamson and Cassius James McCoy. Both parents attended teachers' colleges, then called "normal schools," her father at Whitewater and her mother at Oshkosh. Both taught school for awhile, but each then chose other fields. For health reasons (rheumatism), James McCoy could not tolerate farm life and became instead a builder of homes and commercial establishments in Madison.

Elizabeth's mother, early in life, became attracted to nursing after a younger sister's illness and death from rheumatic heart disease. As Elizabeth puts it, "Mother was probably a frustrated medic; she very much wanted to attend Rush Medical College in Chicago, but her family discouraged it and she settled for nursing at Illinois Training School." This much the family could accept; nursing was respectable, and the training was strict. She practiced nursing for six years, was an early Red Cross nurse, active in the Well Baby Clinic under Dr. Dorothy Mendenhall, saw active duty during World War I for a time, and was active in the Methodist Hospital Nursing School affairs. For six years she kept Cassius McCoy waiting. After they were married they settled in Madison near Lake Wingra, where Elizabeth was born on February 1, 1903.

Elizabeth remembered the neighborhood as a wonderful place in which to grow up. She said there were other children to play with, an abundance of wildlife, Indian relics along the lake and real Indians in a nearby camp. In addition she had the farm to explore. On three occasions the family spent the summer months on the farm. During one of these summers, Elizabeth was thought to be in danger of developing tuberculosis and was required to sleep in a tent under the apple tree. She loved it, and never did contract the disease nor even become tuberculin positive.

Her progressive grade school allowed her to skip fifth grade, permitting her to study with some memorable teachers in junior high school. Elizabeth particularly remembered her English teacher for the literary club and debating team she organized and for her use of Shakespeare for parsing and diagramming. Elizabeth took four years of Latin (and some Greek in college) so, as she said, "I never have had trouble spelling the names of bacteria." She also was well versed in mathematics and chemistry.

Early Influences

By the time she graduated from high school, Elizabeth knew very well what she wanted to study in college: her mind was set on bacteriology. An early incident introduced her to infection: Dr. William Dodge Frost, a family friend and bacteriologist at the University of Wisconsin, drove out one day to visit the McCoys in a cart drawn by a Shetland pony with a colt running alongside. In trying to pet the colt, Elizabeth was bitten by the animal. Dr. Frost took her to the drug store for peroxide, but a few days later, when her arm was swollen and the bite painful, Elizabeth was taken to the family physician, who scraped the wound open and applied iodine. The physician, and subsequently Elizabeth's mother, explained bacterial infection to the youngster. She also learned from her mother about household hygiene, about bacteria in canning, and about respiratory diseases. Many in the vicinity contracted and died from tuberculosis and even more from pneumonia; one of her father's employees lost four of his family to tuberculosis. Quarantine was obligatory for scarlet fever at that time, and the great influenza pandemic following World War I made a lasting impression on Elizabeth, taking both parents of a family she knew.

She learned about bacteriology on the farm as well. The tuberculosis eradication program in cattle and the cooling of milk were explained by her father. In fact her father found his daughter so apt a student and so intensely interested in farming, that it was she who was taught how to manage the farm rather than her brother, who had other interests. It was also she, years later, who took over the management of the farm from her father.

With such background and orientation of interest, it was natural that Elizabeth McCoy chose general bacteriology in the College of Agriculture rather than medical bacteriology in the School of Medicine. For the period of her B.S. major, she was a student of Dr. Frost, the same man whose pony had "introduced" her to bacteriology. Professor Edwin G. Hastings was then chairman of the Department of Agriculture Bacteriology at the University of Wisconsin. Dean Harry L. Russell was in and out of the department during those years, although much occupied with the deanship. In January of her senior year at the university, Elizabeth met Dr. Edwin B. Fred, a decisive encounter in her life. He interviewed her, among others, for a research associate position. Elizabeth got the job and, because she had so few credits left to complete, she was allowed to double-register in the graduate school. This was not a simple decision for her to make, for she already had been offered a position in Washington, D.C., in the Bureau of Home Economics. After her interview with Dr. Fred, Professor Hastings dropped by her laboratory and remarked that Dr. Fred was the genius of the department, that she would be lucky to get the job. McCoy said that she had been eternally grateful that she made the decision to work with Dr. Fred. He served as her advisor for both her M.S. and Ph.D. degrees and was an invaluable aid and guide throughout her career. She fully believed that the coincidence of his leaving the department to go into university administration gave her the opportunity for responsibility and promotion within the department.

Part of the Team

She said that she had never felt any sex discrimination in her career, and was, in fact, given all the responsibility and support she could use. She further stated that she always thought of the department as a team and that she saw herself as very much a member of that team. It is evident that this was true, since in later years she represented the department and even the university in many assignments. One of the most amusing examples came when she was appointed by the dean of the College of Agriculture to be the Wisconsin representative on a United States Department of Agriculture Regional Committee on Farm Animal Manure, which involved her in the planning for the 12-state midwest region. Following this appointment, she served on the regional research review committee as the only bacteriologist, and only woman on the committee, serving the entire time, she explains, without any evidence of prejudice against her. Within the university, her general standing and her progress were attained without evidence of bias. Dr. McCoy was the second woman at the University of Wisconsin to attain the rank of full professor outside the departments of home economics and nursing. She received a Ph.D. in 1929, became an assistant professor of bacteriology in 1930, and by 1943 had become full professor.

As a graduate student of E. B. Fred, she became involved in research problems which occupied her interest for many years to come. She began research on acetone butyl alcohol fermentation and an investigation of root nodule bacteria as well. The latter interest she pursued as a National Research Council Fellow at the Rothamsted Experimental Station in Harpenden, Herts, England, and at the Botanical Institute at Karlova University in Prague, Czechoslovakia, in 1929–1930. She published the results of some of this research in the *Proceedings of the Royal Society* of 1932.[1] In 1933 (with Keith Lewis) McCoy published further work on root nodule bacteria using bean root tissue culture for study of the phenomenon of nodule formation *in vitro*.[2] She later (1939) published a monograph with Fred and Baldwin entitled *Root Nodule Bacteria and Leguminous Plants*.[3]

Studies of Acetone Butyl Alcohol Fermentation

However, her first publication, in 1926,[4] concerned a cultural study of the acetone butyl alcohol organism. In this publication reference is made to the state of confusion concerning the names and classifications of the "anaerobic butyric acid bacteria," resulting from research with incompletely identified cultures. Although these organisms were well known for their metabolic products, the species were virtually unknown; Chaim Weizmann, "a subject of Great Britain and Ireland," who later became the first president of Israel, had in 1919 obtained a patent for the "production of acetone and butyl alcohol by bacteriological processes" without attempting to name the organism used. The name *Clostridium acetobutylicum* was proposed by McCoy, based on a relatively homogeneous group, 11 strains which they had studied. At a later time, McCoy noted that recognition of this species had been delayed through unusual circumstances and it still was not included in the taxonomy of the spore-bearing anaerobes in, for example, Lehmann and Neumann's treatise on bacterial classification or in Bergey's *Manual of Determinative Bacteriology* for 1934. The information deficit on these organisms was soon remedied by a series of 13 papers authored by McCoy and McClung dealing with the butyl-butyric clostridia. Seven of these publications were authored by Elizabeth McCoy and Leland McClung,[5] and two by McCoy and Sjolander. They characterized the organisms studied on media optimal for growth, determined fermentation products, and serological relations among the group of spore-bearing anaerobes. In a review of the last subject appearing in Volume 1 of *Bacteriological Reviews*,[6] McClung and McCoy presented an evaluation of serological data dealing with the group, relating the butyric clostridia to clostridial species in general. They noted that serology was a great aid in taxonomy but did not solve all the problems of classification within the group. Over a period of ten years (1928–1938), McCoy published at least 14 additional papers, some (co-authored with graduate students), on spore-forming anaerobes of this group.[7]

During this period, she spent a year (1936–1937) as an associate in medicine at the University of California's George Williams Hooper Foundation in San Francisco in the laboratory of Karl F. Meyer. And in 1940 she was sent by the University of Wisconsin to Arroyo, Puerto Rico, to put into successful operation a butyl alcohol fermentation plant, a United States government cooperative. The problem, a bacteriophage outbreak ruining the fermentation, was solved by her own culture—for which she later received a United States patent assigned to the Wisconsin Alumni Research Foundation and sold to Puerto Rico.

Pollution Research

During the same period McCoy delved into other research areas. She spent several summers with Birge and Juday (one of them with A. T. Henrici) at Trout Lake Station in the Northern Wisconsin lake district and later directed the bacteriological laboratory there for about eight years. In 1934 she published, with F. T. Williams, on the role of microorganisms in precipitation of calcium carbonate in marl deposits of fresh water lakes.[8] With Wayne Umbreit she published on Micromonospora in inland lakes—reporting their finding, contrary to conventional opinion, that fungi and actinomycetes were lacking in aquatic flora,[9] and, later, with A. Colmer documented the role of micromonosporae.[10] In 1938 Henrici and McCoy further studied the distribution of heterotrophic bacteria in bottom deposits of some lakes.[11] Several other publications appeared during the next few years on the bacteria of fresh waters. In 1969 she obtained a Sea Grant for study of bacterial flora of Lake Michigan, with particular regard to alewife and Coho salmon spawning in polluted rivers and returning to open lake water. In response to demand, her research understandably shifted to the problems of pollution. In 1967 she and W. B. Sarles participated in a National Academy of Science Symposium on Eutrophication, presenting a paper on bacteria in lakes: populations and functional relations.[12] She also became chairman of a graduate school committee of 11 members which supervised research projects on the University Bay area of Lake Mendota.

An Interest in Antibiotics

Dr. McCoy became involved with antibiotics during World War II as part of a team searching for high-yielding strains of Penicillium. They tested their own isolates and thousands of others sent to their laboratories at the University of Wisconsin. McCoy had the good fortune to detect Strain X1612, the high-yielding mutant strain obtained from Dr. Demerec, which allowed the release of penicillin for civilians—and she had the pleasure of mailing the first cultures to industrial companies.

She continued to study other antibiotics, devising screening methods for new antibiotics later used, in principle, by industry, and in the course of these investigations discovered the still marketed oligomycin, an important enzyme inhibitor, in exploring the mitochondrial phosphorylation mechanism. Her patent on oligomycin was also assigned to the Wisconsin Alumni Research Foundation. She published a number of papers dealing with research on the genetic nature of antibiotic resistance. Her work with sulfonamides in nutritional studies of the chick[13] led to studies of changes in host flora subsequent to administration of antibiotics.[14]

Her work on antibiotic resistance extended to mastitis, including the rare Bacteriodes mastitis in dairy cattle, a serious problem in Wisconsin.[15] Later (1960), an outbreak of staphylococcal food poisoning in Puerto Rico traced to Wisconsin milk alerted McCoy and others and resulted in her three-year project with the Dairy Department and Dry Milk Institute, culminating in an ecological study of survival and growth of staphylococci in dairy barns, manure, and soils. She and her co-workers published two papers in 1962 and 1963 on the results of their studies, one paper was written with Smith of the Centers for Disease Control in Atlanta, which included identification of staphylococci in dried milk with FA (fluorescent antibody) technique.[16] The other paper was written with Fred and was on a method for purification of type B staphylococcal enterotoxin.[17]

Following research with K. F. Meyer at the Hooper Foundation (1936–1937), McCoy ventured into studies and short projects on botulinum food poisoning. Some studies, such as that involving survival of type A toxin in canned bread, were done under contract with the United States Army in cooperation with the Department of Dairy and Food Industry at the University of Wisconsin Madison.[18] After an outbreak of type C toxin in pheasants in Wisconsin, McCoy became involved in development of a type C vaccine. The finding of type E toxin in smoked fish prompted McCoy to begin investigation of that problem also.

Her interest in bacteriophage developed in 1940, from her experience with butyl alcohol fermentation in Puerto Rico, and then followed problems of phage interference in commercial production of antibiotics (streptomycete phages) and butylene glycol fermentation (*Bacillus polymyxa* phages). She and her students also studied phage characterizations by serology, phage-host patterns, and the phage growth cycle on complex multicellular actinomycete hosts. She and her co-workers produced some of the early electron microscopy of phage size and morphology and investigated host resistance to phage.[19] Publications during the 1950s and early 1960s dealt with phages of *Streptomyces griseus, Agrobacterium radiobacter,* as well as *Bacillus polymyxa.*

Critical Interest in Taxonomy

An interest in taxonomy and critical, specific characterization of microorganisms used in research were a concern of McCoy's from her very first publication. Her interest in speciation of clostridia involved her in a patent lawsuit in 1932, a test case (in Wilmington, Delaware) establishing the validity of bacterial patents. As a consequence, McCoy was invited to write the section on the genus Clostridium for two editions of Bergey's *Manual.* She also served as an industrial consultant on new species of actinomycetes. She studied *Zoogloea ramigera* (involved in activated sludge settling characteristics) re-isolating the organism to create the neotype, since no cultures were obtainable. Then she fully characterized the organism and, in 1967, proposed strain I-16M as neotype via proposal to the International Committee on Nomenclature of the International Association of Microbiological Societies.[20]

Elizabeth McCoy's research was not finished in 1973 when she retired. She became a very active emeritus professor, deeply involved in a small-scale waste management project as part of a large cooperative effort funded by the State of Wisconsin and the Environmental Protection Agency. The work involved the bacteriology, soil science, law, agricultural engineering, and civil engineering departments. And again she was the only woman "in the lot of us," as she said. She served on the University Bay Committee of the graduate school, exploring research on water quality in Lake Mendota. The committee was awarded $160,000 to protect the lake water and improve its quality. Being a woman did not interfere with her chairing the 11-member committee.

Despite her immense research accomplishments, which resulted in three books and 103 publications,[21] Dr. McCoy spoke of her graduate students as her proudest endeavor and greatest satisfaction. They numbered 47 Ph.D. and at least 110 M.S. graduates. Her teaching encompassed a broad range of courses in microbiology: advanced general microbiology, microbial physiology, soil bacteriology, food bacteriology; her fields of research included industrial microbiology plus taxonomy and nomenclature.

Neither her professional university occupations nor her farm completely absorbed all her time and interest. She served as editor of "Biological Abstracts" in the Food and Industrial Section, for many years, beginning in 1937. She was a member of the editorial board of *Journal of Bacteriology* and was, from 1971 on, as editor for *Transactions* of the Wisconsin Academy of Sciences, Arts and Letters. After achieving emeritus status she became more active in the Academy Council and, in 1976, assumed the academy presidency.

A Personal Legacy

Elizabeth McCoy was most generous. For the Wisconsin Academy, she made possible the remodeling of Steenbock Center, the first permanent home of the academy. To the Wisconsin Alumni Research Foundation for the university, she donated her family farms, including one of the state's most historic ones.

Dr. McCoy was long a member and once president of the Wisconsin section of Sigma Xi. She was a fellow of the American Academy of Microbiology, the American Public Health Association, and the American Association for the Advancement of Science; a national honorary member of Sigma Delta Epsilon and Graduate Women in Science, Inc.; and an honorary member of the American Society for Microbiology.

She was the recipient of the Pasteur Award of the Society of Illinois Bacteriologists in 1968 and received a Distinguished Service Award from the Wisconsin Alumni Association in 1971. She also had to her credit a 25-year Award from the Madison, Wisconsin, Grade A Milk Producers.

President emeritus E. B. Fred of the University of Wisconsin, early mentor and lifelong friend of Elizabeth McCoy, said ". . . as a student, teacher and research investigator, she must be counted among the half dozen most important women in the history of bacteriology in this country. Possessing an unusual combination of practical statesmanship and diplomacy, she has the wholehearted cooperation of everyone with whom she works." He added ". . . moreover she is a thoroughly delightful and interesting person." Countless colleagues, former students, and friends echo that assessment.

Elizabeth McCoy died on March 24, 1978, while en route to a hospital from her farm on Syene Road south of Madison. Her colleague in the Department of Bacteriology at the University of Wisconsin, William B. Sarles, wrote of her "She was recognized throughout the world as a truly great microbiologist. . . . At the time of her death she was working actively, despite her retired status, on microbiology of lakes and streams and on the actions of microorganisms in the treatment of sewage. . . . Her achievements in research, teaching, scholarly affairs, and public service were great, but she was always deeply involved in humanitarian services . . . her life, her work and her attainments were exemplary."[22]

On May 21, 1978, Dr. Elizabeth McCoy was awarded posthumously the Honorary Doctor of Science degree from the University of Wisconsin-Milwaukee.

CHAPTER XVIII

Cornelia Mitchell Downs

". . . Engaged in secret, wartime "biological warfare"; expert on tularemia, developer of fluorescent antibody staining technique."

During World War II, a secret operation was set up at Fort Detrick in Frederick, Maryland, drawing top scientists from all across the country. One of the scientists called to serve the nation was Dr. Cornelia Mitchell Downs. Well known for her tularemia research, she was pressed into service early in the operation. In August 1943, she took leave from her position at the University of Kansas Department of Bacteriology to embark on a secret mission. By the fall of 1944 with the project well underway, she was interrupted by a reminder from her department chairman, Dr. Noble P. Sherwood, that she should return to the university for the fall semester to give her course in immunology. This letter presented a real dilemma to Cora Downs, for the research she was engaged in was classified and neither the nature nor the importance of it could be revealed. The impasse was finally resolved by issuing secret clearance for the chancellor of the University of Kansas, Dean M. Malott, who then arranged for a continuation of Downs' leave from the university for national service of a classified nature.

This secret operation, which in time acquired the pejorative designation "biological warfare," produced many advances in medical microbiology and in some measure brought to a fitting close the era of descriptive bacteriology begun by Louis Pasteur and Robert Koch. Cora Downs and her associates (S. S. Chapman, Lewis L. Coriell, Henry T. Eigelsbach, Barbara J. Owen, and Gifford B. Pinchot) did much to fill out the picture on tularemia started in 1912 by McCoy and Chapin. Downs made significant contributions to the understanding of tularemia, its pathogenesis, immunology, host range, vectors, and characterization of the causative organism itself. She remained two years at Detrick with frequent but brief returns to the University of Kansas. After completing her service at Fort Detrick, she returned to her teaching and research at the University of Kansas, but continued as a consultant at Detrick until 1967.

A Distinguished Family

Cornelia Mitchell Downs (better known as Cora Downs) was born in Wyandotte, Kansas (now part of Kansas City), in 1892 and obtained her early education there. After high school graduation she traveled by interurban trolley to Lawrence for her undergraduate education at the University of Kansas, graduating in 1915 with an A.B. degree in bacteriology, then a relatively new field in a new department at the university. She was well motivated toward medical science by her father, a Kansas City physician. He had started his medical education at the University of Kansas, but owing to an all too successful Halloween prank, he was obliged to continue elsewhere. Thus it was that he went to the University of Michigan, where he met and married Lily Campbell, Cornelia Downs' mother. She had received her early education in Germany, where her mother, Cornelia's maternal grandmother, had accompanied her brother, Walton Murphy, following his appointment by President Lincoln as Consul General at Frankfurt am Main.

Cornelia Downs' paternal grandmother and namesake, Cornelia Mitchell Downs, was a prominent person in her day. A writer on public issues for journals and newspapers, she became the first woman to be appointed regent at the University of Kansas in 1882. Both of Cora's grandfathers were successful businessmen.

After obtaining her master's degree in 1920, Cora Downs spent two summers at the University of Chicago studying physiology with Professor H. Gideon Wells. She also took a course in biochemistry. Her plans to continue at the university were interrupted by the illness of her mother which obliged her to return to Lawrence. She resumed her teaching position in the Department of Bacteriology while completing the requirements for the Ph.D. degree which she received in 1924. She was promoted to associate professor in the same year. It was also the year in which she became interested in tularemia after hearing Edward Francis speak at the 1924 annual meeting of the Society of American Bacteriologists.

Tularemia Research Initiated

During her early years at the university, Downs published on a variety of topics. Her first publication in 1919 (with Noble P. Sherwood) concerned streptococci.[1] She published several papers on typhoid fever, then prevalent in Kansas, and several others dealing with various aspects of immunology: anaphylaxis, the antigenicity of fibrinogen, and diagnostic serology. She was, as she herself says, searching for feasible research projects that could be done with minimal funds. Many in similar circumstances abandoned research. Downs persevered, and in 1930 she published her first paper on tularemia, a report of three cases in the *Journal of Kansas Medicine* for May 1930.[2]

During the Depression, many people hunted for food, and rabbits were plentiful in Kansas. One successful hunter contracted a strange illness with general malaise, enlarged lymph glands, and a persistent draining lesion from a finger. It was from this lesion that *Pasteurella tularensis* was isolated. At that time the diagnostic bacteriology laboratory for the Lawrence area was located in the Bacteriology Department at the university. Suspicion prompted Downs to send a duplicate specimen to Thomas Francis, at the University of Michigan, who phoned back warning her to be cautious until he had confirmed the diagnosis of tularemia. The diagnosis was, in fact, confirmed and the cultures were used in subsequent research. During the next 13 years, until she went to Detrick, Downs published ten additional papers dealing with tularemia.

They included a study of the course of the disease in guinea pigs and in rabbits;[3] immunologic studies of tularemia in rabbits, in which she followed the rise in antibody titer after experimental infection;[4] studies of antigens produced by *P. tularensis;*[5] a description of cultural characteristics of the organisms;[6] and the effect of certain antibiotics (gramacidin and tyrocidin) on *P. tularensis.*[7]

In 1939 Downs spent a sabbatical year at the Rockefeller Institute. Kenneth Goodner, who had obtained his master's degree with Downs, and then gone on to take a Ph.D. with Zinsser, was at the institute. He assisted Downs in arrangements at the Rockefeller Institute, planned as a prelude to a visit later that year to the Pasteur Institute in Paris, France. Dr. Downs lived in a French-speaking pension in New York City, studied the language, and availed herself of all opportunities to prepare for completing her sabbatical at the Pasteur Institute. Then came World War II. With considerable disappointment, she arranged to remain at the institute for the rest of her sabbatical. Her research involved the popular quest of the times, antibiotics, in addition to some of her own work with tularemia. She returned to the University of Kansas in 1940. In 1943 she was called to Fort Detrick.

For three years after Downs went to Fort Detrick, no publications appeared. Then in 1946 four papers or abstracts on tularemia appeared in the *Journal of Bacteriology* on: antibiotic sensitivity of *P. tularensis,*[8] the immunization of rats against tularemia,[9] cultivation of *P. tularensis* in eggs,[10] and the comparative susceptibility of various laboratory animals to tularemia.[11] Two publications on immunization of rats[12] and mice[13] against *P. tularensis* appeared in 1947. These continued her studies on immunization of animals and included the first of her papers on pathogenesis of the infection.[14] There were no publications in 1948, but in the following year Downs published five papers dealing with tularemia, three of them continued the series of pathogenesis and immunity in tularemia.[15] In the same year, 1949, The Proceedings of the Fourth Annual Meeting of the International Northwestern Conference on Diseases of Nature Communicable to Man were published.[16] Downs was invited by K. F. Meyer to speak on tularemia at this conference.

When Downs first returned to the University of Kansas, she was assigned a naval officer to assist her with the research which could be carried out at the university. During the war, this entailed extensive travel, but her top secret clearance at Detrick expedited her trips and, on a mission to Fairbanks, Alaska, in 1947, made it possible for her to reach her destination by displacing a full colonel from the flight. The Alaskan trip, made with a team from the Zoology and Entomology Departments of the University of Kansas, under a contract with the Office of Naval Research, was made to evaluate the status of tularemia in Alaska. Downs studied strains of *P. tularensis,* notably a strain of reputed low virulence considered a candidate strain for vaccines. Other members of the group investigated tularemia sensitization.

The Search for a Human Vaccine

Several low virulence strains had been collected by Foshay and others and tested as immunizing agents, but none at that time would produce an immunity protective against challenge infection. Woodward, in Downs' laboratory, had found that low doses of one strain of *P. tularensis* produced solid immunity in mice against challenge with fully virulent strains.[17] Downs and others had demonstrated that killed vaccines were not sufficiently protective.

The Russians were said to have a low virulence strain which produced an immunity protective against challenge and was safe for use in a human vaccine. After World War II, the first delegation to Russia included Dr. K. F. Meyer, who obtained the Russian strain and passed it on to Downs. At Detrick, Downs and her collaborators confirmed the efficacy of the Russian strain as an immunizing agent and developed strains which could be successfully used as a living vaccine in man.

The final paper on her wartime Detrick research anticipated her next field of research endeavor. This was a paper presented to the Kansas Academy of Science reviewing "Wartime Advances in Yellow Fever and the Rickettsial Infections."[18] During the 1950s Downs began publishing on rickettsiae, which she had worked on with Cox in Missoula during the summer of 1941, not long after Cox's discovery of the Q fever agent. Downs had been struck by the resemblance between the Q agent and tularemia, viz., clinical manifestations, animal and arthropod vectors, and transovarial transmission of the agent in arthropods. Her interest in this group of organisms was augmented by Dr. David Paretsky, newly arrived in the department in 1951, later chairman of the Department of Microbiology. Together they published five papers on rickettsiae.[19] In addition, Downs published with others, many of them her students, seven papers and six abstracts on the organisms, their vectors, and the pathogenesis and immunology of the infection.[20] Among her important contributions is the definition of conditions for growth of *Coxiella burnetii* in tissue culture using L strain mouse fibroblasts. During this period her research was well supported by grants from Detrick, the Office of Naval Research, the Office of the Surgeon General, the National Science Foundation, and the National Institutes of Health.

Fluorescent Antibody Staining Techniques

Another area of interest to Cora Downs during the late 1950s and 1960s was fluorescent antibody staining techniques, first described by Coons using isocyanate as the bonding agent, which proved both difficult to use and unstable in solution. With J. L. Riggs and others at the University of Kansas, Downs perfected the fluorescent antibody technique using isothiocyanate as bonding agent. The introduction of a sulfhydryl group into the fluorescein and rhodamine B combination gave a stable dye easily coupled to immune or normal serum. This work, published in the *American Journal of Pathology,*[21] enabled the fluorescent antibody technique to be widely used as a diagnostic and research tool. It brought her recognition in the form of a review in the *Saturday Review of Literature* and the *Kansas City Star,* an invitation to present her work at Walter Reed Hospital, and a profile entitled, "Bacteriologist Cora Downs is Adding New Scope to a Microscope." Her profile with photographs appeared in "Friends," a Chevrolet publication for September 1962. In 1976 this scientific paper was listed in *Current Contents* as being among the 100 most quoted pathology articles, having been cited 546 times in the 15-year period 1961–1974. In 1978, *Citation Classics* featured the article.[22]

Cora Downs has enjoyed a long and fruitful life marked by many honors. During her creative years she enriched her life with travel, frequently accompanied by her brother Harry, who like Cora never married. She frequently returned to England for which she has a great affinity. In 1959–1960 she spent a sabbatical as a United Stated Public Health Service Fellow at the Sir William Dunn School of Pathology, Oxford, England, under the auspices of Lord Howard Florey. A year of great promise, which started so auspiciously, ended in great sadness with the sudden death of her brother, as he and Cora were returning to England from the continent.

A Lifetime of Accomplishment Honored

Despite official retirement in 1963 at age 70, she continued to pursue research interests actively through 1967. Her latest paper was published in 1970. It was a joint project with researchers at the Czechoslovak Academy of Sciences, including at the time David Paretsky, who was on sabbatical. The publication defines the selective aspects of L cell tissue cultures on *Coxiella burnetii.*[23] In 1972 Cora Downs was named Sommerfield Distinguished Professor of Bacteriology at the University of Kansas. This appointment was particularly gratifying to her, for the founder of the chair is reputed to have said that no woman would ever receive it for none would ever deserve it. She was awarded the University of Kansas Distinguished Service Award in 1964.

Her research was recognized in the design of the 1966 University of Kansas Centennial Medal, which symbolized the work of many distinguished faculty members of the University of Kansas. Downs' work is symbolized by the fluorescent antibody work. In 1971 she received the Crumbine Medal from the Kansas Public Health Association. She was particularly pleased in 1972 to be elected to honorary membership in the American Society of Microbiology. Her photograph has been placed in the U.S.S.R. International Gallery of Medical Honor. In 1980 the Missouri Valley Branch of the American Society for Microbiology voted unanimously to rename its annual graduate student award for Cora M. Downs. The Missouri Valley Branch represents microbiologists from Kansas, Nebraska, Oklahoma, Missouri, and Iowa.

When interviewed by the *Lawrence Journal World* in 1980, Cora Downs modestly remarked, "I'm a woman who has done something she has very much wanted to do." She probably was fortunate in her choice of microbiology as a major field; microbiology certainly is fortunate in having her among its scientists for she produced many advances in this field.

CHAPTER XIX

Pearl Louella Kendrick

*". . . Standardized whooping cough vaccine;
recognized worldwide for her efforts."*

Variable products are likely to produce variable results. Vaccines prepared by different methods cannot be expected to give comparable results. During the early phase of whooping cough (pertussis) vaccine development, it happened that the American-made vaccine was quite effective in protecting children against the disease. At the same time in England, in 1942, the locally prepared vaccine seemed to offer little or no protection. Dr. Pearl Kendrick of the Michigan State Public Health Laboratory was called upon for consultation because she was the originator of the American vaccine. She was invited to become a member of the Whooping Cough Immunization Committee of the Medical Research Council of Great Britain to compare the two vaccines. The results of that comparison were decisive. The variables in the British vaccine were found and corrected. As a consultant with the World Health Organization (WHO), Dr. Kendrick was able to exert her influence and promote uniform standards for vaccine production in many countries of the world while research continued to improve the vaccines.

Pearl Louella Kendrick was born in 1890 in Wheaton, Illinois, where her father, a Free-Methodist preacher, was attending a theological seminary. When she was about three years old, her father was called to Utica, New

York, as a Church District Elder. He remained there for a couple of years before accepting a call from Herkimer, New York. It was in Herkimer that Pearl started school, an event she had eagerly anticipated, for her father had prepared her well in reading and given her a good start with arithmetic. As a consequence, she was so well trained that the first year was quite a disappointment. However, subsequent years proved more challenging.

During those early years, Mr. Kendrick was called to serve a number of churches. Consequently, Pearl attended grade school in Rome, Cortland, and Norwich, New York, and high school in Norwich and Sherburne. During the family's stay in Norwich, Pearl's younger sister died from intestinal tuberculosis. At the time of their move to Sherburne, Pearl herself was ill and coughing, presumably from tuberculosis, and she was out of school most of the year. In Sherburne her health improved. Her father had retired to a farm near a rural church he could serve. The high school was too far away for Pearl to walk, so each week her father drove her to town with food supplies for a week. She and another farm girl shared a room in a home where they could prepare their own meals.

After graduation from high school in 1908, Pearl began teaching in a nearby one-room rural school (1908–1909). The next two years she taught the upper grades and was principal of a two-room school. She saved her earnings to help her brother through college, and he in turn helped her out financially while she attended Greenville College in Illinois (1910–1911), and, later, Syracuse University, where she graduated in 1914 with a B.S. degree in science. She then accepted a position as teacher of science and mathematics and principal of the high school in St. Johnsville, New York. In 1918 she moved to Johnstown, New York, and there taught biology and chemistry. During a summer session, she attended Columbia University, where she studied bacteriology with Hans Zinsser and protozoology with Gary Calkins. This background enabled her to take the next, most decisive step: to become a bacteriologist. She spent one year at the New York State Department of Health Laboratory (1919–1920), and then in 1920 moved to the Michigan State Department of Health Laboratory, where the new director, Dr. C. C. Young, was reorganizing and developing the Michigan Department of Health Laboratories.

Work at the Michigan State Laboratory

During the next six years, in the central laboratory in Lansing, she was involved with all of the diagnostic laboratory procedures. That was a time of typhoid epidemics. Diphtheria also was rampant, and the search for carriers was an important part of the laboratory work, often requiring preparation of media at night for the next day's visit to the schools, with a physician, to make throat swabbings.

For several of those six years in Lansing, Pearl Kendrick worked with Dr. R. L. Kahn, who was developing his precipitation methods for laboratory diagnosis of syphilis.

In 1926, as associate director of laboratories, in charge of the newly established Western Michigan Division Laboratory, Kendrick moved to Grand Rapids. This development was needed to meet the growing demands of the Grand Rapids local area and western Michigan. An old, condemned building on City Hospital grounds, where the Sunshine Tuberculosis Sanatorium had been located, was provided for the laboratory. The place was remodeled, certain rooms were designated for specific services, and furniture, equipment, glassware, and other supplies were ordered as required for the needs of the anticipated laboratory examinations.

An apartment was provided for the bacteriologist-director on the upper floor to make 24-hour laboratory service possible. During the night, physicians frequently requested direct examinations of specimens from suspected diphtheria and pneumonia. For some time, the director's only company during the night was a terrier dog.

As the diagnostic laboratory services in the Grand Rapids Laboratory became better organized and fell into routine, Pearl Kendrick made plans to continue her education. The summer of 1928 she carried out a research problem with Professor Philip Hadley, Department of Bacteriology, University of Michigan Medical School. In 1929, on leave from the Grand Rapids Laboratory, she started a doctoral program at the School of Hygiene and Public Health at the Johns Hopkins University. The summer of 1931 she studied pathology at the University of Michigan Medical School. That fall she returned to Johns Hopkins University to complete work for a doctorate of science in public health, which she obtained in 1932. Her thesis research dealt with the antigenic properties of bacteriophage lysates of *Salmonella suipestifer*. She published a series of papers on this research; however, these were not her first publications. Nine papers on improved laboratory methods had preceded them.

Fruitful Collaboration with Grace Eldering

Soon after she returned to Grand Rapids, Dr. Kendrick was joined by Grace Eldering. Grace had graduated from the University of Montana in 1927, and in the fall of 1928 had come to the Michigan State Laboratories in Lansing as a volunteer worker. A vacancy occurred soon after her arrival and she was hired as a bacteriologist. In 1932 she was transferred to the branch laboratory in Grand Rapids. Her assignment there was most fortuitous both for Pearl Kendrick and for her. Under the skillful guidance of Dr. Kendrick, Grace Eldering soon became an expert in public health laboratory diagnosis. In time, she followed Kendrick's route to Johns Hopkins University and obtained her Sc.D. there in 1941. When, in 1951, Dr. Kendrick became resident lecturer in public health laboratory practice in the Department of Epidemiology at the University of Michigan, Ann Arbor, Dr. Eldering took over the Grand Rapids Laboratory as director. The Kendrick-Eldering research collaboration was most fruitful. They shared research problems, became fast friends, and for many years jointly owned a home outside Grand Rapids and a vacation home, a log cabin which they had built on Drummond

Island, overlooking the Straits of Mackinac between Lake Huron and Lake Michigan.

When Pearl Kendrick returned from Johns Hopkins University in 1932, she was thoroughly committed to studying a single disease. Measles was a great challenge to her, but the incidence of the disease was low at that particular time. Whooping cough, on the other hand, was one of the most prevalent and dreaded diseases. In the United States, in 1930, nearly 6,000 deaths from pertussis were reported, 95 percent of them in children under five years of age.[1]

Kendrick obtained approval from director C. C. Young to study this serious disease. His one-line memorandum of approval became an elastic clause to follow any path of investigation that appeared promising. At first no special resources, funds, or personnel were requested. During the early stages of the research, Drs. Kendrick and Eldering were able to fit the research work into extra hours at night and in the early morning. The first trial began appropriately with a study of the etiologic agent, then called *Hemophilus pertussis* but later changed to *Bordetella pertussis.* Although Bordet and Gengou had identified the organism in 1906 as the causative agent of whooping cough, questions had been raised during the early 1930s as to the possible involvement of a virus, either alone or in combination with the bacterium.[2]

Research on Whooping Cough

When Pearl Kendrick decided to study the organism, neither she nor anyone else in her laboratory had ever seen a culture of *H. pertussis.* According to Dr. Eldering,[3] they prepared cough plates by published methods, with some modification, and collected specimens from children with whooping cough who were referred to them by the city and county departments of health and by pediatricians. After the day's work at the laboratory was completed and the laboratory closed, she and Dr. Kendrick went out to collect specimens. Those were the days of the Depression, when many families lived in pitiful conditions, the parents unable to find work. Specimens were often collected by the light of kerosene lamps from coughing, strangling children. From most of the cases in the early stage, the pertussis organisms were isolated. These cultures were saved for further study and comparison. The studies amply confirmed the bacterial etiology of pertussis.

The next logical step was the preparation of an effective vaccine. Attempts to prepare vaccines had been made soon after the discovery of the organism in 1906.[4] The methods of preparation had not been precisely described. Some vaccines had been tested on a small number of children with no control group, and the results varied widely. It was difficult to assess the worth of these vaccines. As noted by Eldering,[5] confidence in the efficacy of a pertussis vaccine decreased to such an extent that, in 1931, pertussis vaccine was removed from the American Medical Association's list of New and Non-Official Remedies. Yet some studies by Madsen[6] in Copenhagen were sufficiently encouraging to promote a continued interest in a pertussis vaccine.

Leslie and Gardner's studies in England[7] emphasized the importance of careful selection of cultures for vaccine production.

Kendrick and Eldering made their first isolation of *Bordetella pertussis* on November 28, 1932. By January of 1933, they had prepared a small quantity of vaccine, which was given to a pediatrician at his request. Dr. Kendrick had the enthusiastic support and cooperation of local practicing physicians, as well as the local health department with its excellent division of trained nurses. The physicians administered the vaccine in a field study, in conjunction with the 18 nursing districts of the City Health Department. Controls of the same age and sex were selected from the same districts where inoculations were carried out.

Production of the test vaccine followed, in general, the published methods of Madsen and Sauer,[8] though sheep blood was substituted for horse or human blood. Only freshly isolated cultures were used, and this was an important consideration. The vaccine was given the usual sterility and safety tests and some lots were tested by Drs. Kendrick and Eldering by self-injection. There was at this time no potency test, but each lot of vaccine was tested for its agglutinability and for its antigenicity in rabbits. For these tests Dr. Kendrick had to set her own standards.

Because of the need for blood in the culture medium, the increasing volume of vaccine required soon necessitated increasing the number of sheep. These animals, which were bled at frequent intervals, were housed in an old barn behind Sunshine Hospital in Grand Rapids. The need for a sterile room was met by a small glassed-in cubicle, which was installed in the middle of the serology laboratory. But the need for additional funds and increased staff soon became acute. Even working after regular hours until midnight was not enough to keep up with the essential chores. The research funds used for carrying out the laboratory research, and the procedures required for the field trials, were incredibly small, particularly in contrast to modern day costs and funding. This is illustrated by a few items mentioned by Dr. Eldering in her historical sketch: the first financial aid was a check for $200 provided by the Grand Rapids City Commission on December 27, 1933; a private citizen gave $250 the following December. In February of 1935 the Federal Relief Agency awarded the laboratory $600 and an additional $1,200 in April of 1935; in November of that year $7,074 was received from the Works Progress Administration. During the period from December 1933 through September 1938, outside funds received amounted to $36,723; the Michigan Department of Health and the local health department contributed $48,089, making a total for the period of $84,812.[9]

Progress Report on the Vaccine

In the fall of 1935, at the annual meeting of the American Public Health Association, Dr. Kendrick presented a progress report on the field trials of the pertussis vaccine. She was cautious in comparing the two groups, the vaccinated and unvaccinated, relating exposure to contraction of the disease in the two groups. There had been remarkably fewer cases in the vaccinated group than in the control group. Following the presentation of this report, Kendrick was invited to discuss the results with the American Public Health Association (APHA) Subcommittee on the Evaluation of Administrative Practices. This committee requested Dr. Wade Frost, director, Department of Epidemiology, School of Hygiene and Public Health, Johns Hopkins University, to review the data. He in turn recommended that a statistical analysis of the data be made, and the APHA subcommittee obtained funds for this purpose.

At about this same time, a field trial of another pertussis vaccine was in progress in Cleveland, under the direction of Dr. James Doull, an epidemiologist. His study, by contrast, showed almost no difference in incidence of whooping cough, between the vaccinated and the controls.[10] Upon learning the results of this study, Dr. Frost called on Dr. George Ramsey of the School of Public Health, University of Michigan, to evaluate all of the results. Dr. Ramsey's recommendation was that the Kendrick vaccine be tested in another geographic location. Thus in 1940–1941 tests were carried out in Binghamton, New York, by J. E. Perkins and E. L. Stebbins.[11] By then pertussis vaccine was in production at the Biologics Products Division of the State Laboratories in Lansing, Michigan. The results of the New York State trial of the Michigan vaccine carried out by Perkins and Stebbins indicated that a high degree of protection was conferred by the vaccine, results very similar to Kendrick's first trial.

Her first field trial included 4,212 children between the ages of eight months and five years, a vaccinated group of 1,815 and a control group of 2,397.[12] There were 400 cases of whooping cough among the 4,212 children during the observation period of 44 months, 52 cases among the vaccinated and 348 among the control group, giving attack rates for the vaccinated of 2.3 per 100 and 15.1 per 100 in the control group. The cases among the vaccinated were less severe; no deaths occurred in either group. In further field trials with combined antigens, alum precipitated diphtheria toxoid, and pertussis, it was found that both antigens gave good protection. Thus the combined antigens came into general use. Tetanus toxoid was added later.

Potency Test Needed

It had become evident to Kendrick early on that a potency test was needed to differentiate effective from ineffective vaccines; otherwise every modification of the vaccine would require a field trial. Many attempts were made to develop a protection test in mice. Different routes of inoculation were used, different immunization doses and schedules were tried, and different routes of challenge in different strains of mice. Even neutralization tests and passive immunization were tried. Most tests showed some protection, but the results were not reproducible with any precision and did not yield definite end points. Then one day Dr. John Norton suggested to Dr. Kendrick that she try intracerebral inoculation of mice for the challenge inoculation. He and Dr. John Dingle were at that time using this method for potency testing of typhoid vaccine at Upjohn

Laboratories.[13] When the intracerebral challenge route was used for *B. pertussis* by Kendrick and Eldering, they found that following graded doses of vaccine, a graded response was obtained and end points were reproducible with a good degree of precision. Kendrick and Eldering, with M. K. Dixon, reported their results in a paper entitled "Mouse Protection Tests in the Study of Pertussis Vaccine: A Comparative Series Using the Intracerebral Route for Challenge."[14] In 1948 the National Institutes of Health issued minimum requirements for pertussis vaccine preparation. Since then, all pertussis vaccines released for distribution by manufacturing laboratories in the United States have been required to pass such a potency test.

Continuing her studies of the mouse potency test, Kendrick studied different strains of *B. pertussis* for antigenicity and virulence. She soon discovered that the choice of the challenge-strain in the first series of tests was most fortunate, since only one in seven of the smooth cultures tested had sufficient virulence for mice to be satisfactory.

As the evidence accumulated that pertussis vaccine offered substantial protection, interest in commercial production developed. The manufacturing laboratories worked out a plan through the Pertussis Study Group of the Committee on Evaluation of Administrative Practices of the APHA whereby funds from industry were channeled through APHA to the Michigan Health laboratories in Grand Rapids. Vaccine samples from the commercial laboratories were tested for density and potency in Kendrick's laboratory. In 1945 a complementary operation was carried out to test the feasibility and reliability of the mouse potency tests used in large-scale testing. Vaccine samples provided by Kendrick's laboratory were distributed to the industrial producers. The results from these tests proved quite satisfactory; agreement among tester laboratories was remarkably good.

Pertussis research was proceeding well here at home, but elsewhere there were problems. A controlled field trial of pertussis vaccine, carried out in England in 1942 at the instigation of the Medical Research Council, showed no evidence of efficacy in their pertussis vaccine.[15] They found no significant difference in severity or incidence of whooping cough between vaccinated and control groups. Later the Medical Research Council set up another field trial, including, among the antigens used, a reference vaccine prepared in the United States by the Michigan Department of Health Laboratories according to methods shown to be effective. Dr. Kendrick was invited to be a member of the Whooping Cough Immunization Committee of the Medical Research Council for the period of the study, and spent some time in England under WHO sponsorship. The results of this second field trial showed a wide variation in efficacy of the vaccines tested.[16] The Michigan vaccine gave good protection. This particular field trial provided the opportunity for comparison of results in children with the potency test in mice. Results showed good correlation between the order of protection in children and the order of potency in mouse protection tests among the vaccines tested.

Following these successful trials, Dr. Kendrick went on to study optimal size and spacing of dosage, the use of booster inoculation, and the stability of vaccines under storage. The investigations of her pertussis study group also extended to comparison of cross protection offered among other species of *Bordetella* and a study of immune globulins in pertussis.

Pertussis Research Brings Worldwide Recognition

Pearl Kendrick became widely known for her expertise with pertussis vaccines and was called upon by foreign nations to assist them. In 1940 she was invited to Mexico to help that country's health department in preparation of pertussis vaccine and to advise on an immunization program. She spent several months there in 1942 and returned later, on several occasions, for consultation.

She had come to Grand Rapids in 1926 as associate director of Michigan State Laboratories and chief of the Grand Rapids Branch, positions she held until 1951. In that year she moved to the University of Michigan School of Public Health as a resident lecturer in public health laboratory practice. Along with her teaching responsibilities, she continued research in collaboration with Dr. Eldering, who had become chief of the Grand Rapids Laboratory, and with the Immunization Committee of the American Public Health Association. Her research continued long after her official retirement, as shown by the 19 publications that appeared between 1960 and 1975. These included studies on application of fluorescent antibody method to *B. pertussis* in collaboration with Dr. Warren Eveland.

The World Health Organization sought Pearl Kendrick's expertise on many occasions. In 1950 she served in South America, as consultant on immunization programs for UNICEF, spending one month each with the ministers of health in Colombia, Chile, and Brazil. She served in 1952 as a member of a WHO Expert Committee on Diphtheria and Pertussis Immunization, which held a week-long meeting in Dubrovnik, Yugoslavia. In 1961 she returned to Mexico as WHO consultant to the Secretariat of Health and Welfare in its program for a nationwide campaign against whooping cough. In the following year she spent a month in the U.S.S.R. as a member of the Immunology Delegation, USPHS, under a U.S.-U.S.S.R. Exchange Agreement. While there, she and the other members of the delegation visited laboratories in Moscow, Rostov on Don, Kiev, Kharkov, and Leningrad, an experience she long remembered. On its return, the group made an official report to the Division of International Health, of the Department of Health, Education and Welfare. From October 1964 through January 1965, she visited laboratories in Central and South America as a Pan-American World Health Organization consultant on control of biologic products. In 1959 Dr. Kendrick participated in the Symposium on Immunization at the International Children's Center in Paris, where she discussed the optimal schedule of immunization against pertussis.

Honors and Awards

Since the early 1920s Pearl Kendrick had been an active participant in the American Public Health Association, of which she was a fellow. She served on the Governing Council for six years, was a member of the Executive Board for three years, vice-president in 1946, and served on a number of APHA committees: Laboratory Section (chairman) and Pertussis Subcommittee of the Committee on Evaluation of Administrative Practices, she was chairman of the Committee on Research and Standards from 1936 to 1954, she also chaired the Committee on Multiple Antigens 1954–1958, and she was a member and for several years chairman of the Committee on Bacteriophage Typing.

At the University of Michigan, she served on a number of academic committees: Scholarship, Student Affairs, and Graduate Student Committee, chairing several of them. She was long a member of Sigma Xi, Delta Omega, Theta Beta Phi, and Phi Kappa Phi, scientific honorary societies. In 1950 she was made an honorary member of the medical staff of Blodgett Hospital in Grand Rapids.

Among her awards are: a diploma from the Government of Mexico (1942) for assistance in whooping cough studies; a resolution of the Michigan State Legislature (1960), acknowledging her contributions to the health of Michigan; an Honorary Life Membership in the Michigan Public Health Association (1961). In the same year, she was made an Honorary Member of the Sociedad de Laboratorio Clinico, Mexico; in 1964, an Honorary Member of Asociacion Panamena de Microbiologia. She received the Sesquicentennial Award from the University of Michigan in 1967. In 1972 she was made an Honorary Member of the American Society for Microbiology.

In 1975, at age 85, she was selected as the Gudekunst Lecturer by the University of Michigan, School of Public Health. The lecture she delivered was entitled "Can Whooping Cough be Eradicated?"[17] She summarized many of her own contributions to the study and provided a historical review of the development of vaccine protection against pertussis. She compared pertussis with smallpox, then thought to be nearing eradication, and noted the similarities between the two diseases which favored eradication: humans are the only known host; there seems to be no reservoir in nature, and no carriers; the only source of infection is the patient with clinical or subclinical infection; the etiological agents appear to be stable with regard to the protective antigen; and a vaccine against each infection is available.

However, she added that the differences between smallpox and pertussis are sufficient to make the eradication of pertussis a low probability in the immediate future. She pointed out that pertussis is still so widespread throughout the world that the practical difficulties in providing vaccine coverage of all infected areas are enormous. Thus the unvaccinated areas will be continuing foci for reintroduction of disease even in generally well-vaccinated areas. She also noted that some of the remaining problems are amenable to research, e.g., improvement of the vaccine and augmentation of the immune response, concomitant with decrease in reactive material which produces the occasional severe reaction. She spoke about the analogous problem which had existed with regard to the smallpox vaccine: the rare untoward reaction to the vaccine.

With pertussis vaccine as with others, the balance of benefit had to be weighed against the hazard. Lastly, she pointed out that pertussis vaccine does not give complete protection and, with time, antibody levels fall. Booster injections must be considered where high risk remains.

In retirement Dr. Kendrick and Dr. Eldering enjoyed their home overlooking the Grand River, and the wooded grounds, which are inviting to birds of many a feather, supplementing Dr. Eldering's activities with the Audubon Society. There Dr. Kendrick assembled her publications and relevant correspondence files for reposit with the Bentley Historical Library, University of Michigan, Ann Arbor.

Both Dr. Kendrick and Dr. Eldering made significant contributions to public health progress. They dispelled the fog of uncertainty and distrust clouding the assorted pertussis vaccines produced through the early 1930s, and brought clarity of understanding to the problems of vaccine production and to standardization of procedures which could be relied upon. Thereafter they continued to refine methods of vaccine production, and to improve early diagnosis of pertussis and other infectious diseases. As a consultant for the World Health Organization, Dr. Kendrick traveled to Mexico, Russia, and other countries to teach and disseminate her skills. The recipient of many professional honors, she retained the love and esteem of her many students and laboratory associates. She was most fortunate in her association with Dr. Eldering, a reciprocal relationship which brought a blessing to the children of the world.

In October 1980 Pearl Kendrick died at age 90.

Mary Bunting with her genetics class, 1956.

CHAPTER XX

Mary Ingraham Bunting

". . . President of Radcliffe College, educational innovator, believer in equal opportunity for women in education."

Adversity alters careers, it produces a decision point where changes must be made. A sudden misfortune in the life of Dr. Mary Ingraham Bunting forced her to use her own resources and allow her native intelligence to come to the fore. She had been a pioneering microbial geneticist at a time when that field was commonly believed to be one of the badlands of microbiology. After the death of her husband she entered the field of women's education just before the awareness of women as people in their own right became a public policy issue. These ventures propelled her into prominence, setting a pattern for others to follow in education as in microbiology.

Born in Brooklyn, New York, in 1910 into a family long associated with education, Mary Ingraham was the oldest of four children. Her brother, Henry Gardner Ingraham, became a lawyer, and her sister, Winifred, attended Smith College before her marriage. Her younger brother, David, majored in music in college and took a master's degree in fine arts before going into the Navy in World War II. Later, he became a lawyer. Her father, Henry Ingraham, was a lawyer who came from several generations of lawyers. He was a graduate of Wesleyan College, where he later became a trustee. Her mother, Mary Shotwell Ingraham, graduated from Vassar. She was a dynamic woman and a professional volunteer, who served as national president of the Young Women's Christian Association (YWCA) for many years. She worked industriously for racial desegregation and the advancement of black women. She also served on the New York City Board of Higher Education under Mayor LaGuardia.

Early Education Belies the Future

Mary Ingraham (later Bunting) always expected to go to college, as far back as she could remember. However, her early education was anything but traditional. Due to a series of illnesses, she missed school most of the time prior to high school. A considerable amount of that time was spent with her mother's parents in Northport, Long Island, where she could indulge her interests in nature and farming. There in Northport and at home, books were readily available. She read widely. Her grandmother, who had once taught arithmetic in the public schools of New York City, tutored her in some of the basics until her parents decided that she should attend high school at Packer Collegiate Institute on a regular basis beginning in the fall of 1923. The entrance exams of the institute included a test on American history, or were supposed to. By mistake, Mary Ingraham was given the test on English history and passed it. Thus she entered high school with some advanced credit which permitted her an elective. She took biology—and didn't much like it. She found chemistry quite exciting, though, and recalls the thrill of looking through her first chemistry book on the trolley car as she returned home from school.

Her mother, Mary Shotwell Ingraham, had loved Vassar and so it followed naturally that her daughter Mary would go there also. Mary Ingraham had by then decided on a career in science and major in physics, judging that it would be good preparation for whatever field she chose later. It was when she studied bacteriology with Professor Anne Benton in her junior year that she found her niche. Here were problems that intrigued her in a field in which she felt she could make a contribution.

Living at Vassar was her first experience of being away from home on her own, and she enjoyed it. Graduating in 1931 with an A.B. in physics, she went to Cornell University for summer school and there began to catch up on chemistry. A Nancy Skinner Clark fellowship from Vassar encouraged her to pursue graduate work in agricultural bacteriology at the University of Wisconsin that fall. At Wisconsin she minored in biochemistry and took agricultural bacteriology (from Elizabeth McCoy, among others). She became interested in genetics, but it was not until later, when she had to teach the subject, that she began to master it.

Mary Ingraham received an M.A. degree in 1932 in bacteriology and continued on an Annie Gorham fellowship for a Ph.D. She served as a research assistant at the University of Wisconsin in 1934–1935, first in agricultural bacteriology and after completing her doctorate in 1934, with Harry Steenbock, in agricultural chemistry. She published three papers on her research at

Wisconsin, one with Steenbock on the relationship of microorganisms to carotenoids and vitamin A,[1] an earlier one with A. C. Baumann on the same subject,[2] and the third on her master's research, "The Bacteriostatic Action of Gentian Violet and Its Dependence on the Oxidation-reduction Potential."[3]

Marriage and Family

In the winter of 1936 she accepted a teaching position at Bennington College, then a new venture receptive to new ideas, offering students freedom to explore various avenues to education. Mary Ingraham taught physiology and genetics there for a year and a half. In June of 1937 she married Henry Bunting, whom she had met at the University of Wisconsin while they were both taking his father's course in pathology. The following year she taught physiology and hygiene at Goucher College while her husband completed an internship at Johns Hopkins University. In 1938 he moved to Yale as a resident in pathology where Mary Bunting obtained a research position working with Leo Roetger. Her formal responsibility was to transfer Roetger's *Lactobacillus acidophilus* cultures. It was a fortunate arrangement, for she was able to continue her own research work in his laboratory for two years before her first child was born. In 1940 she made the decision, quite customary at the time, to drop out and devote full time to her family. She stayed away, maintaining this role, for six years. During that period she had four children, Mary, Charles, William and John.

Between the third and fourth child, World War II ended and her husband, Dr. Henry Bunting, was able to take a sabbatical to pursue postdoctoral research at Harvard and Massachusetts Institute of Technology. Mary Bunting resumed her career by teaching a bacteriology course at Wellesley College. Upon returning to Yale University, where Henry Bunting was a member of the Medical School faculty in the Department of Pathology, Mary Bunting obtained a position as a research assistant, later lecturer, in microbiology, a position she retained until 1955.

She published four papers in the early 1940s based on the research she had done earlier at Yale with *Serratia marcescens.*[4] In 1945 she was invited to present her research at the Cold Spring Harbor Symposium on Quantitative Biology, despite the fact that her research had been interrupted for several years and dated from "the prehistoric era before Beadle and Tatum had isolated the first mutant strain of Neurospora," as she said in her presentation, titled "The Inheritance of Color in Bacteria, with Special Reference to *Serratia marcescens.*[5]

Color Variations in Bacteria

In her presentation, she noted that color had been a useful genetic marker in Drosophila. The change from red eye to white eye was conspicuous and made it easy for the geneticist to discover the laws of segregation and dominance governing transmission of the character, but no such regularity was revealed to the bacteriologist. Dealing with colonies rather than individuals, one had the impression that variations were continuous rather than discrete. "Small wonder that the bacteriologist called things by names of his own invention," she said.

Earlier studies by others working with *S. marcescens* had categorized the variations into color types, some rather stable on subculture. But quantitative studies of the phenomenon were conspicuous by their absence. Little advantage had been taken of the fact that the color variants are easy to detect and easy to count, and that, by counting them under controlled conditions, one might obtain information about rates of variation. Mary Bunting took advantage of these factors to find out what she could about the mechanism involved in production of variants.

Using American Type Culture Collection (ATCC) strain #274 of *S. marcescens* grown on beef extract peptone agar, she obtained a multitude of variants, but the color variation was continuous from deep red to white. Following the observations of others[6] that color distinction was better under acid conditions, she used a highly buffered ammonium citrate glycerol agar medium, from which she selected individual colonies for dilution and subculture onto the same type of medium. From a series of subcultures, she observed that the dark red type was most stable, producing 98 percent dark red colonies. It was also apparent that there were colonies of at least four types, the so-called dark red, bright pink, pale pink, and white types, that all contained a number of cells capable of reproducing the parent type, but that none of these was stable and, furthermore, that all variations were reversible. The organisms were unstable with respect to color, but the specific rates of variation were remarkably constant. She found that selective replating over a period of six months did not modify the stability of any type. All the evidence from the plating experiments indicated that specific variants were produced at constant rates.

She then followed the changes in color types in rapidly growing cultures that were maintained at logarithmic growth rates in a well buffered liquid medium. Although there were no detectable differences in the rates of growth of cultures inoculated with cells from dark red, bright pink, or light pink colonies, all of the cultures tended to come to equilibrium after ten to 15 days, with approximately 97 percent of cells of the dark red and three percent of cells of the bright pink types, as revealed by plating on the buffered agar medium. Evidence that the pale pink type gave rise, primarily, to cells of the bright pink type was indicated from the fact that the proportion of bright pink cells peaked after about four days, in the cultures inoculated with cells from pale pink colonies. From the dark red: bright pink equilibrium, she could estimate the rates of variation to those two types, concluding that in rapidly growing cultures, one in 10,000 dark red cells produced a bright pink variant in a two-day interval, whereas 32 in 10,000 bright pink cells produced dark red variants in the same interval. Very different results were obtained in aging cultures where population changes were due primarily to differences in rates of multiplication or survival of the different color types.

When other strains of *S. marcenscens* were tested (25 strains were studied), many behaved quite differently though characteristically for each strain. Ten strains were found to resemble strain #274, the original obtained from ATCC. Thus she concluded that these were heritable variations, that they were independent and reversible and tended to occur in sequence. She stated that, in these respects, the variations are analogous to gene mutations in higher organisms. She noted that there might be nongenic, or cytoplasmic, factors involved. She also added that uncritical acceptance of the concept at that time might tend "to blind our sight to other discoverable mechanisms that might produce heritable bacterial variants or influence their production."

When she returned to Yale in 1948, this early research of hers was sufficiently well accepted for her to receive a grant from the American Tuberculosis Association to study the genetics of Mycobacteria, analyzing factors involved in pathogenicity. Later, she received a grant from the Atomic Energy Commission to the study of the effects of radiation on the genetics of *S. marcescens*.

Life Outside the Laboratory

In 1954 her husband died. This misfortune completely changed the direction of her career. With four young children to support, she could no longer indulge herself in the leisurely pursuit of a research and teaching career which held such uncertain rewards. In 1955 she became dean of Douglass College and professor of bacteriology at Rutgers University, a step related to her extra-curricular and volunteer activities as much as to her professional career. During the six "inactive" years at home with her growing family and later, she had become active in many community functions. She had helped to organize the Public Health Nursing Association and had become a member of the Board of Directors, and had also been on the planning committee for the Regional School District in Bethany, Connecticut (1950–1953). She was secretary and chairman of the Educational Policies Committee of the Regional High School Board (1953–1955), a member of the Bethany School Board (1952–1955), a member of the Board of the Bethany Library Association (1952–1954), and a 4-H Club leader (1942–1955). As a member of the Regional Planning Committee and the Board, she had been involved in persuading citizens of the towns of Orange, Woodbridge, and Bethany to vote for a bond issue, and had participated in selecting an architect, developing plans, choosing contractors, choosing a principal, developing a budget, and assisting with the start-up of the school. Although only a volunteer, she had been exposed to public education and shown her interest in it.

In New Brunswick, at Douglass College, Bunting continued her volunteer activities with civic and social affiliations. She was a director of the Visiting Nurses Association there (1956–1959) and the United Fund of New Brunswick (1958); chairman of the Schools and Colleges Committee (1958–1959) and trustee of the YWCA (1958–1959); and a director and a trustee of the Middlesex General Hospital, New Brunswick, New Jersey (1959).

During this same period she was very much involved with professional organizations. She was chairman, Commission on Education of Women, American Council on Education (1958–1959); member, Commission on the Education of Women (1957–1959); member, Committee on Statistical Information and Research, American Council on Education (1956–1958); member, Divisional Committee for Science Personnel and Education, National Science Foundation (1957); and member, Board of Directors, New Jersey Association of Colleges and Universities (1956–1959). She also served on the James J. Kerrigan Memorial Scholarship Selection Committee for Merck and Company (1956–1959); and was an active member of the National Association of Deans of Women, Phi Beta Kappa (president, Rutgers Chapter, 1957–1958), Sigma Xi, and the American Society for Microbiology.

The Presidency of Radcliffe College

In 1960 she became the fifth president of Radcliffe College, a position she held until 1972. Paradoxically, as dean of Douglass College, she had had her own faculty, whereas as president of Radcliffe, she did not because the faculty for Radcliffe was Harvard University faculty.

For the first five years at Radcliffe, Bunting taught a freshman seminar on microbial genetics, in which some six to eight students pursued related but independent projects involving color-variation in *S. marcescens*. It was a popular course, which made it difficult to select among the applicants. Hoping one year to ease the decision process, she decided that she would not take any student who had not done well on college boards in chemistry. To her chagrin, she found that all the male applicants had taken board exams in chemistry and had done well, but only one of the 16 women applicants had chosen to take the exam. So she looked further into the matter to find out why there was a difference. A check of the women's folders revealed that all had taken chemistry in high school and had done quite well. On interviewing these women, she discovered that in each case someone—a teacher, a parent, a friend—had advised them that women don't do as well as men on science examinations. Although these women were all superior students in science, they had let generalizations based on slight differences in averages determine their personal decisions. Such norms and such advice have undoubtedly affected the career decisions of countless women.

While still at Douglass College, Bunting's interest in women's careers had been sparked by a statistic discovered in the course of a post-Sputnik study on the flow of talent into science. The National Science Foundation (NSF) study made by the Committee on Scientific Personnel, of which she was a member, was designed to find out which able high school graduates did not go on to college. What the committee discovered was that at least 97 percent of those who did not go on to college were female. It was a surprising statistic to Bunting and disturbing, all the more so because the statistic was suppressed. It was then that she began to realize that women were not expected to contribute anything really important to science or to many other intellectual frontiers. All too often academic advisors did not consider the loss of a young female scholar to be of any real significance.

Bunting came to Radcliffe sensitized to the problems of lack of expectations for women, all the subtle dissuaders, the inflexible requirements for fellowships (full-time) and for college faculty, even in women's colleges. Given her background as a microbiologist, her approach to the problem was experimental.

An Educational Experiment

She set up the Radcliffe Institute for Independent Study as a laboratory. Her first experiment was fairly simple: to offer financial assistance to women who had projects but lacked resources, time, or were in other, subtler ways isolated. The objective was to find out whether, if roadblocks were removed, women would be productive, would move ahead on their own—and, if so, if that would change attitudes and expectations in general. The experiment was designed for, but not restricted to, married women with children. The experiment was highly successful; virtually all of the some 300 women assisted by the Radcliffe Institute between 1961 and 1973 continued in their chosen professions.[7]

The Radcliffe Institute had been established in 1960, and supported by gifts from a few foundations, corporations, and individuals, as a laboratory in which to discover and provide the kinds of assistance that able and motivated women need to work more effectively in their chosen professions. Married women were given special consideration since they constituted the great majority and had had the most difficulty fulfilling their career goals. The announcement of the opening of the Radcliffe Institute made the front page of the *New York Times,* and a deluge of letters of inquiry and applications were received at the institute. This underlined the fact that almost no effort had been made in this country to further the careers of professional women. This program for independent study proved highly instructive and quite productive. Other programs followed, each set up to meet the needs of certain groups of women who for one reason or another had been prevented from moving ahead. Many participants were Ph.D.s with small children who needed the opportunity to continue their research in order to establish themselves as independent scholars. Some were medical women unable to get residencies because family responsibilities prevented their working full-time. Also, many hospitals had not hesitated to import non-English speaking male interns while being rigid about not hiring part-time women graduates of top medical schools. Radcliffe fellowships were given to part-time interns and graduate students whose records proved the value of the experiment.

Bunting notes that in the beginning many questions were raised by the "establishment" about the Radcliffe venture. Some questioned whether such women really existed as those whom the institute aimed to assist. There was also skepticism about their future, what these women would do after a year or two at Radcliffe. The next question could be anticipated: what would the effect be on husbands and children? In large part the answers were found to be positive: such women existed in large numbers, virtually all continued in their chosen fields (they were highly motivated), and in many cases part-time work could be carried on without disrupting the family at a time when full-time work would have made it difficult and unwise. Ultimately public recognition of the Institute's success came with the question "To what extent is the Institute exportable?" Many of the specific remedies were exportable and the waste of talent and early education was thereby greatly reduced.

Presidential Appointee

At the request of President Lyndon Johnson, Mary Bunting served with the Atomic Energy Commission during 1964–1965, taking leave from Radcliffe for that year. In 1972 she resigned from the presidency of Radcliffe and accepted a request from the president of Princeton University to serve as assistant for special projects, a position she retained until her retirement in 1975.

While president of Radcliffe College, Mary Bunting had served on President Kennedy's Commission on the Status of Women (1961–1963) and on the National Science Board (1965–1970). She became a trustee of the Population Council in 1971 and served on the Board of the College Retirement Equities Fund (CREF) from 1970 to 1978. After leaving Radcliffe she became a director of the New England Electric System, the Sperry & Hutchinson Company, and Arthur D. Little, Inc., as well as the Kaiser Foundation Hospital/Health plans.

In 1973 the New York Academy of Sciences sponsored a conference on "Successful Women in the Sciences. Analysis of Determinants" (Dr. Ruth Kundsin, convener), in which Mary Bunting participated. Her topic of discussion was "Education: A Nurturant if Not a Determinant of Professional Success."[8] In her presentation she noted that there was little evidence in the life histories presented at the conference that formal educational experiences or influences were critical determinants in career decisions or eventual success of the women participants. Education seemed to be a resource they used well. She emphasized the critical factor of motivation with two references of remarkable achievement: the small town of Northbrook, Illinois, had developed speed skaters using talent on hand with no special recruiting; at Merck Institute the remarkable record of their animal caretakers, many of them high school dropouts, who had been hired in the 1930s. Of the first 12 hired, all became productive scientists, 11 of them going on to obtain a Ph.D. or M.D. degree. Bunting also remarked that in 1973 there was a new era. She expressed the belief that the climate of unexpectation for women was changing; the rigid, entrenched practices and attitudes so detrimental to women's education and career success were becoming more enlightened and more democratic.

Commenting on her own career, Bunting emphasized the importance of freedom for exploration and discovery in her own development. First, in her childhood, when she had an extraordinary opportunity to explore nature as well as the classics, to follow where her curiosity led. Second, at Yale, during the early years of her marriage, when she was able to pursue her own research interests full-time. Later on, these experiences served her well in her experimental approach to the Radcliffe Institute.

Mary and her husband Henry felt free to experiment at home as well as in their laboratories. A few weeks before the birth of their fourth child the family moved into the basement of the house they were building on fifteen acres of submarginal farm land in Bethany, Connecticut. Goats, chickens, ponies, bees, and a variety of other animals, as well as gardens and orchards, kept everyone busy. They spent four or five happy years in the basement before the "upstairs" was completed, including a wing for Henry's father. Neighboring grandmothers babysat when Mary and Henry were in New Haven, but when they were home, the family preferred to be together, sharing whatever chores or projects needed doing. Even at Douglass College, after Henry's death, the family preferred to spend evenings together.

In 1979 Mary Bunting married Dr. Clement A. Smith, a neonatologist. They had known each other for many years. His first wife, who died in 1960, had been on the trustee committee that selected Bunting for the presidency of Radcliffe.

Mary Bunting has had a distinguished career building successive steps on her previous experience. She made germinal contributions to microbial genetics and to the field of women's education and her talents have been widely utilized. However, it well may be that she has contributed more by example than by precept.

FOOTNOTES

FOREWORD

1. Cole, R. M. 1984. Bacteriology and Mycology. In by D. Stetten, Jr., and W. T. Carrigan, 114–40: *NIH: An account of its research in laboratories and clinics,* New York: Academic Press.
2. O'Hern, Elizabeth M. 1975. Rebecca Craighill Lancefield, pioneer microbiologist. *ASM NEWS* 41: 805–810.
3. O'Hern, Elizabeth M. 1979. Women in the Biological Sciences. In *Expanding the role of women in the sciences,* Ed. Anne M. Briscoe and Sheila M. Pfafflin. Ann. N. Y. Acad. Sci. 323; 110–24.

CHAPTER I   Sara Josephine Baker

1. Baker, S. J. 1939. *Fighting for life.* New York: Macmillan, Chapt IV.
2. Ibid.
3. Ibid., p. 132.
4. Ibid., p. 138.
5. Ibid., p. 139.
6. Ibid., Chapter X.
7. Ibid., p. 200.
8. Baker, S. J. 1920. *Healthy babies.* Minneapolis: Federal Publishing Co., pp. 209.
9. ———. 1920. *Healthy mothers.* Minneapolis: Federal Pub. Co., pp. 187.
10. ———. 1920. *Healthy children.* Minneapolis: Federal Pub. Co., pp. 230.
11. ———. 1923. *The growing child.* Boston: Little Brown, pp. 230.
12. ———. 1925. *Child hygiene.* New York, London: Harper, pp. 534.
13. Baumgartner, L. 1971. Sara Josephine Baker. In *Notable American women,* Ed. Barbara Sicherman. Cambridge: Belknap Press of Harvard Univ Press, pp. 85–86.

CHAPTER II   Anna Williams

1. Park, William H., and Anna W. Williams. 1914. *Pathogenic microorganisms.* Baltimore: Williams and Wilkins; Park and Williams. 1929. *Who's who among the microbes.* New York: The Century Co.
2. From *The man who lived for tomorrow* by W. W. Oliver, Copyright 1941, 1969 by W. W. Oliver. Reprinted by permission of the publisher, E. P. Dutton, p. 95.
3. Ibid., p. 96.
4. Ibid., p. 103.
5. Ibid., p. 104–105.
6. Williams, Anna W. 1934. Group work in public health laboratories. *Med Women's J* 43: 151–3.
7. Oliver, p. 109.
8. Ibid., p. 155.
9. Ibid., p. 174–177.
10. Williams, Anna W. 1904. The rapid diagnosis of rabies by the examination of smears of brain tissue. *Ann Rept of Board of Health:* New York 1: 470–1.
11. Oliver, p. 223.
12. Williams, A. W. 1905. Negri bodies, with special reference to diagnosis in suspected rabies. *Coll Studies Res Lab Dept Health:* New York 2: 479–82.
13. Williams, A. W. and T. Flournoy. 1902. Report of studies on the etiology of vaccinia and variola. *Ann Rept Board of Health:* New York 2: 356–7.
14. Report of the medical commission for the investigation of acute respiratory diseases of the department of health of the city of New York. 1905. Part I. Studies on the pneumococcus. *J Exp Med* 7: 401–632.
15. Avery, O. T., H. T. Chickering, R. Cole, and A. R. Dochez. 1917. Acute lobar pneumonia: prevention and serum treatment. *Rockefeller Inst Med Res Monograph* No. 7.
16. Williams, A. W., and M. M. Lowden. 1906. The etiology and diagnosis of hydrophobia. *J Infect Dis* 3: 452–83.
17. Special report on typhoid fever. 1905. *Ann Rept Board of Health:* New York 1: 365.
18. Park, W. H. 1907. The role of ice in the production of typhoid fever. *JAMA* 49: 731–732.

19. Williams, A. W. 1908. Recent studies on scarlet fever. *Am J Obstet* 58: 152–156.
20. Williams, A. W. 1912–1913. A study of trachoma and allied conditions in the public school children of New York City. *Coll Stud Res Lab Dept Health:* New York 7: 159–247.
21. Williams, A. W. 1914. Chronic conjunctival afflictions in childhood. *Arch Ped* 31: 895–9.
22. Oliver, pp. 346–7, 351.
23. Williams, A. W. 1916–1919. Studies on the etiology of poliomyelitis. *Coll Stud Res Lab Dept Health:* New York 9: 330–333; Neal, J. B., P. L. Du Bois, H. L. Abraham, et al. 1916–1919. Report of the 1916 epidemic of poliomyelitis from a clinical and laboratory standpoint. *Coll Stud Res Lab Dept Health:* New York 9: 77–142.
24 Oliver, pp. 383–6.
25. Williams, A. W., H. M. Hatfield, A. G. Mann, and H. D. Hussey. 1916–1919. The etiology of influenza. *Monthly Bull Dept Health:* New York 8: 284–8.
26. Park, W. H., and A. W. Williams. 1919. Studies on the etiology of the pandemic of 1918. *Am J Public Health* 9: 45–9.
27. Park, W. H. 1919. Bacteriology of recent pandemic of influenza and complicating infections. *JAMA* 73: 318–21.
28. Park, W. H., A. W. Williams, and C. Krumwiede, Jr. 1921. Microbial studies on acute respiratory infection with especial consideration of immunological types. *J Immunol* 6: 1–4.
29. Williams, A. W., M. Nevin, and C. R. Gurley. 1921. Studies on acute respiratory infections. I. Methods of demonstrating microorganisms, including "Filtrable Viruses" from upper respiratory tract in "Health," and in "Common Colds," and in "Influenza" with the object of discovering "Common Strains." *J Immunol* 6: 5–24.
30. Williams, A. W., A. Unneberg, A. Goldman, and H. Hussey. 1921. Studies on acute respiratory infections. III. Relationship to upper respiratory infections of streptococci producing a green zone on standard blood agar plates. *J Immunol* 6: 53–64.
31. Park, W. H., A. W. Williams, and M. Wilson. 1927. The relationship of the Tunnicliff and Ferry diplococci to measles. *Am J Public Health* 17: 460–5.
32. Dick, G. F., and G. H. Dick. 1924. A skin test for susceptibility to scarlet fever toxin and antitoxin. A preliminary report. *JAMA* 82: 265–6.
33. Williams, Anna W. 1929. Relationship of the streptococci causing erysipelas. *Am J Public Health* 19: 1303–8.
34. Williams, A. W. 1929. Exotoxins of hemolytic streptococci. Their complexity and relationships. *JAMA* 93: 1544–5.
35. Park, W. H., and M. C. Schroeder. 1928. Practical points about active immunization against diphtheria and scarlet fever. *Am J Public Health* 18: 1455–64.
36. Park, W. H., A. W. Williams, and A. G. Mann. 1920–1926. Immunological studies on types of diphtheria bacilli. 1. Protective value of standard monovalent antitoxin. *Coll Stud Res Lab Dept Health:* New York 10: 82–8.
37. Oliver, p. 429.
38. Oliver, p. 431.
39. Park, W. H., and A. W. Williams. 1929. *Who's who among the microbes.* New York: The Century Co.
40. Williams, A. W. 1932. *Streptococci in relation to man in health and disease.* Baltimore: Williams and Wilkins Co.
41. Tunick, Irene and Janet Selig. 1940. *Panorama of gallant american women* (Program Supervision by Eva Hansl; Historical Consultant, Mary R. Beard and Eugenie Leonard). Washington: Office of Education, Federal Security Agency.
42. Oliver, p. 449.
43. Oliver, pp. 456–7.
44. Robinson, Elizabeth D. 1974. A tribute to women leaders in laboratory section of the American Public Health Association. *Am J Public Health* 64: 1006–7.

CHAPTER III   Florence Sabin

1. McMaster, P. D., and M. Heidelberger. 1960. *Florence Rena Sabin. Biographical memoirs,* National Acad Sci 34: 271–318.
2. Sabin, F. R. 1934. *Franklin Paine Mall: The story of a mind.* Baltimore: Johns Hopkins Press, p. 342.
3. McMaster and Heidelberger, p. 65.
4. Sabin, F. R. 1897. On the anatomical relations of the nuclei of reception of the cochlear and vestibular nerves. *Johns Hopkins Hospital Bull* 8: 253–9.
5. Sabin, F. R. 1901. *An atlas of the medulla and midbrain. A laboratory manual.* Baltimore: Friedenwald Co.
6. See note 4 above.
7. See note 1 above.

8. Sabin, F. R. 1920. Studies on the origin of blood-vessels and of red-corpuscles seen in the living blastoderm of chicks during the second day of incubation. *Carnegie Inst Contrib Embryol* 9: 213–62.
9. Sabin, F. R., R. S. Cunningham, S. Sugiyama, and J. A. Kindwall. 1925. The role of the monocyte in tuberculosis. *Johns Hopkins Hosp Bull* 37: 231–80
10. Corner, G. W. 1964. *A history of the rockefeller institute 1901–1953,* Rockefeller Institute Press, New York p. 635.
11. Sabin, F. R. 1927. The biological reactions in rabbits to the protein and phosphatide fractions from the chemical analysis of human tubercle bacilli. *J Exp Med* 46: 645–70.
12. Corner, p. 239.
13. Sabin, F. R., C. A. Doan, and C. E. Forkner. 1930. The reactions of the tissues to the lipoid fractions of the tubercle bacillus, strain H-37. *Am Rev Tuberc* 21: 290–304.
14. Sabin, F. R., F. R. Miller, C. A. Doan, and B. K. Wiseman. 1931. A study of the toxic properties of tuberculo-proteins and polysaccharides. *J Exp Med* 53: 51–80.
15. Sabin, F. R. 1939. Cellular reactions to a dye-protein with a concept of the mechanism of antibody formation. *J Exp Med* 70: 67–82.
16. McMaster and Heidelberger, p. 292.
17. Ibid., p. 293.
18. See note 2 above.
19. Sabin, F. R. 1936. Women in science. *Science* 83: 24–6.
20. McMaster and Heidelberger, p. 283.
21. Sabin. F. R. 1950. *The extension of the full-time plan of teaching to chemical medicine.* See: McMaster and Heidelberger, p. 285.
22. Sabin, F. R. 1927. Research in medical schools. *Science* 65: 308–11.
23. McMaster and Heidelberger, p. 299.
24. Ibid., p. 300.
25. *Rocky Mountain News,* 1 March 1951.
26. *Denver Post,* 9 October 1951.
27. Bluemel, E. 1959. *Florence Sabin: Colorado woman of the century.* Boulder: *Univ Colorado Press,* p. 222.
28. *Rocky Mountain News* 18 June 1959.
29. Corner, p. 242.
30. See note 29 above.

CHAPTER IV   Florence Seibert

1. Seibert, F. B. 1968. *Pebbles on the hill of a scientist.* St. Petersburg: Petersburg Printing Co, p. 162.
2. Bourn, J. and F. B. Seibert. 1925. The cause of many febrile reactions following intravenous injections. II. The bacteriology of twelve distilled waters. *Am J Physiol* 71: 652–9.
3. Seibert, F. B. 1926. the isolation of a crystalline protein with tuberculin activity. *Science* 63: 619–620.
4. See note 1 above.
5. Seibert, F. B., K. O. Pedersen, and A. Tiselius. 1938. Molecular weight electrochemical and biological properties of tuberculin protein and polysaccharide molecules. *J Exp Med* 68: 413–38.
6. ———. 1938. Molecular weight electrochemical and biological properties of tuberculin protein and polysaccharide molecules. *Rev Tuberc* 38: 399–405.
7. Heilman, D. H. and F. B. Seibert. 1946. The effect of purified fractions of tuberculin on tuberculin-sensitive tissue. Quantitative studies on tissue cultures. *Am Rev Tuberc* 53: 71–82.
8. Diller, E. C., A. J. Donnelly, and M. E. Fisher. 1967. Isolation of pleomorphic, acid-fast organisms from several strains of mice. *Cancer Res* 27: 1402–8.
9. Seibert, F. B., F. K. Farrelly, and C. C. Shepherd. 1967. DMSO and other combatants against bacteria isolated from leukemia and cancer patients. *Ann NY Acad Sci* 141: 175–201.

CHAPTER V   Rebecca Lancefield

1. Montague, Peter. 1894. *History and geneology of Peter Montague of Nansemond and Lancaster Counties, Virginia 1621–1894.* Amherst, Mass.: Press of Carpenter and Morehouse.
2. Dochez, A. R., O. T. Avery, and R. C. Lancefield. 1919. Studies on the biology of streptococcus. I. Antigenic relationships between strains of *Streptococcus haemolyticus. J. Exp Med* 30: 179–213.

3. Lancefield, R. C. 1925. The immunological relationships of *Streptococcus viridans* and certain of its chemical fractions. I. Serological reactions obtained with antibacterial sera. *J Exp Med* 42: 377–96.
4. Lancefield, R. C. 1928. The antigenic complex of *Streptococcus haemolyticus*. I. Demonstration of a type-specific substance in extracts of *Streptococcus haemolyticus*. *J Exp Med* 47: 91–103. II. Chemical and immunological properties of the protein fractions. Ibid., 469–80. III. Chemical and immunological properties of the species-specific substance. Ibid., 481–91. IV. Anaphylaxis with two non-type specific fractions. Ibid., 843–55. V. Anaphylaxis with the type-specific substance. Ibid., 857–75.
5. Hirst, G. K. and R. C. Lancefield. 1939. Antigenic properties of type-specific substances derived from group A hemolytic streptococci. *J Exp Med* 69: 425–45.
6. Lancefield, R. C. 1933. A serological differentiation of human and other groups of hemolytic streptococci. *J Exp Med* 57: 571–99.
7. Lancefield, R. C. 1934. A serological differentiation of specific types of bovine hemolytic streptococci (Group B). *J Exp Med* 59: 441–58.
8. Hare, R., and L. Colbrook. 1933. The biochemical reactions of haemolytic streptococci from the vagina of febrile and afebrile parturient women. *J Path Bact* 39: 429–42.
9. Lancefield, R. C., and V. P. Dole. 1946. The properties of T antigens extracted from group A hemolytic streptococci. *J Exp Med* 84: 449–71.
10. Lancefield, R. C. 1940–41. Specific relationships of cell composition to biological activity of hemolytic streptococci. Harvey Lectures, Ser. 36, 251–90.
11. See note 2 above.
12. Markowitz, M., and A. G. Kuttner. 1965. *Rheumatic fever: Diagnosis, management and prevention.* Philadelphia: J. B. Saunders Pub., p. 242. Markowitz, M., and L. Gordis. 1972. *Rheumatic fever: Diagnosis, management and prevention.* Second Edition. Philadelphia: J. B. Saunders Pub., p. 307.
13. Hook, E. W., R. R. Wagner, and R. C. Lancefield. 1960. An epizootic in Swiss mice caused by a group A streptococcus, newly designated type 50. *Am J Hyg* 72: 111–19.
14. Lancefield, R. C. 1959. Persistence of type-specific antibodies in man following infection with group A streptococci. *J Exp Med* 110: 271–92.
15. McCarty, M., and R. C. Lancefield. 1955. Variation in the group specific carbohydrate of group A streptococci. I. Immunochemical studies on the carbohydrates of variant strains. *J Exp Med* 102: 11–28.
16. Swanson, J., and M. McCarty. 1969. Electron microscopic studies on opaque colony variants of group A streptococci. *J Bact* 100: 505–11.
17. Curtis, S. N., and R. M. Krause. 1964. Antigenic relationships between group B and G streptococci. *J Exp Med* 120: 629–37.
18. Lancefield, R. C., and F. Perlmann. 1952. Preparation and properties of a protein (R antigen) occurring in streptococci of group A, type 28, and in certain streptococci of other serological groups. *J Exp Med* 96: 83–97.
19. Lancefield, R. C., M. McCarty, and W. N. Everly. 1975. Multiple mouse-protective antibodies directed against group B streptococci. *J Exp Med* 142: 165–79.
20. Wannamaker, Lewis W. 1981. Obituary: Rebecca Craighill Lancefield. *ASM News* 47: 555–9.

CHAPTER VI   Gladys Hobby

1. Hobby, G. L., K. Meyer, and E. Chaffee. 1942. Activity of penicillin *in vitro. Proc Soc Exp Biol Med* 50: 277–80.
2. Dawson, M. H., and G. L. Hobby. 1944. The clinical use of penicillin: Observations in one hundred cases. *JAMA* 124: 611–22.
3. Dawson, M. H., and T. H. Hunter. 1945. Treatment of subacute bacterial endocarditis with penicillin, results in 20 cases. *JAMA* 127: 129–37.
4. Finley, A. C., G. L. Hobby, S. Y. Pan, P. P. Regna, J. B. Routein, D. B. Seeley, G. M. Shull, I. A. Sobin, I. A. Solomons, J. W. Vinson, and J. H. Kane. 1950. Terramycin[R], a new antibiotic. *Science* 111: 85.
5. Hobby, G. L. 1962. Primary drug resistance in tuberculosis. A review: Part I. *Am Rev Resp Dis* 86: 839–46.
6. Hobby, Gladys L. 1951. Microbiology in relation to antibiotics. *J Hist Med & Allied Sciences* 3: 369–87.
7. Hobby, G. L. 1949. The mode of action of streptomycin. In *Streptomycin* Ed., S. A. Waksman. Baltimore: Williams and Wilkins Co., p. 618.
8. Hobby, G. L. 1950. Terramycin. In *Therapeutics in internal medicine.* New York: Nelson and Sons.
9. Hobby, G. L. 1954. Synergism, antagonism and hormesis. In *Antibiotic therapy.* Ed. H. Welch. New York: Medical encyclopedia, Inc.

10. Hobby, G. L. 1960. Antibiotics. In *Encyclopedia of science and technology.* New York: McGraw-Hill, pp. 464–8.
11. Hobby, G. L. 1960. Viomycin. Ibid., p. 327.
12. Hobby, G. L. 1963. Antimicrobial susceptibility tests. In *Diagnostic procedures and reagents,* Fourth Edition. American Public Health Association.

CHAPTER VII   Rhoda Benham

1. Benham, R. W. 1931. Certain monilias parasitic on man; their identification by morphology and by agglutination. *J Infect Dis* 49: 183–215.
2. Benham, R. W. 1932. Monilias, yeasts and cryptococci; their pathogenicity, classification and identification. *Am J Public Health* 22: 502–4.
3. Benham, R. W. 1945. Pathogenic fungi. In *Agents of disease and host resistance,* Ed. Gay, et al. Springfield: Charles C. Thomas.
4. Conant, N. F., D. T. Smith, R. D. Baker, and J. L. Callaway. 1971. (Third Ed) *Manual of clinical mycology.* Philadelphia: W. B. Saunders Co.
5. Emmons, C. W., C. H. Binford, and J. P. Utz. 1963. *Medical mycology.* Philadelphia: Lea & Febiger.
6. Benham, R. W., and B. W. Kesten. 1932. Sporotrichosis: its transmission to plants and animals. *J Infect Dis* 50: 437–58.
7. Benham, R. W. 1934. The fungi of blastomycosis and coccidiodal granuloma. *Arch Derm Syph* 30: 385–400.
8. DeLamater, E. D., and R. W. Benham. 1938. Experimental studies with the dermatophytes. 1. Primary disease in laboratory animals. *J Invest Dermat* 1: 451–67.
9. DeLamater, E. D., and R. W. Benham. 1938. Experimental studies with the dermatophytes. 2. Immunity and hypersensitivity provoked in laboratory animals. *J Invest Dermat* 1: 469–88.
10. Silva, M., B. M. Kesten, and R. W. Benham. 1955. *Trichophyton rubrum* infections: a clinical, mycologic and experimental study. *J Invest Dermat* 25: 311–28.
11. Benham, R. W. 1947. Biology of *Pityrosporum ovale.* In *Biology of pathogenic fungi,* Ed. W. Nickerson. Ann Cryptogam Phytopathol VI. Waltham, Mass: Chronica Botanica Publ. Co.
12. Hopkins, J. G., R. W. Benham, and B. W. Kesten. 1930. Asthma due to a fungus, Alternaria. *JAMA* 94: 6–10.
13. Benham, R. W. 1931. *Phoma condiogena,* an excitant in asthma: some observations on the development and cultural characteristics. *Bull Torrey Bot Club* 58: 203–14.
14. Benham, R. W., and L. Georg. 1948. *Allescheria boydii,* causative agent in a case of meningitis. *J Invest Dermat* 10: 99–110.
15. Benham, R. W., S. M. Aronson, and A. Wolf. 1953. Maduromycosis of the central nervous system. *J Neurophysiol and Expt Neuropathol* 12: 158–68.
16. Benham, R. W. 1956. The genus Cryptococcus. *Bact Rev* 20: 189–200.
17. Benham, R. W. 1957. Species of Candida most frequently isolated from man: methods and criteria for their identification. *J Chronic Dis* 5: 460–72.
18. Pollack, J. D., and R. W. Benham. 1957. The chlamydospores of *Candida albicans:* comparison of three media for their induction. *J Lab Clin Med* 50: 313–17.
19. Silva, M., and E. Hazen. 1957. Rhoda Williams Benham, 1894–1957. *Mycologia* 49: 596–602.

CHAPTER VIII   Elizabeth Hazen

1. Bacon, W. S. 1976. Elizabeth Lee Hazen 1885–1975. *Mycologia* 48: 961–69.
2. Ibid.; Hazen, E. L. 1938. Two strains of *Clostridium botulinum* Type E: Incitants of human botulinism. *Science* 87: 414.
3. Hazen, E. L., and F. C. Reed. 1955. *Laboratory identification of pathogenic fungi simplified.* Charles C. Thomas, Springfield, Ill. p. 253. Hazen, E. L., and M. A. Gordon. 1970. Idem.
4. Hazen, E. L. 1947. *Microsporum audouini:* The effect of yeast extract, thiamine, pyradoxine, and *Bacillus weidmaniensis* on the colony characteristics and macroconidia formation. *Mycologia* 39: 200–9.
5. Hazen, E. L. 1951. Effect of nutrition on the colony characteristics and macroconidial formation of *Microsporum audouini. Mycologia* 43: 284–96.
6. Georg, L. K. 1950. The nutritional requirements of the faviform trichophytons. *Ann NY Acad Sci* 50: 1315–47.
7. Hazen, E. L. 1957. Effect of temperature and nutrition upon macroconidial formation of *Microsporum audouini. Mycologia* 49: 11–19.
8. Hazen, E. L., and R. Brown. 1950. Two antifungal agents produced by a soil actinomycete. *Science* 112: 423.
9. See note 1 above.

10. Brown, R., and E. L. Hazen. 1955. Two antifungal agents produced by *Streptomyces noursei*. In *Therapy of fungus diseases: An international symposium*. Boston: Little, Brown & Co., pp. 199–204.

11. Mariat, F., E. L. Hazen, J. Le Beau, and E. Testard. 1955. Nocardiose humaine a abces cerebraux multiples: Etude bacteriologique. *Ann Inst Pasteur* 89: 256–61.

12. Cullen, J. H., E. L. Hazen, and R. Scholdager. 1956. Two cases of histoplasmosis acquired in felling a decayed tree in the Mohawk valley. *New York State J Med* 56: 3507–10.

13. Edwards, G. A., M. R. Edwards, and E. L. Hazen. 1959. Electron microscopic study of Histoplasma in mouse spleen. *J Bact* 77: 429–38.

CHAPTER IX   Leona Baumgartner

1. Sherwood, N. P. and L. Baumgartner. 1926. Studies on the Dick test and agglutination reactions in a series of university students. *J Immunol* 11: 323–30; Sherwood, N. P., C. Nigg, and L. Baumgartner. 1926. Studies on the Dick test and natural immunity to scarlet fever among American Indians. *J Immunol* 11: 343–60; Baumgartner, L. 1927. Agglutinins in human sera for scarlet fever streptococci. *Am J Pub Health* 17: 414–17.

2. Baumgartner, L., E. J. King, and I. H. Page. 1929. Die abnahme der Knochenphosphatase bei Uberfutterung mit bestrahlem Ergosterin. Biochem Zeitschr, Sonderabdruck aus 213 Bd. 1–3, Heft, pp. 170–76.

3. Baumgartner, L. 1932. Leonardo Da Vinci as a physiologist. *Ann Med Hist* n. s. 4: 155–71.

4. Baumgartner, L. 1935. Edwin Klebs, a centennial note. *New Eng J Med* 213: 60–3.

5. Baumgartner, L., and J. F. Fulton. 1935. *A bibliography of the poem Syphilis Morbus Gallicus by Girolamo Fracatoro of Verona*. New Haven: Yale U. Press, p. 157.

6. Baumgartner, L., and E. M. Ramsey. 1933. Johann Peter Frank and his "System Einer Vollstandigen Medicinischen Polizey." *Ann Med Hist* n. s. 5: 525–32 and 6: 69–90.

7. Baumgartner, L. 1937. John Howard and the public health movement. *Bull Inst Hist Med* 5: 489–508.

8. Baumgartner, L. 1939. John Howard (1726–1790), hospital and prison reformer: a bibliography, with Introduction by Arnold M. Muirhead. *Bull Hist Med* 7:486–534, 595–626. (Also published as a book by Johns Hopkins Press, Baltimore, p. 79.)

9. Baumgartner, L. 1940. Harvey Cushing as book collector and litterateur. *Bull Hist Med* 8: 1055–66.

10. Baumgartner, L. 1943. Arnold Carl Klebs (1870–1943). *Bull Hist Med* 14: 201–16.

11. Baumgartner, L. 1944. Arnold Klebs as humanistic scholar. *Bull Med Lib Assn* 32: 85–95.

12 Baumgartner, L. 1938. Old dogs and new tricks, the story of Ivan Pavlov. *Hygeia* 16: 150–52, 189–90.

13 Baumgartner, L. 1934. Age and antibody production. II. Further observations on qualitative changes in antisera associated with age. *J Immunol* 27: 417–29.

14. Baumgartner, L. 1934. The relationship of age to immunological reactions. *Yale J Biol and Med* 6: 403–34.

15. Baumgartner, L. 1935. Pituitary basophilism, pituitary tumors and hypertension. *Yale J Biol and Med* 7: 327–54.

16. Baumgartner, L., and D. M. Angevine. 1936. Lipoid pneumonia and conditions that may favor its occurrence. *Am J Med Sci* 192: 252–56.

17. Baumgartner, L. 1937. Age and antibody production III. Quantitative studies on the precipitin-reaction with antisera produced in young and adult rabbits. *J Immunol* 33: 477–88.

18. Frank, J. B. 1977. A personal history of Dr. Leona Baumgartner covering the years 1902–1962. Yale University Thesis.

19. Evans, A. C., F. H. Robinson, and L. Baumgartner. 1938. Studies on chronic brucellosis. IV. An evaluation of the diagnostic laboratory tests. *Public Health Rept* 53: 1507–25; Angle, F. E., W. H. Algie, and L. Baumgartner, and W. F. Lunsford. 1938. Skin testing for brucellosis (undulant fever) in school children. *Ann Internal Med* 12: 495–502.

CHAPTER X   Ida Bengston

1. Bengston, Ida A. 1918. The nature of contaminations of biological products. *U.S. Hygiene Laboratory Bulletin* No. 112: 14–36.

2. Bengston, I. A. 1922. Preliminary note on a toxin producing anaerobe isolated from larvae of *Lucilia caesar*. *Public Health Rept* 37: 164–70.

3. Bengston, I. A., and S. E. Steward. 1931. The official U.S. and international unit for standardizing gas gangrene antitoxin (histolyticus). *Public Health Rept* 51: 1263–72.

4. Stewart, S. E., and I. A. Bengston. 1939. Studies on standardization of gas gangrene antitoxin (Sordelli). *Public Health Rept* 54: 1435–41.

5. Noguchi, H. 1928. The etiology of trachoma. *J Exp Med* 48 (Suppl 2): 1–22. Part II.

Experimental production of chronic granular conjunctivitis in *Macacus rhesus* and chimpanzee with *Bacterium granulosis,* n. sp. Ibid., 23–32. Part III. Transmission of experimental granular conjunctivitis from animal to animal. Ibid., 33–44. Part IV. Bacterium granulosis and the experimental and human lesions. Ibid., 45–53.

6. Bengston, I. A. 1932. Etiology of trachoma with reference to relationship of *Bacterium granulosis* (Noguchi) to the disease. *Public Health Rept* 47: 1914–35.

7. Ibid.

8. Bengston, I. A. 1932. *Bacterium granulosis* conjunctivitis compared with that produced from human trachoma. Transmissibility of the granular condition induced in *Macacus rhesus* monkeys by inoculation with culture of *B. granulosis* contrasted with that induced by the same species by direct transfer from human trachoma. *Public Health Rept* 47: 2281–86.

9. Bedson, S. P. 1959. The psittacosis-lymphogranuloma group of infective agents. *J Roy Inst Public Health and Hyg* 22: 67–78.

10. Moulder, J. W. 1964. The psittacosis group as bacteria. New York, London, Sydney: John Wiley & Sons Inc., p. 95.

11. Bengston, I. A. 1940. The question of the rickettsial nature of trachoma. Proc Third Intl Congr Micro, pp. 395–404.

12. Cole, R. M. 1984. Bacteriology and mycology. In *NIH: An account of research and its laboratories and clinics,* by D. Stetten, Jr., and W. T. Carrigan, pp. 114–40. New York: Academic Press.

13. Bengston, I. A. 1935. Cultivation of the virus of Rocky Mountain spotted fever in the developing chick embryo. *Public Health Rept* 50: 1489–98.

14. Bengston, I. A. 1937. Cultivation of rickettsiae of Rocky Mountain spotted fever in vitro. *Public Health Rept* 52: 1329–35.

15. Bengston, I. A. 1941. Immunological relationships between rickettsiae of Australian and American Q fever. *Public Health Rept* 56: 272–81.

16. Bengston, I. A. 1941. Studies on active and passive immunity in Q fever infected and immunized guinea pigs. *Public Health Rept* 56: 327–45.

17. Bengston, I. A., and N. H. Topping. 1942. Complement fixation in rickettsial disease. *Am J Public Health* 32: 48–58.

18. Brigham, G. D., and I. A. Bengston. 1945. A study of complement fixation and Weil-Felix reactions in wild rats as related to the isolation of the virus of endemic typhus. *Public Health Rept* 60: 29–46.

19. Bengston, I. A., and N. H. Topping. 1941. The specificity of complement fixation test in endemic typhus fever using rickettsial antigens. *Public Health Rept* 56: 1723–27.

20. Topping, N. H., I. A. Bengston, R. G. Henderson, C. C. Shepherd, and M. J. Shear. 1945. Studies of typhus fever. *NIH Bull* 183: 1–110.

21. Evans, A. C. 1953. Obituary: Ida Albertina Bengston. *J Washington Acad Science* 43: 239–40.

CHAPTER XI   Alice Evans

1. Evans, Alice C. 1963. Memoirs. National Library of Medicine, p. 107. Addendum, 1969, p. 36.

2. Rogers, L. A., W. M. Clark, and A. C. Evans. 1914. The characteristics of bacteria of the colon type found in bovine feces. *J Infect Dis* 15: 100–23.

3. Evans, A. C. 1916. The bacteria of milk freshly drawn from normal udders. *J Infect Dis* 19: 437–76.

4. Evans, A. C. 1915. *Bacillus abortus* in market milk. *J Wash Acad Sci* 5: 122–25.

5. Evans, A. C. 1918. Further studies on *Bacterium abortus* and related bacteria. I. The pathogenicity of *Bacterium lipolyticus* for guinea pigs. *J Infect Dis* 22: 576–79. II. A comparison of *Bacterium abortus* with *Bacterium bronchisepticus* and with the organism which causes Malta fever. Ibid., 580–93. III. *Bacterium abortus* and related bacteria in cow's milk. Ibid., 23: 354–72.

6. Eyre, J. 1936. Undulant fever, a retrospect. *London J State Med* 44: 64–8.

7. Smith, R. 1929. Undulant fever: its relation to new problems in bacteriology and public health. *Medicine* 8: 193–209; Zinsser, H. 1936. Theobald Smith, 1859–1934. *Biographical Memoirs of the National Academy of Science* 17: 261–303.

8. Evans, A. C. 1923. The serological classification of *Brucella melitensis* from human, bovine, caprine, porcine and equine sources. *Public Health Rept* 38: 1948–63.

9. Dalrymple-Champneys, W. 1950. Undulant fever, a neglected problem. *Lancet* 21: 429–35, 477–85.

10. Simpson, W. M., and E. Frai. 1929. Undulant fever: report of 63 cases occurring and about Dayton, Ohio. *JAMA* 93: 1958–63.

11. Evans, A. D. 1934. Chronic brucellosis. *JAMA* 103: 665–7.

12. Cole, R. M. 1984. Bacteriology and Mycology. In *NIH: An account of research in its laboratories and clinics,* by D. Stetten, Jr., and W. T. Carrigan, pp. 114–40. New York: Academic Press.

13. Evans, A. C. 1937. The distribution of *Brucella melitensis* variety *melitensis* in United States. *Public Health Rept* 52: 295–303.
14. Evans, A. C. 1941. Cross protection between heterologous agglutinogenic types of beta hemolytic streptococci. *J. Immunol* 42: 15–34.
15. Eddy, B. E. 1976. Obituary: Alice Catherine Evans. *ASM News* 166–68.

CHAPTER XII Sara Branham

1. Branham, S. E., L. Robey, and L. A. Day. 1928. A poison produced by *Bacterium enteritidis* and *Bacterium aertryke* which is active in mice when given by mouth. *J Infect Dis* 43: 507–15.
2. Dopter, C. 1909. Étude de quelques germes isolés du rhino-pharynx voisin de méningocoque (Paramentingococcus). *Compt Rend Soc Biol* 67: 74–6.
3. Flexner, S. 1913. The results of the serum treatment in thirteen hundred cases of epidemic meningitis. *J Exp Med* 17: 553–76.
4. Gordon, M. H., and E. D. G. Murray. 1915. Identification of the meningococcus. *J Roy Army Med Corps* 25: 411–25.
5. Rake, G., and H. W. Scherp. 1933. Studies on meningococcus infection. III. The antigenic complex of the meningococcus—a type specific substance. *JAMA* 58: 341–60.
6. Laybourn, R. L. 1931. A study of epidemic meningitis in Missouri: Epidemiological and administrative considerations. *Southern Med J* 24: 678–86.
7. Branham, S. E. 1937. The significance of serologic types among meningococci. *JAMA* 108: 692–6.
8. Branham, S. E., and M. Pittman. 1940. A recommended procedure for the mouse protection test in evaluation of antimeningococcus serum. *Public Health Rept* 55: 2340–46.
9. Noble, A. 1927. A rapid method for the macroscopic agglutination test. *J Bact* 14: 287–300.
10. Branham, S. E. 1935. Laboratory diagnosis of meningococcus meningitis and identification of the meningococcus. In *Yearbook Supplement, Am J Public Health* 25: 143–46.
11. Miller, C. P. 1938. Experimental meningococcal infection in mice. *Science* 78: 340–41.
12. See note 8 above.
13. Flosdorf, E. W., and S. J. Mudd. 1935. Procedure and apparatus for preservation in "lyophile" form of serum and other biological substances. *J Immunol* 29: 389–425.
14. Branham, S. E. 1935. Protection of mice against meningococcis infection by polyvalent antimeningococcic serum. *Public Health Rept* 50: 768–78.
15. Branham, S. E., and S. M. Rosenthal. 1937. Studies in chemotherapy V. Sulphanilamide, serum and combined drug and serum therapy in experimental meningococcus and pneumococcus infections in mice. *Public Health Rept* 52: 685–95.
16. Branham, S. E., and M. F. Wormald. 1954. The use of the chick in titration of diphtheria antitoxin. *J Immunol* 72: 478–84.
17. Branham, S. E., and G. A. Hottle, and D. B. Riggs. 1954. Studies with *Shigella dysenteriae* (Shiga). V. Factors involved in the preparation of toxoid. *J Immunol* 73: 199–204.
18. Branham, S. E., and K. Habel. 1946. Preparation and evaluation of an irradiated toxoid from the toxin of *Shigella dysenteriae* (Shiga). *J Immunol* 54: 305–14.
19. Branham, S. E., and S. A. Carlin. 1948. Studies with *Shigella dysenteriae* (Shiga). I. Infection and toxin action in mice. *J Infect Dis* 83: 60–5.
20. Branham, S. E., K. Habel, and R. D. Lillie. 1949. Studies with *Shigella dysenteriae* (Shiga). III. Infection and intoxication in *Macacus mulatta* monkeys. *J Infect Dis* 85: 295–303.
21. Branham, S. E. 1951. Potency testing of dysentery antitoxic serum (Shiga). *Bull WHO* 4: 11–118.
22. Branham, S. E., G. M. Dack, and D. B. Riggs. 1952. Studies with *Shigella dysenteriae* (Shiga). IV. Immunological reactions in monkeys to the toxin in isolated intestinal pouches. *J Immunol* 70: 103–13.
23. Branham, S. E., and S. A. Carlin. 1950. The antigenicity of *Shigella sonnei*. *J Immunol* 65: 407–17.
24. Murray, R., and S. E. Branham. 1951. Effect of cortisones and ACTH on adrenals in experimental diphtheria, Shiga, and meningococcus intoxication. *Proc Soc Exp Biol Med* 78: 750–3.
25. Branham, S. E., C. W. Hiatt, A. D. Cooper, and D. B. Riggs. 1959. Antigens associated with the toxin of the *gravis* type of *Corynebacterium diphtheriae*. *J Immunol* 82: 397–408.
26. Branham, S. E., C. W. Hiatt, and D. B. Riggs. 1960. Properties of diphtheria antitoxin produced in guinea pigs with use of Freund's adjuvant. *Proc Soc Exp Biol Med* 104: 484–6.
27. Branham, S. E. 1928. The chemistry of antigens. In *Newer Knowledge of Bacteriology and Immunology*. Ed. E. O. Jordan and I. S. Falk. Chicago: the University of Chicago Press, pp. 710–20.
28. See note 10 above.

29. Branham, S. E. 1936. Laboratory diagnosis of meningococcus meningitis and identification of the meningococcus. *The Yearbook Supplement, Am J Public Health* 26: 170–84.
30. Branham, S. E. 1941 (First Ed.). 1945 (Second Ed.). Diagnosis of meningococcus infections and identification of the meningococcus. In *Recommended procedures and reagents*. New York: American Public Health Association.
31. Branham, S. E. 1948. Meningitis. *Encyclopaedia Britannica*.
32. Branham, S. E., H. E. Alexander, C. R. Falk, M. H. Lepper, and L. Weinstein. Bacterial Meningitis. In *Diagnostic procedures and reagents* (Fourth Ed.). Ed. A. H. Harris, and M. B. Colman, pp. 426–61. New York: American Public Health Association, Inc.
33. Stitt, E. R., P. W. Clough, and S. E. Branham. 1945. *Practical Bacteriology, Hematology and Parasitology* (Tenth Ed.). New York: The Blakiston Co.
34. Murray, E. D. G., and S. E. Branham. 1948. Genus I. *Neisseria* Trevisan. *Bergey's manual for determinative bacteriology* (Eighth Ed.), Ed. R. S. Breed, E. D. G. Murray, and A. P. Hitchems, pp. 295–302. Baltimore: Williams and Wilkins Co.
35. Branham, S. E., and M. J. Pelezar. 1957. Genus I. *Neisseria* Trevisan, 1885. *Bergey's manual of determinative bacteriology* (Seventh Ed.), Ed. R. S. Breed, E. D. G. Murray, and N. R. Smith. Baltimore: Williams and Wilkins Co.
36. Branham, S. E. 1958. Reference strains for the serologic groups of meningococcus (Neisseria meningitidis). *Intl Bull Bact Nomenc Taxon* 8: 1–15.
37. Branham, S. E., Secretary of the Committee. 1954. Preliminary report of the Committee on the Family Neisseriaceae. Interim report of the sub-committee on the Family Neisseriaceae. *Intl Bull Bact Nomenc* 4: 102–8.
38. Pittman, M. 1976. Sara Elizabeth Branham (Mathews): A biographical sketch. *ASM News* 42: 420–22.
39. Branham, S. E. 1960. A defense of Epimetheus: Development of knowledge concerning the meningococcus. *J Am Women's Assn* 15: 571–5.

CHAPTER XIII   Bernice Eddy

1. Enders, J. F., T. H. Weller, and F. C. Robbins. 1949. Cultivation of the Lansing strain of poliomyelitis virus in cultures of various human embryonic tissues. *Science* 109: 85–7.
2. Eddy, B. E., and S. E. Stewart. 1959. Physical properties, hemagglutinating and cytopathogenic effects of the SE polyoma virus. *Proc Third Canadian Cancer Conf.* New York: Academic Press, pp. 307–24.
3. Hull, R. M., J. R. Minner, and C. C. Mascoli. 1958. New Viral agents recovered from tissue cultures of monkey kidney cells. III. Recovery of additional agents both from cultures of monkey tissues and directly from tissues and excreta. *Am J Hyg* 68: 31–4.
4. Kirschstein, R. L. 1984. I. The virus and poliomyelitis vaccine. In *NIH: An Account of Research and Its Laboratories and Clinics,* by D. Stetten, Jr., and W. T. Carrigan, pp. 380–6. New York: Academic Press.
5. Sweet, B. H., and M. R. Hillman. 1960. The vacuolating virus, SV40. *Proc Soc Exp Biol Med* 105: 420–7; Hsiung, G. D., and W. A. Gaylord, Jr. 1961. the vacuolating viruses of monkeys. I. Isolation, growth characteristics and inclusion body formation. *J Exp Med* 114: 975–86.
6. Hull, R. N. 1957. New viral agents recovered form tissue cultures of monkey kidney cells. *N.Y. Acad Sci* 64: 413–23.
7. Melnick, J. L., and S. Stinebaugh. 1962. Excretion of vacuolating S-V 40 virus (papova virus group) after ingestion as a contaminant of oral poliovaccine. *Proc Soc Exp Biol Med* 109: 965–8.
8. Mortimer, E. A., Jr., M. L. Lepow, S. Gold, F. Robbins, G. J. Burton, and J. G. Fraumeni. 1981. Long-term follow-up of persons inadvertently inoculated with SV40 as neonates. *N Eng J Med* 305: 1517–18.
9. *Congressional Record.* 15 October 1971.
10. *Congressional Record.* 8 December 1971.
11. Kauffmann, F., K. Lund, and B. E. Eddy. 1960. Proposal for a change in the nomenclature of *Diplococcus pneumoniae* and a comparison of the Danish and American type designations. *Intl Bull Bact Nomenclature and Taxonomy* 10: 31–40.
12. Eddy, B. E. 1947. A study of influenza virus vaccines by a serum virus neutralization test and by active immunization. *J Immunol* 57: 195–202.
13. Ward, T. G., and B. E. Eddy. 1950. An antigenically distinct subtype of influenza virus which is virulent for mice in primary passage of allantoic fluid. *Science* 112: 501–3.
14. Stewart, S. E., B. E. Eddy, A. M. Gochenour, N. G. Borgese, and G. E. Grubbs. 1957. The induction of neoplasms with a substance released from mouse tumors by tissue culture. *Virology* 3: 380–400.
15. Stewart, S. E., B. E. Eddy, and N. G. Borgese. 1958. Neoplasms in mice inoculated with a tumor agent carried in tissue culture. *J Natl Cancer Inst* 20: 1223–43.

16. Eddy, B. E., and S. E. Stewart. 1959. Characteristics of the SE polyoma virus, and a virus that induces malignant tumors in mice, hamsters and rats and benign growths in rabbits. *J Am Public Health* 49: 1488–92.
17. Eddy, B. E., S. E. Stewart, and R Touchette. 1959. Effect of immunization of adult female hamsters on the latency of infection in offspring inoculated with SE polyoma virus. *Fed Proc Part 1,* 18: 565.
18. DiMayorca, G. A., B. E. Eddy, S. E. Stewart, W. S. Hunter, C. Friend, and A. Bendich. 1960. Isolation of infectious deoxyribonucleic acid from SE polyoma-infected tissue culture. *Proc Natl Acad Sci* 45: 1805–8.
19. Eddy, B. E. 1960. The polyoma virus. In *Advances in Virus Research* 7: 91–102.
20. Eddy, B. E. 1965. Virus and cancer. In *McGraw-Hill Yearbook of Science and Technology,* pp. 11–17.
21. Eddy, B. E. 1966. Oncogenic viruses. In *Basic Medical Virology,* pp. 471–501. Baltimore: Williams and Wilkins Co.
22. Eddy, B. E. 1967. Virus diseases. In *Encyclopedia of Biochemistry,* pp. 823–5. New York: Reinhold Publ. Corp.
23. Eddy, B. E. 1969. Polyoma virus. Monograph 7: 1–114. Wein/New York: Springer-Verlag, Inc.
24. Eddy, B. E. 1970. Infection with oncogenic viruses. In *Infectious agents and host reactions.* Ed. Stuart Mudd, pp. 572–91. Philadelphia: W. B. Saunders Co.
25. Eddy, B. E., G. S. Borman, W. H. Berkeley, and R. D. Young. 1961. Tumors induced n hamsters by injection of rhesus monkey cell extracts. *Proc Soc Exp Biol Med* 107: 191–7.
26. Eddy, B. E., G. W. Borman, G. E. Grubbs, and R. D. Young. 1962. Identification of the oncogenic substance in rhesus monkey kidney cell cultures as simian virus 40. *Virology* 17: 65–75.
27. Eddy, B. E., R. D. Young, and G. E. Grubbs. 1966. Resistance to viral-induced tumors. In *Viruses inducing cancer.* Ed. Walter J. Burdette, pp. 403–14. Salt Lake City: University of Utah Press.
28. Eddy, B. E. 1972. Viral infectivity or oncogenicity due to viruses in hamsters. In *Hamster Pathology.* Ed. Freddie Homburger, 6: 454–96. Basel/New York: Karger.
29. Eddy, B. E. 1972. Problems in the detection of the oncogenic potential of viruses in cell culture. In *Progress in immunobiological standardization* 5: 216–225. Basel/New York: Karger.
30. Li, C. P., N. M. Tauraso, B. Prescott, B. E. Eddy, R. C. Haye, E. C. Martino, G. Caldes, and G. Gorschboth. 1972. Intratumor therapy in rodents with aqueous clam extracts. *Cancer Res* 32: 1201–5.
31. Li, C. P., N. M. Tauraso, B. Eddy, B. Prescott, and E. C. Martino. 1972. Studies on inhibition of viral oncogenesis. III. Effect of clam extracts and methotrexate on tumor formation in male and female hamsters induced by virulent and attenuated adenovirus 12. *Arch Gesamte Virusforsch* 36: 284–95.

CHAPTER XIV   Sarah Stewart

1. Stewart, S. E. 1953. Leukemia in mice produced by a filterable agent present in AKR leukemic tissues with notes on a sarcoma produced by the same agent. *Anat Rec* 117: 532.
2. Stewart, S. E. 1955. Neoplasms in mice inoculated with cell free extracts of filtrates of leukemic mouse tissues. I. Neoplasms of the parotid and adrenal glands. *J Nat Cancer Inst* 15: 1391–1415.
3. Stewart, S. E., B. E. Eddy, and N. G. Borgese. 1958. Neoplasms in mice inoculated with tumor agent carried in tissue culture. *J Nat Cancer Inst* 20: 1223–43.
4. Eddy, B. E., S. E. Stewart, M. F. Stanton, and M. J. Marcotte. 1959. Induction of tumors in rats by S. E. polyoma virus embryo tissue culture preparations. *J Nat Cancer Inst* 22: 161–71.
5. Stewart, S. E. 1963. The mammalian oncogenic viruses. *J Am Med Woman's Assoc* 18: 129–36.
6. Polyoma cancer virus work progresses. No. 232 in a series. *NIH Record XI*(20) 1959. pp. 2–3.
7. *Time,* July 27, 1959. pp. 52–6.
8. Stewart, S. E., and F. E. Durr. 1967. Brain lesions in experimental animals produced with an agent from Burkitt tumor cultures. In *Perspectives in Virology* 5: 167–181. Ed. Morris Pollard. New York: Harper and Row.
9. Stewart, S. E., and A. E. Ferreira. 1967. Studies on the herpes-like virus recovered from the SL₁ line of the Burkitt tumor. In *Carcinogenesis: A broad critique,* pp. 121–124. Baltimore: Williams and Wilkins Co.
10. Stewart, S. E., E. Lovelace, J. J. Whang, and V. A. Ngu. 1965. Burkitt tumor: tissue culture, cytogenetic and virus studies. *J Nat Cancer Inst* 34: 319–27.
11. Stewart, S. E., D. E. Glazer, M. I. Stevenson, and B. J. Lloyd, Jr. 1967. Method for culture of the Burkitt herpes-types virus and the antigenic identity of three lines isolated. *Proc Third Intl Symp Comp Leukemia Res,* Paris, pp. 303–11. Basel/New York: Karger.

12. Stewart, S. E. 1967. The isolation of a myxo type virus from two human sarcomas. *Proc Third Intl Symp Comp Leukemia Res,* Paris, pp. 333–4. Basel/New York: Karger.
13. Stewart, S. E., J. Landon, E. Lovelace, and J. McBride. 1964. Viruses in cultures of human leukemia cells. In *Att del Symp sul Tema* I. Virus nelle Leucemie de Mammiferi. 364: 271–287.
14. Stewart, S. E., D. Glazer, T. Ben, and B. J. Lloyd, Jr. 1968. Studies on the hamster-brain passage virus recovered from human lymphoma cultures. *J Nat Cancer Inst* 40: 423–8.
15. Stewart, S. E. 1969. Studies on the herpes-type virus recovered from the Burkitt's tumor and other human lymphomas. In *Advances in virus research.* Ed. K. N. Smith, M. S. Lauffer, and F. B. Band, pp. 290–305. New York: Academic Press.
16. See note 14 above.
17. Stewart, S. E., G. Kasnic, Jr., G. Draycott, W. Feller, W. Golden, E. Mitchell, and T. Ben. 1972. Activation in vitro by 5-iododeoxyuridine of a latent virus resembling C-type viruses in a human sarcoma cell line. *J Nat Cancer Inst* 48: 273–7.
18. Stewart, S., G. Kasnic, Jr., C. Draycott, and T. Ben. 1972. Activation of viruses in human tumors by 5-iododeoxyuridine and dimethylsulfoxide as virus activating agents in human tumors. *Science* 175: 198.
19. Stewart, S. E., G. Kasnic, Jr., and C. Draycott, 1973. Characterization of C-type viruses activated in human tumors by modified 5-iododeoxyuridine technique. *Perspectives in Virology* VIII: 103–117. New York: Academic Press.
20. Spoken by H. L. Stewart on the occasion of the memorial service for the late Sarah Elizabeth Stewart on May 23, 1977 at the Bethesda Presbyterian Church.
21. Gross, L. 1951. Spontaneous leukemia developing in C3H mice following inoculation, in infancy, with AK-leukemia extracts, or AK-embryos. *Proc Soc Exper Biol Med* 76: 27–32.

CHAPTER XV   Margaret Pittman

1. Pittman, M., and I. S. Falk. 1930. Studies on respiratory diseases. XXXIV. Some relations between extracts, filtrates and virulence of pneumococci. *J Bact* 19: 327–61.
2. Pittman, M., and M. A. Southwick. 1930. Studies on respiratory diseases. XXXV. The pathology of pneumococcus infections in mice. *J Bact* 19: 363–74.
3. Pittman, M. 1933. The action of type-specific *Hemophilus influenzae* antiserum. *J Exper Med* 58: 683–706.
4. Pittman, M. 1931. Variation and type specificity in the bacterial species *Hemophilus influenzae.* *J Exper Med* 53: 471–92.
5. Ouchterlony, O. 1949. Antigen-antibody reactions in gels. *Arch Kemi Mineral Geol* B26: 1–9.
6. Pittman, M., S. E. Branham, and E. M. Sockrider. 1938. A comparison of the precipitation reaction in immune serum agar plates with the protection of mice by antimeningococcus serum. *Pub Health Rept* 53: 1400–8; Branham, S. E., M. Pittman, G. Rake, and H. W. Scherp. 1938. A proposed mouse protection unit for anti-meningococcus serum. *Proc Soc Exp Biol Med* 39: 348–50.
7. Pittman, M., and H. F. Fraser. 1940. A recommended procedure for the mouse protection test in evaluation of antimeningococcus serum. *Pub Health Rept* 55: 915–25; Pittman, M. 1941. A study of certain factors which influence the determination of the mouse protective action of meningococcus antiserum. *Pub Health Rept* 56: 92–110; Pittman, M. 1943. Mouse protective values of antimeningococcus serum in comparison with precipitation in immune serum agar plates. *Pub Health Rept* 58: 139–42.
8. Pittman, M. 1946. A study of fluid thioglycollate medium for the sterility test. *J Bact* 51: 19–32.
9. Probey, T. F., and M. Pittman. 1945. The pyrogenicity of bacterial contaminants found in biologic products. *J Bact* 50: 397–411.
10. Pittman, M. 1953. A study of bacteria implicated in transfusion reactions and of bacteria isolated from blood products. *J Lab Clin Med* 42: 273–88.
11. Pittman, M., and J. E. Lieberman. 1948. An analysis of the Wilson-Worcester method for determining the median effective dose of pertussis vaccine. *Am J Pub Health* 38: 15–21.
12. Pittman, M. 1974. Highlights of the development of requirements for pertussis vaccine and the effectiveness and safety of the vaccine. World Health Organization Panel Review, pp. 1–34.
13. Pittman, M. 1952. Influence of preservatives, of heat, and of irradiation on mouse protective activity and detoxification of pertussis vaccine. *J Immunol* 69: 201–16.
14. See note 12 above.
15. Pittman, M. 1970. *Bordetella Pertussis*—Bacterial and Host Factors in the pathogenesis and prevention of whooping cough. In *Infectious Agents and Host Reactions.* Ed. S. Mudd, pp. 239–70. Philadelphia: W. B. Saunders Co.
16. See note 12 above.

17. Mosley, W. H., J. C. Feeley, and M. Pittman. 1971. The interrelationships of serological responses in humans, and the active mouse protection test to cholera vaccine effectiveness. Intl Symp Immunobiol Standards 15: 185–196. Basel/Munchen/New York: Karger.
18. Pittman, M., R. W. Kolb, M. F. Barile, M. C. Hardegree, E. B. Seligmann, Jr., R. MacLennan, and F. D. Schofield. 1970. Immunization against neonatal tetanus in New Guinea—V. Laboratory assayed potency of tetanus toxoids and relationship to human antitoxin response. *Bull WHO* 43: 469–78.
19. Pittman, M., and H. J. Bohner. 1966. Laboratory assays of different types of field trial typhoid vaccines and relationship to efficacy in man. *J Bact* 91: 1713–23.
20. Felix, A., and R. M. Pitt. 1934. Virulence of *B. typhosus* and resistance to O antibody. *J Path Bact* 38: 409–20.
21. Wong, K. H., J. C. Feeley, and M. Pittman. 1972. Effect of a Vi-degrading enzyme on potency of typhoid vaccines in mice. *J Infect Dis* 125: 360–6.
22. Parfentijev, I. A., and M. A. Goodline. 1948. Histamine shock in mice sensitized with *Hemophilus pertussis* vaccine. *J Pharm Exp Ther* 92: 411–13.
23. Pittman, M. 1954. Variability of the potency of pertussis vaccine in relation to the number of bacteria. *J Ped* 45: 57–69.
24. Stronk, M. G., and M. Pittman. 1955. The influence of pertussis vaccine on histamine sensitivity of rabbits and guinea pigs and on the blood sugar in rabbits and mice. *J Infect Dis* 96: 152–61.
25. Manclark, C. R., C. T. Hansen, P. E. Treadwell, and M. Pittman. 1975. Selective breeding to establish a standard mouse for pertussis vaccine bioassay. II. Bioresponse of mice susceptible and resistant to sensitization by pertussis vaccine HFS. *J Biol Standardization* 3: 353–63.
26. Pittman, M. Hemophilus Infections in *Diagnostic Procedures and Reagents,* Fourth Ed., pp. 414–25. New York: American Public Health Association.
27. See note 15 above.
28. Pittman, M. 1970. Pertussis Vaccine Testing. Proc Round Table Conference on Pertussis, Bilthoven, Holland, 1969. *Symp Series Immunobiol Stand* 13:65–68 Basel/New York: Karger.
29. Pittman, M. 1979. Pertussis toxin: the cause of the harmful effects and prolonged immunity of whooping cough: a hypothesis. *Reviews of Infect Dis* 1: 401–12.
30. Pittman, M., B. L. Furman, and A. C. Wardlaw. 1980. *Bordella pertussis* respiratory tract infection in the mouse: pathophysiological responses. *J Infect Dis* 142: 56–66.

CHAPTER XVI   Bernice Eddie

1. Meyer, K. F., and B. Eddie. 1934. Psittacosis in the native Australian budgerigars. *Proc Soc Exper Biol Med* 31: 917–20.
2. Meyer, K. F., B. Eddie, and L. Foster. 1935. Cytology of psittacosis virus in the sparrow (Zonotrichia). *Proc Soc Exper Biol Med* 32: 1656–8.
3. Lazarus, A. S., B. Eddie, and K. F. Meyer. 1937. Ultrafiltration of psittacosis virus. *Proc Soc Exper Biol Med* 36: 437–8.
4. Meyer, K. F., B. Eddie, and I. M. Stevens. 1935. Recent studies on psittacosis. *Am J Pub Health* 25: 571–79; Geiger, J. C., A. B. Crowley, K. F. Meyer, and B. U. Eddie. 1939. Administrative problems in connection with psittacosis and the importation of Australian parrots. *JAMA* 113: 1479–81.
5. Meyer, K. F., B. Eddie, and H. Yanamura. 1939. Complement-fixation test with tissue-culture-antigens as aid in recognizing latent avian psittacosis (ornithosis). *Proc Soc Exper Biol Med* 41: 173–6.
6. Eddie, B., and T. Francis, Jr. 1942. Occurrence of psittacosis-like infection in domestic and game birds of Michigan. *Proc Soc Exper Biol Med* 50: 291–5.
7. Eddie, B., F. J. Radovsky, D. Stiller, and N Kumada. 1969. Psittacosis-lymphogranuloma venereum (PL) agents (Bedsonia, Chlamydia) in ticks, fleas, and native mammals in California. *Am J Epidemiol* 90: 449–60.
8. Meyer, K. F., B. Eddie, and H Yanamura. 1942. Active immunization to the Microbacterium multiforme psittacosis in parakeets and ricebirds. *J Immunol* 44: 211–17.
9. Quan, S. F., K. F. Meyer, and B. Eddie. 1950. Attempts to cure parakeet psittacosis carriers with aureomycin and penicillin. *J Infect Dis* 86: 132–5.
10. Meyer, K. F., and B. Eddie. 1955. Chemotherapy of natural psittacosis and ornithosis. Field trial of tetracycline, chlortetracycline and oxytetracycline. *Antibiotics and Chemother* 5: 289–99.
11. Meyer, K. F., and B. Eddie. 1951. A review of psittacosis for the years 1948 to 1950. *Bull Hyg* 26: 1–8.
12. Meyer, K. F., and B. Eddie. 1942, 1956, 1964. Psittacosis. *Diagnostic procedures for viral and rickettsial diseases.* First, Second, and Third Ed. New York: American Public Health Assn.

13. Meyer, K. F., and B. Eddie. 1954. Field trails of antibiotic treatment of psittacosis and ornithosis. *All Pets* 25: 96–102.
14. Fleischner, E. D., K. F. Meyer. 1917. Observations on the presence of *Bacillus abortus bovinus* in certified milk. Preliminary notes. *Am J Dis Child* 14: 157–73.
15. Meyer, K. F., and E. G. Shaw. 1920. A comparison of the morphologic, cultural and biochemical characteristics of *B. abortus* and *B. melitensis*. Studies of the genus *Brucella* nov. gen. *Int J Infect Dis* 27: 173–84.
16. Meyer, K. F., and B. Eddie 1929. Further studies on the pathogenicity of *Br. abortus* and *Br. Melitensis* for monkeys. *Proc Soc Exper Biol Med* 27: 222–4.
17. Meyer, K. F., and B. Eddie. 1930. Notes on the bacteriology of the Brucella group. *J Lab Clin Med* 15: 447–56.
18. Meyer, K. F., B. Stewart, L. Vassis, and B. Eddie. 1934. Brucella phagocytic index text. *Proc Soc Exper Biol Med* 32: 284–6.
19. Meyer, K. F., and B. Eddie. 1935. The problem of caprine Brucella infections in the United States. *J Am Vet Med Assn* 86: 286–303.
20. Stewart, B., B. Eddie, F. Paxton, and K. F. Meyer. 1935. Blood cultures in Brucella infections (a new method). *Calif & Western Med* 43: 112–13.
21. Meyer, K. F., and B. Eddie. 1941. Laboratory infections due to brucella. *J Infect Dis* 68: 24–32.
22. Meyer, K. F., and B. Eddie. 1949. Observations on difficulties encountered in the serological diagnosis of brucellosis and Q fever. *Calif Med* 70: 292–3.
23. Meyer, K. F., and B. Eddie. 1965. Sixty-five years of human botulism in the United States and Canada. Epidemiology and tabulations of reported cases 1899 through 1964. The George Williams Hooper Foundation, Univ Calif San Francisco Medical Center, p. 78.
24. Meyer, K. F., and J. Gunnison. 1928. *Cl botulinum* type D Sp. N. *Proc Soc Exp Biol Med* 26: 88–9.
25. Meyer, K. F., and J. Gunnison. 1928. Susceptibility of Maccus rhesus monkeys to botulinum toxin type B, C, and D. *Proc Soc Exp Biol Med* 26: 89–90.
26. Marshall, M. S., J. Gunnison, A. S. Lazarus, E. L. Morrison, and M. C. Shevsky. 1947. *Applied Medical Bacteriology.* Philadelphia: Lea & Fabiger.
27. Gunnison, J. B., E. Kunishige, V. R. Coleman, and E. Jawetz. 1955. The mode of action of antibiotic synergism and antagonism: the effect in vitro on bacteria not actively multiplying. *J Gen Microbiol* 13: 509–18.
28. Meyer, K. F., Eddie, and B. Anderson-Stewart. 1938. Canine, murine, and human leptospirosis in California. *Proc Exper Biol Med 38,* 17–19.
29. Howitt, B. F. 1934. Hyperimmune antipoliomyelitis horse serum. *Science* 80: 621–2.
30. Daggett, Emerson L., (Ed.). 1970. *California's Health.* Centennial Issue 1870–1970. Berkeley: University of California.
31. Meyer, K. F., and B. Eddie. 1938 Persistence of sylvatic plague. *Proc Soc Exper Biol Med* 38: 333–4.
32. Cavanaugh, D. C. 1974. K. F. Meyer's work on plague. *J Infect Dis 129* (Supplement): 510–12.
33. Heller, H. H. 1921. Principles concerning the isolation of anaerobes. Studies on pathogenic anaerobes. *J Bact* 6: 445–70.

CHAPTER XVII Elizabeth McCoy

1. McCoy, E. 1932. Infection by *Bacterium radicicola* in relation to the microchemistry of the host's cell walls. *Proc Roy Soc, B,* 110: 514–33.
2. Lewis, K. H., and E. McCoy. 1933. Root nodule formation of the garden bean, studies by a technique of tissue culture. *Bot Gaz* 95: 316–29.
3. Fred, E. B., I. L. Baldwin, and E. McCoy. 1939. Root nodule bacteria and leguminous plants. University of Wisconsin Studies in Science—No. 5. Supplement, Univ Wisc Press.
4. McCoy, E., E. B. Fred, W. H. Peterson, and E. G. Hastings. 1926. A cultural study of the acetone butyl alcohol organism. *J Infect Dis* 39: 457–83.
5. McCoy, E., and L. S. McClung. 1936. Studies on anaerobic bacteria. IX. Antigenic relations of *Clostridium bifermentans* and *Clostridium centrosporogenes. J Bact* 31: 557–68.
6. McCoy, E., and L. S. McClung. 1938. Serological relations among spore-forming anaerobic bacteria. *Bact Rev* 2: 47–97.
7. Langlykke, A. F., W. H. Peterson, and E. McCoy. 1935. Products from the fermentation of glucose and arabinose by butyric anaerobes. *J Bact* 29: 333–47.
8. Williams, F. T., and E. McCoy. 1934. On the role of microorganisms in the precipitation of calcium carbonate in the deposits of fresh water lakes. *J Sedim Petrol* 4: 113–26.
9. Umbreit, W. W., and E. McCoy. 1940. The occurrence of actinomycetes of the genus Micromonospora in inland lakes. In *Symposium on Hydrology,* pp. 106–14.

10. Comer, A. R., and E. McCoy. 1950. Some morphological and cultural studies on lake strains of micromonosporae. *Trans Wisc Acad Sciences, Arts, and Letters* 40: 49–70.

11. Henrici, A. T., and E. McCoy. 1938. The distribution of heterotrophic bacteria in the bottom deposits of some lakes. *Trans Wis Acad Sci, Arts, Lett* 31: 323–61.

12. McCoy, E., and W. B. Sarles. 1969. Bacteria in lakes: populations and functional relations. Eutrophication: Causes, Consequences, Correctives Symposium, 11–15. 1967. Natl Acad Science, pp. 331–339.

13. Moore, P. R., A. Evenson, T. D. Luckey, E. McCoy, C. A. Elvehjem, and E. B. Hart. 1945. Use of sulfasuxidine, streptothricin, and streptomycin in nutritional studies with the chick. *J Biol Chem* 165: 427–41.

14. McCoy, E. 1954. Changes in the host flora induced by chemotherapeutic agents. *Ann Rev Microbiol* 8: 257–72.

15. Simon, J., and E. McCoy. 1958. Bovine mastitis attributed to *Bacteroides* species. *J Am Vet Med Assn* 133: 165–8.

16. Smith, P. B., E. McCoy, and J. B. Wilson. 1962. Identification of staphylococci in nonfat dry milk by the fluorescent antibody technique. *J Dairy Sci* 45: 729–34.

17. Frea, J. I., E. McCoy, and F. M. Strong. 1963. Purification of type B staphylococcal enterotoxin, *J Bact* 86: 1308–13.

18. Weckel, K. G., R. Hawley, and E. McCoy. 1964. Translocation and equilibration of moisture in canned frozen bread. *Food Technol* 18: 234–36.

19. Roslycky, E. B., O. N. Allen, and E. McCoy. 1963. Physiochemical properties of phages of *Agrobacterium radiobacter. Can J Microbiol* 9: 119–209; ———. 1963. Serological properties of phages of *Agrobacterium radiobacter. Can J Microbiol* 9: 709–17.

20. Crabtree, K., and E. McCoy. 1967. *Zoogloea ramigera* Itzigsohn, identification and description. *Intl J Sys Bact* 17: 1–10.

21. McCoy, E., and L. S. McClung. 1931. *The Anaerobic bacteria and their activities in nature and disease.* A subject bibliography. Two vols., 295 pp. and 602 pp. Univ Calif. Supplement.; Witzel, S. A., E. McCoy, O. J. Attoe, L. B. Polkowski, and K. Crabtree. 1969. A study of farm waste: Farm animal waste characterization, handling, utilization. Washington: GPO.

22. Sarles, W. B. 1978. Obituary: Elizabeth McCoy. *ASM News* 44: 266–7.

CHAPTER XVIII   Cornelia Mitchell Downs

1. Sherwood, N. P., and C. M. Downs. 1919. Further studies of Pleomorphic streptococci—biologic reactions. *J Infect Dis* 24: 133–44.

2. Downs, C. M., A. M. Fortney, and E. R Edmiston. 1930. Three cases of tularemia. *J Kan Med* (May).

3. Downs, C. M. 1931. Studies of tularemia infection in rabbits and guinea pigs. *J Bact* 21: 47.

4. Downs, C. M. 1932. Immunologic studies on tularemia in rabbits. *J Infect Dis* 51: 460–8.

5. Bond, G. C., and C. M. Downs. 1935. Antigenic studies of the genus pasteurella. *Bull Kan Acad Science* 38: 87–92.

6. Downs, C. M., and G. C. Bond. 1935. Studies on the cultural characteristics of *Pasteurella tularense. J Bact* 30: 485–90.

7. Downs, C. M. 1942. The lethal effect of certain substances on *Pasteurella tularense. J Bact* 43: 102.

8. Chapman, S. S., C. M. Downs, and S. F. Kowal. 1946. Studies on the bacteriostatic and bactericidal action of streptomycin on *Bacterium tularense. J Bact* 51: 606.

9. Coriell, L. L., C. M. Downs, H. T. Eigelsbach, G. B. Pinchot, B. Owen, B. Hamilton, G. R. Spencer, and L. Buchele. 1946. The immunization of white rats against tularemia. *J Bact* 51: 623.

10. Downs, C. M., L. L. Coriell, S. S. Chapman, and A. Klauber. 1947. The cultivation of *Bacterium tularense* in embryonated eggs. *J Bact* 53: 89–100.

11. Downs, C. M., L. L. Coriell, G. B. Pinchot, S. S. Chapman, and B. Owen. 1947. Studies on Tularemia I. The comparative susceptibility of various laboratory animals. *J Immunol* 56: 217–28.

12. Downs, C. M., L. L. Coriell, H. T. Eigelsbach, K. F. Plitt, G. B. Pinchot, and B. J. Owen. 1947. Studies on tularemia II. Immunization of white rats. *J Immunol* 56: 229–43.

13. Coriell, L. L., C. M. Downs, and M. P. Clapp. 1957. Studies on tularemia III. Immunization of white mice. *J Immunol* 56: 245–53.

14. Downs, D. M., L. Buchele, and B. J. Owen. 1947. Studies on the pathogenesis and immunity in tularemia I. The course of infection with *Bacterium tularense* as seen in the normal vaccinated and recovered white rate. *J Bact* 54: 83–4.

15. Downs, C. M., L. Buchele, and E. P. Edgar. 1949. Studies on the pathogenesis of tularemia in the white rat. *J Immunol* 63: 117–33.; Downs, C. M., and L. Buchele. 1949. Studies on pathogenesis and immunity in tularemia II. Immune response of the white rats to *Bacterium*

tularense. J Immunol 63: 135–45; Downs, C. M., and J. M. Woodward. 1949. Studies on pathogensis and immunity in tularemia III. Immunogenic properties for the white mouse of various strains of *Bacterium tularense. J Immunol* 63: 147–63.

16. Downs, C. M. 1949. Tularemia. Proc Fourth Annual Meeting Intl Northwest Conference on Diseases of Nature Communicable to Man, pp. 80–3.

17. Downs, C. M., and J. M. Woodward. 1949. Immunogenic properties for the white mouse of various strains of *Bacterium tularense*. Proc 49th Ann Meeting Soc Am Bact, pp. 85–6.

18. Downs, C. M. 1949. Wartime advances in yellow fever and the rickettsial infections. *Trans Kan Acad Science* 52: 407–15.

19. Paretsky, D., C. M. Downs, R. Consigli, and B. Joyce. 1958. Studies on the physiology of rickettsiae I. Some enzyme systems in *Coxiella burnetii. J Infect Dis* 103: 6–11.

20. Roberts, A. M., and C. M. Downs. 1959. A study of the growth of *Coxiella burnetii* in the L strain mouse fibroblast. *J Bact* 77: 194–204; Bobb, D., and C. M. Downs. 1962. The phase antigens of *Coxiella burnetii. Can J Micro* 8: 687–702.

21. Riggs, J. L., R. J. Seiwald, J. H. Burckhalter, C. M. Downs, and T. G. Metcalf. 1958. Isothiocyanate compounds as fluorescent labelling agents for immune serum. *Am J Pathol* 34: 1081–97.

22. Riggs, et al. 1978. *Citation Classics* 17: 8.

23. Kordova, N., P. R. Burton, C. M. Downs, D. Paretsky, and E. Kovacova. 1970. The interaction of *Coxiella burnetii* phase I and phase II in Earle's cells. *Can J Micro* 16: 125–33.

CHAPTER XIX   Pearl Kendrick

1. Eldering, G. 1971. Symposium on pertussis immunization, in honor of Dr. Pearl L. Kendrick in her eightieth year: historical notes on pertussis immunization. *Health Lab Sci* 8:200–5.

2. McCordock, H. A., and M. G. Smith. 1934. Intranuclear inclusions. *Am J Dis Child* 47: 771–9.

3. See note 1 above.

4. Bordet, J., and O. Gengou. 1906. Le microbe de la coqueluche. *Ann Inst Pasteur* (Paris) 20: 731–41.

5. See note 1 above.

6. Madsen, T. 1933. Vaccination against whooping cough. *JAMA* 101: 187–8.

7. Leslie, P. H., and A. D. Gardner. 1931. The phases of *Hemophilus pertussis. J Hyg* 31: 423–34.

8. Sauer, L. W. 1933. Whooping cough: resume of a seven years' study. *J Ped* 2: 740–9.

9. See note 1 above.

10. Doull, J. A., G. S. Shibley, and J. E. McClelland. 1936. Active immunization against whooping cough. Interim report of the Cleveland experience. *Am J Public Health* 26: 1097–1105.

11. Perkins, J. E., E. L. Stebbins, H. F. Silverman, R. A. Lembcke, and B. M. Blum. 1942. Field trial of the prophylactic value of pertussis vaccine. *Am J Public Health* 32: 63–72.

12. Kendrick, P. L., G. Eldering, and A. Borowski. 1939. A study in active immunization against pertussis. *Am J Hyg* 29: 133–53.

13. Norton, J. F., and J. H. Dingle. 1935. Virulence tests for typhoid bacilli and antibody relationships in antityphoid sera. *Am J Public Health* 25: 609–17.

14. Kendrick, P. L., and G. Eldering, with M. Dixon, and J. Misner. 1947. Mouse protection tests in the study of pertussis vaccine. A comparative series using the intracerebral route for challenge. *Am J Public Health* 37: 803–10.

15. McFarlan, A. M., and E. Topley. 1945. Trial of whooping cough vaccine in city and residential nursery groups. *Brit Med J* 2: 205–8.

16. Medical Research Counsel (Great Britain). 1951. Report of committees on whooping cough immunization: the prevention of whooping cough by vaccination. *Brit Med J* 11: 1464–72.

17. Kendrick, P. L. 1975. Can whooping cough be eradicated? *J Infect Dis* 132: 707–12.

CHAPTER XX   Mary Ingraham Bunting

1. Ingraham, M. A., and H. Steenbock. 1935. The relation of microorganisms to carotenoids and vitamin A. II. The production of carotenoids by *Mycobacterium phlei. Biochem J* 29: 2553–62.

2. Ingraham, M. A., and C. A. Bauman. 1934. The relation of microorganisms to carotenoids and vitamin A. *J Bact* 28: 31–40.

3. Ingraham, M. A. 1933. The bacteriostatic action of gentian violet and its dependence on the oxidation-reduction potential. *J Bact* 26: 573–98.

4. Bunting, M. I., and L. J. Ingraham. 1943. The distribution of color variants in aging broth cultures of *Serratia marcescens. J Bact* 43: 585–91.
5. Bunting, M. I. 1945. The inheritance of color in bacteria, with special reference to *Serratia marcescens. Cold Spr Harb Symp Quant Biol* 11: 25–32.
6. Reed, G. B. 1937. Independent variation of several characteristics in *S. marcescens. J Bact* 34: 255–66.
7. Bunting, M. I. 1973. Education: A nurturant if not a determinant of professional success. *Ann N Y Acad Sci* 208: 194–9.
8. Ibid.

GLOSSARY

A

Abscess—Localized collection of pus in a cavity formed by disintegration of tissue.

Absorbed antiserum—Antiserum made more specific by absorption with an antigen.

Achorion—Obsolete genus of dermatophyte; now Trichophyton.

ACTH—Adrenal corticotrophic hormone.

Actinomycetes—Gram positive branching bacteria, some pathogenic.

Adenovirus—DNA (deoxyribonucleic acid) virus multiplying in cell nucleus, many types, can cause acute respiratory disease.

Aerobic—A bacterium requiring atmospheric oxygen for growth.

Agar—A gelatinous substance from certain algae, used as solidifying agent in culture media.

Agglutinin—An antibody demonstrated by agglutination of antigen (usually bacteria or cells)-antibody complex.

Agrobacterium—Gram negative, motile soil bacterium which can produce plant tumors.

Amoeba—A single-celled protozoan, some pathogenic.

Anaerobic—Bacteria multiplying in the absence of atmospheric oxygen.

Anaphylaxis—Severe systemic reaction to antigen in a hypersensitive individual.

Anatomy—Study of normal body structure.

Antibody—A globulin produced in response to an antigen and reacting specifically with that antigen.

Antigen—A macromolecule which can stimulate production of corresponding antibodies and can react with these antibodies.

Antiserum—Serum containing antibodies.

Arthroderma—A dermatophyte genus, the perfect form of Trychophyton.

B

Bacillus—A rod-shaped bacterium.

Bacterial culture medium—Nutrient broth or agar for growth of bacteria.

Bacteriophage—A bacterial virus.

Bacterium—Formerly used as genus name for many organisms.

BCG—Bacillus of Calmette and Guerin, a nonpathogenic tubercle bacillus.

Blastomyces—Dimorphic fungus, can produce systemic disease, blastomycosis.

Blastospore—A spore produced by budding, as in yeasts.

Bone marrow—The soft material that fills most of the cavities of the bones.

Branhamella—Bacterial genus: Gram negative cocci, nonpathogenic.

Brucella—Bacterial genus: Gram negative cocco-bacilli, three species, all pathogenic.

C

Candida—A yeastlike fungus, one species a primary pathogen, several species opportunistic.

Capsule—A hyaline mucopolysaccharide sheath on the wall of a cell or spore.

Ceratostomella—Fungus genus: one species causes Dutch elm disease, arthropod transmitted.

Chlamydospore—A thick-walled, intercalary, or terminal vegative cell which has become modified by thickening of the wall into a resting spore.

Clostridium—Bacterial genus: Gram positive, spore forming anaerobic bacilli producing toxins, many pathogenic, can cause botulism, tetanus, and gas gangrene.

Coccidioides—Dimorphic fungus: soil organism, can cause systemic disease, coccidioidomycosis.

Coccus—Spherical bacterium.

Complement—A heat-labile serum component affecting membranes when activated by antigen-antibody complex.

Complement fixation—A test using lysis of red blood cells as an indicator of antigen-antibody complex which binds (fixes) complement.

Corynebacterium—Bacterial genus: Gram positive club-shaped rods, many species, only one pathogenic, can cause diphtheria.

Coxiella—A rickettsial bacterium; one species can cause Q fever.

Cryptococcus—Fungus genus, a yeast, one species pathogenic, can cause cryptococcosis.

D

Dermatophyte—A fungus capable of living as a parasite on skin, hair, or nails.

Dimorphic (fungus)—Having two forms, as the hyphal and yeast forms of *Histoplasma capsulatum*.

Drosophila—A fly used for genetic studies.

E

Edema—Accumulation of fluid in connective tissue.

Electrophoresis—A process of separating molecules by electric charge.

Endospore—A fungus spore borne within a cell.

Epidermophyton—A dermatophyte, one species, pathogenic.

Epstein-Barr virus—An enveloped DNA virus which can cause infectious mononucleosis or Burkitt lymphoma.

Erythrocyte—A red blood cell derived from hemopoietic stem cell in bone marrow.

Etiologic agent—The causative organism.

F

Fluorescent antibody stain—chemically tagged antibody readily visible under special microscope.

Fluorescent hair—A hair which fluoresces under ultraviolet light owing to spores of certain dermatophytes.

Francisella—Bacterial genus (formerly Pasteurella): small Gram negative rods, one species can cause tularemia.

G

Gamma globulin—A serum protein which may contain antibodies.
Glabrous—A smooth surface.
Gram stain—A bacterial stain used to differentiate bacteria.

H

Hemolytic streptococcus—A streptococcus (colony) producing lysis of red blood cells in the medium.
Hemopoietic cells—Blood forming cells.
Herpes virus—A DNA virus, can cause gingival or genital herpes.
Heterologous—Having a different origin; a different kind.
Histology—Microscopic study of normal tissues.
Histoplasma—Dimorphic fungus, can cause histoplasmosis, a pulmonary, sometimes disseminated, disease.
Homologous—Having the same origin.
Hypersensitivity—An allergy to specific antigen(s).
Hypha (ae)—One of the tubular, usually branching and septate, cells which make up the vegetative portion or mycelium of fungi.

I

Immunoglobulin—Globulin containing antibodies.
Imperfect stage—A phase of fungus life cycle in which there is no sexual reproduction.
In vitro—Outside the living animal, as in a test tube.
In vivo—Within the living organism, human or animal.
Inflammation—A pathologic condition characterized by redness, pain, heat, and swelling.
Influenza virus—An RNA (ribonucleic acid) virus, three types, can cause influenza; antigenic variants continually emerge, can cause epidemics.
Intracellular—Within a cell.
Intradermal—Within the substance of skin.

L

Lactobacillus—Bacterial genus: Gram positive rods, several species, non-pathogenic, can be found in milk, important in cheese production.
Leprosy bacillus—*Mycobacterium leprae,* an acid fast organism which causes leprosy.
Leptospira—Bacterial genus: spiral motile bacterium, some pathogenic species, can cause leptospirosis.
Lesion—Any hurt, wound, or local degeneration.
Leucocyte—White blood cell which derives from hemopoietic stem cells of bone marrow; end cells with limited life span.
Lymph—Fluid taken up and discharged by the lymphatics.
Lymphatics—Vessels containing or conveying lymph.
Lymphatic system—The system of lymph vessels and lymph glands.
Lymphocyte—A type of white blood cell derived from a stem cell but matured in lymphatic system. Key specificity-determining cells in immune response.

M

Macroconidia—Large spores borne externally in various ways on specialized hyphae.

Macrophage—White blood cell of tissue and organs; binds, ingests, and degrades antigens, bacteria, and debris.

Matt colony—Coarse surfaced bacterial colony.

Meningococci—Bacteria of genus Neisseria, can cause meningitis.

Metastasis—Spread from one organ to other parts of the body.

Microsporum—Dermatophyte genus, can cause ringworm of the scalp.

Monoclonal antibody—Antibodies derived from a single clone of cells, a single progenitor cell.

Mouse protection test—Test for effectiveness of vaccine against specific organism.

Mouse strain—Inbred mice selected for certain characteristics.

Murine sarcoma virus—Mouse virus producing sarcoma tumors.

Mycobacterium—Bacterial genus: Acid-fast organisms, several species, *Mycobacterium tuberculosis* can cause tuberculosis.

Mycosis—A fungous disease.

N

Nanizzia—Dermatophyte genus; perfect stage of Microsporum.

Necrosis—Death of tissue.

Negri bodies—A colony of rabies viruses within certain nerve cells, visible with special stain under microscope.

Neisseria—Bacterial genus: Gram negative cocci, several species; two pathogenic. Can cause meningitis or gonorrhea.

O

Oncogenic virus—A virus which can cause cancer.

Onychomycosis—Fungous disease of the nails.

Opsono-phagocytic index—Measure of macrophage ingestion (phagocytosis) of antibody-coated bacteria or other particles.

P

Parasite—Organism that lives on and gets its food from another living organism.

Pasteurella—Bacterial genus: Gram negative rods, primarily animal pathogens. Genus formerly included organisms now found in Francisella and Yersinia.

Pathogen—Any disease-producing microorganism.

Pathology—The study of abnormal tissues and organs.

Perfect stage—Sexual stage of fungi; part of life cycle in which spores are formed after sexual mating and nuclear fusion.

Phoma—A soil fungus which can form brackets on trees.

Pityrosporum—A yeast-like fungus, seldom pathogenic.

Pneumococcus—Bacteria of genus Streptococcus, Gram positive cocci, usually encapsulated, many types, can cause pneumonia.

Pneumonitis virus—RNA virus related to mumps and measles viruses.

Poliomyelitis virus—RNA virus, three types pathogenic. Replicate only within cells but remain infectious for long periods in foods.

Polyclonal antibody—Antibody derived from several cells.

PPD—Purified protein derivative of tuberculin.

Precipitin—Antibody demonstrated by precipitation of antigen-antibody complex.

Proteus—Bacterial genus: Gram negative motile rods, may be pathogenic.

Pseudomycelium—Loosely united chain of cells formed by budding from the tip, which when elongated resemble mycelial hyphae.

Puerperal sepsis—Infection following childbirth.

R

Rickettsia—Small cocco-bacilli multiplying only intracellularly, several pathogenic species, transmitted by arthropods, can cause typhus fever.

Root nodule bacteria—Bacteria found in nodules on certain plant roots, usually provide nutrient to the plant.

S

Saccharomyces—Yeast genus: used in making bread and alcohol.

Salmonella—Gram negative motile bacilli, can cause food poisoning or paratyphoid fever.

Saprophyte—Free living organism.

Septate—Cells or hyphae divided by cross-walls.

Serological methods—Use of blood serum in diagnosis of disease and identification of microorganisms; antibody diagnosis.

Serratia—Gram negative bacilli producing pigmented colonies. Nonpathogenic.

Serum sickness—A severe allergic reaction to heterologous serum such as diphtheria antitoxin prepared in horses.

Schick test—Skin test used to determine susceptibility to diphtheria.

Shigella—Bacterial genus: Gram negative rods, several species, some pathogenic, can cause bacillary dysentery.

Sporotrichum—Dimorphic fungus of genus Sporothrix, found in soil and rotting wood, can cause sporotrichosis.

Staphylococcus—Bacterial genus: Gram positive cocci, characteristically in clusters, some pathogenic species, can cause abscesses, osteomyelitis.

Streptococcus—Bacterial genus: Gram positive cocci characteristically in chains, many serological types; can cause variety of diseases.

Streptomyces—Bacterial genus: branching organisms with aerial spores, found in soil, produce antibiotics.

SV40—Simian virus #40, a helper virus in tissue culture of certain defective adenoviruses. DNA virus, oncogenic for some animals.

T

Tinea capitis—Ringworm of the scalp.

Tissue culture—Growth of cells in culture used for propagation of viruses.

Trichophyton—Dermatophyte genus: many species, most are pathogenic, can cause ringworm.

Tubercle bacillus—*Mycobacterium tuberculosis,* cause of tuberculosis.

Tuberculin—Antigen of tubercle bacilli.

V

Vaccination—Immunization procedure used to increase resistance to infectious agents through production of antibodies.

Vaccine—A preparation of microorganisms or their products used for protection against a specific disease.

Vaccinia virus—Cowpox virus, a DNA virus.

Variola virus—Smallpox virus, a DNA virus.

Viral plaque—An area on tissue culture showing lysis or other cytopathic evidence of viral growth.

Viridans streptococci—Streptococci producing a green halo around colony on blood agar.

Virulence—Degree of pathogenicity.

Virus—Very small living organisms dependent upon intracellular replication.

W

Weil-Felix test—A serological test for rickettsial disease.

Widal test—A serological test for typhoid fever.

Willia—Yeast genus, nonpathogenic.

Y

Yersinia—Bacterial genus: Gram negative rods, can cause plague.

INDEX

Index of Names

Altman, Benjamin, 82
Anderson, R. J., 51
Anderson-Stewart, Belle, 139, 190
Arkwright, J. A., 82
Avery, Oswald T., 71, 72, 74, 75
Azzi, Azzo, 136

Baehr, Grandmother, 104
Baker, Jennie, 21
Baker, Orlando, 21
Baker, Sara Josephine, 21–30, 39, 110
   Honors & Awards, 21, 30–31
Bang, Bernhart, 136
Bang, Olaf, 136
Banting, Frederick G., 106
Barile, M. F., 176
Bauman, A. C., 225
Baumgartner, Abraham, 103
Baumgartner, David, 100
Baumgartner, Leona, 103–115
   Honors & Awards, 111, 113, 114
Baumgartner, Olga Leisy, 104, 105
Baumgartner, William J., 103, 105
Bayne-Jones, Stanhope, 122, 142–143
Beadle, George W., 227
Belcher, Sarah, 34
Bengston, Ida Albertina, 119–124, 137, 162
   Honors & Awards, 123, 124
Benham, George, 87
Benham, James Tyler, 87
Benham, James Tyler Jr., 87
Benham, Rhoda Williams, 87–93, 96, 100
   Honors & Awards, 93
Benham, Sarah Brower, 87
Benham, Victor, 87
Bensel, Walter, 23
Benton, Ann (Reiboth), 82, 225
Besredka, Alexander, 75
Biggs, Herman, 34, 35
Billings, Frank, 38
Birge, Edward A., 199
Blackwell, Elizabeth, 22, 34
Blackwell, Emily, 22
Bluemel, Elinor, 55
Bouquet, Paul, 62
Bordet, Jules, 136, 216
Botsford, Anna (Comstock), 128
Bourn, Janet, 61
Branham, Sara Elizabeth, 135–137, 141–148
   Honors & Awards, 146, 147
Brown, Rachel, 93, 98, 99
Bruce, David, 132, 137
Bruce, Mary, 132
Buba, Joy, 55
Buchanen, Robert, 136
Bunting, Charles, 227
Bunting, Henry, 227, 229
Bunting, John, 227
Bunting, Mary, 227
Bunting, Mary Ingraham, 225–233
   Honors & Awards, 230, 231
Bunting, William, 227
Byram, Mary Wortley Montague, 70

Calkins, Gary, 214
Calmette, Albert, 136
Campbell, Charlotte, 93

Catt, Carrie Chapman, 52
Chapman, S. S., 206
Clark, William M., 130
Cole, Rufus, 173
Colmer, A., 199
Comstock, John Henry, 128
Conant, Norman, 90
Coons, Albert, 209
Coriell, Louis, 206
Cox, H. R., 124, 208
Craighill, William E., 70
Cram, Eloise, 135
Cushing, Harvey, 109

da Vinci, Leonardo, 107
Dalldorf, Gilbert, 97
Dalrymple-Champneys, Weldon, 134, 137
Danforth, Samuel, 21
Darlington, Thomas, 24
Dawson, M. H., 82, 83
Delamater, E. D., 91
Demerec, M., 200
Dick, George, 42
Dick, Gladys, 42
Diller, Irene, 65
Dingle, John, 218
Dixon, M. K., 219
Doan, Charles, 51
Dochez, A. R., 71, 74, 75
Dodge, B. O., 88, 89
Dopter, C., 143
Downs, Cornelia Mitchell, 104, 205–210
   Honors & Awards, 210
Downs, Cornelia M. (Grandmother), 206
Downs, Harry, 209
Downs, Lily Campbell, 206
Doull, James, 218
Dozier, Carrie Castle, 191
Dublin, Louis, 110
Dyer, Rolla, 122

Eddie, Bernice Ulah, 185–193
   Honors & Awards, 193
Eddie, Hamilton, 185
Eddie, Louise Marcelin, 185
Eddie, Marceline (Cannon), 186
Edwards, G. A., 100
Edwards, M. R., 100
Eddy, Bernice Elaine, 151–159, 161
   Honors & Awards, 158, 163
Eddy, Nathan, 151
Eigelsbach, Henry T., 206
Eisenhower, President Dwight, 114
Eldering, Grace, 215, 216–221
Elias, Nathaniel, 110, 114
Eliot, Martha, 111
Evans, Alice Catherine, 108, 124, 127–138
   Honors & Awards, 133, 135, 138
Evans, Anne, 128
Evans, William Howell, 128
Eveland, Warren, 220
Eyre, John, 137

Falk, I. S., 173
Feeley, John C., 176
Flexner, Simon, 51
Flick, Lawrence F., 62

Florey, Howard, 209
Florio, Lloyd, 53
Foster, Lucile, 191
Fracastoro, Giralomo, 107
Francis, Arlene, 111
Francis, Edward, 206
Francis, Thomas, 207
Frank, Johann Peter, 107
Franklin, Benjamin, 66
Fred, Edwin B., 197, 198, 202
Freund, Jules, 108
Friedman, Lorraine, 202
Frost, Wade, 218
Frost, William D., 196, 197
Fulton, John, 107
Furman, Brian L., 179

Gardner, A. D., 217
Garrett, Mary, 48
Gay, Frederick P., 72–73
Gengou, O., 216
Georg, Lucile, 92, 97
Gilbert, Ruth, 96
Golgi, Camillo, 37
Goodner, Kenneth, 207
Gordon, M. A., 96
Gordon, M. H., 143
Gougerot, Henri, 90
Grad, Frank, 112
Green, Henry, 65
Griffith, Fred, 75, 82, 137
Guerin, Camille, 62, 136
Gunnison, Janet, 189, 190

Haas, Victor, 163
Hadley, Philip, 215
Hamilton, Fowler, 114
Hardagree, Carolyn, 176
Harper, R. A., 88
Harriman, Mrs. J. Bordon, 29
Harrington, Mark Henry, 54
Hastings, Edwin G., 129, 197
Hatfield, Hazel, 41
Hazen, Elizabeth Lee, 90, 95–100
    Honors & Awards, 93, 100
Hazen, Tracey, 88
Hektoen, Ludwig, 132
Heller, Hilda Hemple, 191
Heller, John R., 164
Henderson, R. G., 123
Henrici, A. R., 199
Hicks, Elias, 202
Hilleboe, Commissioner, 90
Hobby, Flora L., 82
Hobby, Gladys Lounsbury, 81–85
    Honors & Awards, 84
Hobby, Theodore, 82
Hoffstadt, Rachel, 136
Hopkins, J. Gardner, 88, 89, 92, 93, 96, 97
Horsfall, Frank, Jr., 63
Howitt, Beatrice, 190
Hussey, Helena, 41
Hylan, Mayor, 27

Ingraham, David, 225
Ingraham, Henry A., 225
Ingraham, Henry Gardner, 225
Ingraham, Mary Shotwell, 225
Ingraham, Winifred, 225

Joblovka, T. V., 65
Johnson, Edith Benham, 88
Johnson, President Lyndon B., 232

Johnson, Rhoda Benham, 88
Johnson, Treat, 51
Jordon, Edwin O., 142
Juday, Chauncey, 199

Kabat, Elvin, 63
Kahn, R. L., 214
Kasnic, George, 167
Kekule, F. A., 137
Kendrick, Pearl, 175, 213–221
    Honors & Awards, 220–221
Kennedy, President John F., 232
Kilham, Lawrence, 156
Klebs, Arnold C., 107, 109
Klebs, Edwin, 107
Knous, W. Lee, 53
Knox, Margaret, 27
Koch, Robert, 34, 47, 62, 132, 206
Kristensen, M., 134
Kuttner, Anne G., 76

LaGuardia, Mayor Fiorello, 44, 110, 112
Laighton, Florence, 22
Lambert, Alexander, 36
Lancefield, Donald, 71, 72
Lancefield, Rebecca Craighill, 69–78
    Honors & Awards, 78
Landsteiner, Karl, 105
Langmuir, Alexander, 114
Larson, Adline, 191
Lasker, Mary, 112
Lautenslager, Karl, 62
Lederle, Ernest J., 23
Ledingham, J. C. G., 136
Leslie, P. H., 217
Lillie, Frank, 105
Lincoln, President Abraham, 206
Lindsay, Mayor John, 84
Linstrom-Lang, 64
Long, Esmond R., 51, 61, 62, 65
Longley, William, 59
Lowenstein, Ernest, 62

Madsen, Thorvald J., 217
Mall, Franklin P., 49, 52
Mallon, Mary, 24, 38
Malott, Dean M., 205
Manclark, C. R., 178
Mankowski, Z. T., 92
Mann, Alice, 40
Mariot, Francois, 100
Marmorek, A., 35
Marshall, General George, 58
Marshall, Max, 190
Mathews, Phillips, 148
McCarty, Maclyn, 77
McClung, Leland, 199
McCollum, Elmer V., 129
McCormick, Cyrus Hall, 172
McCormick, E. G., 172
McCoy, Casius J., 134
McCoy, Elizabeth, 195–202, 224
    Honors & Awards, 202
McCoy, Esther, 196
McCoy, George, 122, 132, 137, 152
McGlone, William, 54
Mendenhall, Dorothy, 196
Mendell, Lafayette, 59
Metz, C. W., 71
Meyer, Karl, 82, 83
Meyer, Karl Friedrich, 186, 188, 191, 193, 199, 200, 208
Miles, Windham, 128

Miller, C. P., 170
Minor, Jessie, 58, 59
Montague, Lady Mary Wortley, 70
Morgan, Thomas Hunt, 71
Morris, J. Anthony, 156
Murphy, Walton, 206
Murray, E. D. G., 143, 147
Murray, Roderick, 180

Nickerson, Walter, 92
Nelson, P. Mabel, 59, 60
Nelson, Walter, 64
Nigg, Clara, 104
Noguchi, Hideyo, 121
Norton, John F., 175, 218
Nourse, William, B. 98

Oliver, Wade W., 37
Osborne, Thomas B., 60
Osler, William, 38, 106
Ouchterlony, Orjan, 174
Owen, Barbara J., 206

Page, Irvine, 106
Paretsky, David, 208, 209
Park, William H., 28, 34, 35, 38, 40, 43, 44, 112, 136, 137
Pasteur, Louis, 106
Pearce, Louise, 143
Pfeiffer, Jules, 173
Phipps, Henry, 62
Pinchott, Gifford, 206
Pinner, Emmy, 62
Pinner, Max, 62
Pittman, Helen, 172
Pittman, James, 172
Pittman, Margaret, 144, 171–181
    Honors & Awards, 178–180
Pittman, Virginia McCormick, 172
Plaut, Felix, 106
Poor, D. W., 37

Rabinowich, Lydia, 136
Ramsey, George, 218
Ranvier, Louise-Antoine, 49
Rawl, B. G., 130
Reed, Frank C., 96
Ribicoff, Abraham, 156
Richards, H. M., 88
Rice, John L., 44, 108, 109
Riggs, J. L., 209
Rivers, Thomas, 108
Rockefeller, John D., 82
Roetger, Leo, 227
Rogers, Lena, 24
Rogers, Lore A., 130
Rood, John, 55
Rosenberg, Anna, 112
Roosevelt, Eleanor, 112
Roosevelt, President Franklin D., 30
Roux, Emile, 34
Russell, Harry L., 197

Sabin, Florence Rena, 44–55, 63
    Honors & Awards, 52, 53
Sabin, George Kimball, 47
Sabin, Mary, 48, 53
Sabin, Serena Minor, 47
Sabin, William, 48
Salk, Jonas, 153
Sarles, W. B., 199, 202
Sauer, Louis, 217
Schick, Bela, 136

Schofield, Frank, 176
Schottmüller, Hugo, 75
Scott, John, 66
Segni, Antonio, 168
Seibert, Barbara Memmert, 58
Seibert, Florence Barbara, 57–67
    Honors & Awards, 64, 66
Seibert, George Peter, 58
Seibert, Mabel, 57, 58, 62, 64
Seibert, Russell, 57, 58, 66
Sherwood, Noble P., 104, 205, 206
Silva-Hutner, Margarita, 92, 100
Sjolander, N. O., 199
Smadel, Joseph, 176
Smith, Clement A., 231
Smith, Erwin, 130
Smith, George H., 107
Smith, Theobald, 132–134
Soper, George, 24
Stebbins, E. L., 218
Steenbock, Harry, 225
Stewart, Arthur, 162
Stewart, George, 162
Stewart, Helen, 162
Stewart Laura, 162
Stewart, Maria Andrade, 162
Stewart, Sarah Elizabeth, 154, 161–169
    Honors & Awards, 168
Stocking, W. A., 129
Stronk, Maria G., 177
Studdiford, William, 24
Svedborg, Theodor, 63
Swift, Homer, 63
Szent-Georgi, Albert, 64

Taliaferro, George, 58
Taliaferro, Lucy Graves, 58
Tatum, Edward L., 227
Tavari, D., 168
Thelander, Hulda, 192, 196
Thomas, M. Carey, 48, 52
Thomson, Annis, 82
Tiselius, Arne, 63
Todd, E. W., 73
Topping, Norman, 125, 126

Umbreit, Wayne, 199

Van Niel, C. B., 137
Van de Velde, Prof., 137
Van Kluyver, Albert, 137
Van Wagonen, Gertrude, 112
Veazie, Lyle, 189
Vivian, Governor, 53
Von Behring, Emil, 34
Von Frisch, Max, 105

Wagner, Mayor Robert, 111
Waksman, Selman, 84
Wald, Lillian D., 24
Wardlaw, A. C., 179
Waterhouse, Alice, 113
Weinberg, M., 136
Weisman, Chaim, 198
Welch, Lillian, 58
Welch, William, 38, 132, 133
Welles, Francis R., 136
Wells, H. Gideon, 61, 206
Wherry, William B., 152
White, Andrew D., 128
Wilder, Burt G., 128
Willetts Rachel Hicks, 195, 196
Williams, Anna Wessels, 33–45, 82, 112
    Honors & Awards, 44

Williams, Amelia Van Saun, 33
Williams, F. T., 199
Williams, Harry, 36
Williams, William, 33
Williamson, William, 196
Wilson, Amelia Williams, 33, 45
Wilson, Julius, 65
Wilson, R. J., 37, 45
Wilson, President Woodrow, 29
Winslow, C. E. A., 107, 108

Winternitz, Charles, 107
Woodward, J. M., 208
Wooley, Bernice Elaine, 156
Wooley, Gerald G., 156
Wooley, Sarah Elizabeth, 156

Young, C. C., 214, 216

Zackrzewska, Marie, 22
Zinsser, Hans, 70, 72, 106, 137, 207, 214

Index of Subjects

Accademia Nazionale dei Lincei, 165
Agency for International Development, 114
All Saints Cathedral, San Francisco, CA, 192
American Academy of Microbiology, 84, 158, 178
American Association for the Advancement of Science, 84, 90, 124, 158, 202
American Association for Cancer Research, 158
American Association of Blood Banks, 61, 66
American Association of Immunologists, 77
American Association of University Women, 66, 135, 138, 177
American Cancer Society, 66
American Child Hygiene Association, 29
American Council on Education, 229
American Design Award, 111
American Heart Association, 78
American Institute of Chemists, 100
American Medical Association, 44, 89, 216
American Medical Women's Association, 30
American Physiological Society, 61
American Public Health Association, 30, 44, 84, 89, 100, 113, 202, 217, 220
American Red Cross, 110
American Society for Microbiology, 138, 158, 180, 210, 221
American Society of Anatomists, 50
American Society of Pathology and Bacteriology, 37
American Society of Tropical Medicine, 132
American Thoracic Society, 84
Antibiotics
    Actidione, 95
    Aureomycin, 187
    Fungicidin, 99
    Nystatin, 95, 99
    Oligomycin, 200
    Oxytetracycline, 83, 84
    Penicillin, 81, 82, 187, 200
    Streptomycin, 82
    Tetracyclines, 187
    Viomycin, 82
Atomic Energy Commission, 230

Baby Health Stations, 26, 43
Bacteria
    Actinomycetes, 98, 199
    Agrobacterium radiobacter, 201
    Anaerobes, 62, 162, 198
    B C G, 136
    Bacillus granulosis, 121
    Bacillus polymyxa, 200, 201
    Bacillus sphaericus, 177
    Bacillus weidmanensis, 97
    Bacteria, coli-aerogenes group, 175
    Bacteria, Gram negative rods, 175
    Bacteria, pseudomonads, 175
    Bacteria, spore formers, 175

Bacterium aertrycke (See Salmonella)Bacterium enteritidis (See Salmonella)
Bacteriodes, 200
Bedsonia *(See Chlamydia)*
Bordetella pertussis, 175, 177, 178, 216–220
Branhamella catarrhalis, 147
Brucella abortus, 130, 131, 134, 188
Brucella melitensis, 130, 131, 134, 137, 188
Brucella suis, 133, 134
Chlamydia, 188
Chlamydia trachomatis, 121
Clostridium acetobutylicum, 198
Clostridium botulinum, 96, 120, 189
Clostridium histolyticum, 120
Clostridium oedematiens, 120
Clostridium perfringens, 120, 162
Corynebacterium diphtheriae, 34, 35, 37, 42, 62, 82, 146
Coxiella burnettii, 209
Francisella tularensis, 207, 208
Hemophilus aegyptius, 178
Hemophilus influenzae, 39, 41, 131, 173, 178
Hemophilus pertussis, *(See* Bordetella)
Lactobacillus acidophilus, 226
Leptospira sp., 190
Meningococci, 131, 137, 141–145
Micromonospora sp, 199
Miyagawanella (*See* Chlamydia)
Mycobacterium tuberculosis, 47, 62, 65, 66
Neisseria catarrhalis (*See* Branhamella)
Neisseria gonorrhoeae, 147
Neisseria meningitidis, 147
Pasteurella pestis (*See* Yersinia)
Pasteurella tularensis (*See* Francisella)
Pneumococci, 38, 72
Proteus vulgarus, 121
Rickettsia prowazekii, 121, 123
Rickettsia tsutsugamushi, 122
Root nodule bacteria (*See* Agrobacterium)
Salmonella enteritidis, 142
Salmonella suipestifer, 215
Salmonella typhi, 24, 35, 177
Serratia marcescens, 228, 229
Shigella dysenteriae, 145
Shigella sonnei, 146
Staphylococci, 200
Streptococci, 35, 207
Streptococcus hemolyticus, 42, 73–78
Streptococcus pyogenes (See S. hemolyticus)
    Streptococcus viridans, 42, 72, 73
Streptomyces griseus, 201
Streptomyces noursei, 98
Vibrio cholera, 35
Yersinia pestis, 191
Zoogloea ramigera, 201
Baltimore Association for Promotion of Education for Women, 52

Bay Pines Veterans Administration Hospital, 66
Bellevue Hospital, New York City, 112
Bergey's Manual of Determinative Bacteriology,
    147, 178, 198
Biological Warfare, 205
Biologics Control Laboratory, 152–153
Birthplace
    Brooklyn, New York, 225
    Cedarhurst, Long Island, New York, 87
    Central City, Colorado, 47
    Chicago, Illinois, 103
    Easton, Pennsylvania, 57
    Fort Wadsworth, Staten Island, New York, 69
    Glendale, West Virginia, 151
    Hackensack, New Jersey, 33
    Harvard, Nebraska 119
    Madison, Wisconsin, 195
    Neath, Pennsylvania, 128
    Oxford, Georgia, 141
    Poughkeepsie, New York, 21
    Prairie Grove, Arkansas, 171
    Rich, Mississippi, 95
    San Francisco, California, 185
    Tecalitlan, Mexico, 162
    Washington Heights, New York City, 81
    Wheaton, Illinois, 213
    Wyandotte, Kansas, 206
Blackhawk, Colorado, 48
Blodgett Hospital, Grand Rapids, MI, 221
British Medical Research Council Fellow, 74
Bureau of Animal Industry, 129
Bureau of Biologics, 64
Bureau of Child Hygiene, 21, 27, 29
Bureau of Municipal Research, 25
Bureau of Plant Industry, 130

California National Canners Association, 189
Cancer, viral etiology, 161
Carlsberg Laboratories, 64
Center for Disease Control, 65, 93, 114, 200
Charles Pfizer Incorporated, 83
Chemical Pioneer Award, 100
Children's Bureau, U.S. Department of Labor, 27,
    110
Cholera Research Laboratory, Dacca, 176, 179
Citation Classics, 209
Civil War, 48, 128, 172
Cold Spring Harbor Symposium on Quantitative
    Biology, 226
College Retirement Equities Fund, 232
Colorado State Board of Health, 54
Colorado State Tuberculosis Hospital, 54
Commercial Solvents Award, 84
Commissioner of Health, New York City, 103
Commonwealth Fellow, 65
Connaught Laboratories Ltd., Toronto, Canada,
    177, 190
Contagious Diseases Hospital, New York City, 39
Cooms Memorial, 66
Crumbine Medal, 210
Czechoslovakia Academy of Science, 209

Daughters of Cincinnati, 70
Denver Children's Hospital, 53
Denver General Hospital, 55
Denver Tuberculosis Hospital, 54
Department of Health Education and Welfare, 154,
    156
Department of Health Education and Welfare,
    Division of International Health, 220
Deutsch Forschungsanstalt fur Psychiatrie, 106
Diphtheria toxin and antitoxin, 35, 36, 43

Diseases
    Adenocarcinoma, 167
    Amebiasis, 39
    Blastomycosis, 91
    Botulism, 162, 200
    Brucellosis, 127, 132, 133, 137, 188–189
    Burkitt lymphoma, 165, 166
    Cholera, 171, 176, 178
    Choriomeningitis, 156
    Coccidioidomycosis, 87, 91
    Conjunctivitis, 39
    Contagious abortion of cattle (See Brucellosis)
    Diphtheria, 34, 36, 42, 144, 214, 215, 218
    Eclampsia, 33
    Encephalomyelitis, 190
    Endocarditis, 83
    Erysipelas, 42
    Gas gangrene, 120, 162
    Gross leukemia, 163
    Hodgkins disease, 165
    Impetigo, 25
    Influenza, 41, 131, 142
    Leprosy, 152, 159
    Leptospirosis, 190
    Leukemia, murine, 163, 169
    Malignancies, animals, 161, 163
        humans, 161, 164, 167
        viral etiology, 161, 163
    Malta fever (See Brucellosis)
    Measles, 36, 42
    Meningitis, 24, 36–38, 40, 141, 143
    Pediculosis, 24, 25
    Pertussis, 171, 216, 221
    Plague, 190, 191
    Pneumonia, 38, 197, 215
    Poliomyelitis, 40, 57, 58, 153, 158, 190
    Psittacosis, 185–187
    Q fever, 121, 189, 208
    Rabies, 35, 37, 171, 185
    Rheumatic fever, 69, 72, 74
    Rickettsial disease, 119–123, 208
    Ringworm, 87
    Rocky Mountain spotted fever, 121–123
    Rous sarcoma, 163
    Sarcoma, human, 65
    Scarlet fever, 42, 49, 104, 197
    Smallpox, 24, 36, 37, 171, 221
    Sporotrichosis, 90
    Syphilis, 81, 214
    Tetanus, 37, 40, 176, 177, 218
    Tuberculosis, 36, 57, 83, 132, 197
    Tularemia, 206–208
    Typhoid fever, 22, 24, 35, 38, 58, 171, 207–208, 214
    Typhus fever, 121, 123
    Undulant fever, (See Brucellosis)
    Whooping cough, (See pertussis)
    Yellow fever, 178
Diseases of Nature Communicable to Man, 208
Division of Biologics Standards, 154, 156, 179
Dry Milk Institute, University of Wisconsin, 200

E. R. Squibb & Sons, 99
Einstein Award, Albert, 113
Elliott, John, Memorial Award, 61
Emergency Maternal and Infant care, EMIC, 110,
    111

Fluorescent antibody test, 209
Fluorescent hair, 91
Ford Foundation, 112
Fort Detrick, 104, 207
Four-H Club leader, 228

Frankfort am Main, Germany, 206
Friday Harbor Marine Station, University of
    Washington, 104
Fungi
    Achorion quinckeanum, 91
    Allescheria boydii, 92
    Alternaria sp, 88
    Arthroderma benhamae, 91
    Aspergillus fumigatus, 99
    Aspergillus niger, 88
    Blastomyces dermatitidis, 91
    Candida albicans, 88–92, 98, 99
    Candida guillermondii, 92
    Candida parasilopsis, 92
    Candida tropicalis, 92
    Ceratostomella ulmi, 99, 100
    Coccidioides immitis, 91
    Cryptococcus neoformans, 88, 91, 92
    Epidermophyton floccosum, 91
    Histoplasma capsulatum, 99
    Microsporum audouinii, 91, 97, 100
    Microsporum felineum (M. canis), 91, 97
    Microsporum gypseum, 97
    Nanizzia sp, 97
    Pityrosporum ovale, 92
    Phoma condiogena, 92
    Saccharomyces sp., 89
    Sporotrichum schenckii (Sporothrix), 90, 100
    Sporotrichum beurmanii, 90
    Trichophyton gypseum (T. mentagrophytes), 91
    Trichophyton rubrum, 91
    Willia sp, 89
Fysikalisk kemiska Institutionen, 63

Gimbel Award, 66
Goodwin House, Alexandria, VA, 138
Guarnieri bodies, 36
Gudekunst lecture, 221
Guggenheim fellowship, 63

Hammersley Papermill Co., 59
Harvey lecture, 75
Health Research Council, 112
Henry Street Settlement, 24
Heterodoxy Club, 30
Hogan Mathematics Medal, 179
Hooper Foundation Laboratory for Medical
    Research, 186, 190, 192, 193, 199, 200
Hooper Newsvector, 193

Indians, American, 104, 196
Influenza Commission, New York City, 41
Influenza pandemic, 131, 197
International Center for Research and Training
    (ICMRT), 192
International Children's Center, Paris, 178
International Congress
    Antibiotics, 1959, Prague, 99
    Bacteriology, 1930, Paris, 135
    Bacteriology, 1936, London, 137
    Botany, 1950, Stockholm, 89
    Dermatology, 1935, Budapest, 88
    Hygiene and Demography, 1894, Paris, 34
    Medicine and Hygiene, 1913, London, 131
    Microbiology, 1950, Rio de Janeiro, 178
    Women, 1938, Edinburgh, 195
International Society of Bacterial Nomenclature,
    147

Jones, Duckett T., Memorial Award, 78

Kaiser Foundation Hospital/Health Plan, 232
Kaiser Wilhelm Institute, Munich, 106

Klebs-Loeffler bacillus *(See Cornyebacterium diph-
    theriae)*
Koch, Institute, Robert, 62
Koch's Postulates, 65, 163

Laboratory of Hygiene, USPHS *(See Hygienic Labo-
    ratory)*
Lake Mendota, Wisconsin, 199, 201
Lasker Award, Albert, 111
League of Nations, 120
League of Women Voters, 30
Lederle Laboratories, 99
Lenghi Prize, 168
Lister Institute, London, 136
Little Mothers League, 27
Lord and Taylor Award, 113
Lübeck tragedy, 136
Lymphatic system, 49, 50
Lyophilization, 144

M. Carey Thomas Award, 52
Madamoiselle Award in Science, 84
Marine Biological Laboratory, Woods Hole,
    Massachusetts, 71
McCalls Pattern Company, 26
Medical Care and Education Foundation of
    Massachusetts, 114
Medical Mycological Society of the Americas, 93
Medical Mycology, 89, 93
Medical Research Council, England, 213, 219
Memorial Hospital, Sloan Kettering, New York
    City, 76, 157
Mennonite Church, 103
Metropolitan Life Insurance Co., 41, 173
Metropolitan Museum of Art, 82
Mexico, Government of, 221
Michigan Public Health Association, 221
Michigan State Board of Health Laboratory,
    Lansing, 213, 215, 218–220
Michigan State legislature, 221
Midwives, 26
Missouri Valley Branch, American Society for
    Microbiology, 210
Mound Park Hospital, 66
Mount Vernon United Methodist Church,
    Washington, D. C., 180
Mouse protection tests, 175, 219
Mulford, H. K. & Co., 51
Mycological Society of America, 90
Mycology Laboratory of Columbia University
    College of Physicians and Surgeons, 92, 100

Naples Table Association, Italy, 50, 52
National Academy of Science, 50, 70, 77, 103
National Academy of Science Committee on Scien-
    tific Personnel, 229
    National Research Council, 132, 133
National Academy of Science, 114
    Institute of Medicine, 66, 114
National Achievement Award of Chi Omega
    Sorority, 52, 66
National Cancer Institute, 163, 164
National Foundation for Infantile Paralysis, 153
National Health Council, 114
National Institute of Allergy and Infectious
    Diseases, 84, 156
National Institutes of Health, 84, 113, 121, 128, 142,
    156, 161, 162, 174, 200
National Institutes of Health Cholera Advisory
    Council, 178
National Microbiological Institute, 163
National Research Council Fellow, 198
    Symposium on Eutrophication, 199

National Science Board, 231
National Science Foundation, 209, 229
National Statuary Hall, U. S. Capitol, 55
National Tuberculosis Association, 50, 51, 63, 64–65
Nature Study Course, Cornell University, 128
Negri bodies, 37
Nevada City, California, 185
New England Electric System, 232
New England Hospital for Women and Children, Boston, 30
New Jersey Association of Colleges and Universities, 229
New Jersey Department of Health, 30
New Jersey Women's Prison Board, 30
New York Academy of Medicine, 26, 30, 90
New York Academy of Science, 84, 90, 232
New York City Bureau of Adult Hygiene, 113
Bureau of Child Hygiene/Health, 39, 43, 108, 110, 111
New York City Commissioner of Health, 111–113
New York City Department of Health, 22, 109
New York City Department of Health Laboratory, 28, 35, 37, 39, 41, 42–44, 82, 112
New York City Sanitary Code, 112
New York Foundation, 111
New York Lung Association, 84
New York Public Health Research Institute, 112
New York Society of Pathology, 37
New York State Department of Health Laboratory, 93, 96–99, 214
New York State Board of Regents, 22
New York Times, 30
North Brother Island, N. Y., 24

Office of Naval Research, 208
Office of Naval Research Laboratory, Berkeley, CA, 104
Office of Strategic Research and Development, 162
Office of the Surgeon General, 209
Old Tuberculin, 57, 62
Olin Mathiesson Chemical Corporation, 99

Page Foundation, 66
Parke Davis Company, 51
Pasteur Award, 202
Pasteur Institute, Paris, 35, 62, 135, 136, 191, 207
Pasteur Institute, Southeast Asia, 192
Pasteur Treatment for rabies, 37
Philadelphia College of Physicians and Surgeons, 28
Phipps, Henry, Institute, Philadelphia, 62–64
Pictorial Review, 52
Population control, 114
Population Council, 232
Post, The Denver, 54
Presbyterian Church, Madison Avenue, New York City, 84
Pure Food and Drug Act, 129

Quakers, 195

Radcliffe Institute, 230
Research Corporation of New York City, 99
Rhoda Benham Award, 93, 100
Ricketts Prize, 61
Rockefeller Foundation, 47, 53, 55, 63, 71, 72, 104, 108, 143, 173, 174, 207
Rothamstead Experimental Station Harpenden Herts, England, 198

Sabin Building for Medical Research, Denver, Colorado, 54
Sabin School in Denver, 54
Schick test, 42

Schiffelein Award, William J., 113
Schools and Academies
Atlanta Girls' School, 142
Girls' Academy of Gallaway College, 172
Hopkins Hall, 70
Lowell High School, San Francisco, 186
Normal School for Teachers, Oshkosh, Wisconsin, 196
Normal School, for Teachers, Whitewater, Wisconsin, 196
Packer Collegiate Institute, 226
Silasm Springs Academy, 172
Susquenanna Institute, 128
The Misses Thomas' School, 22
Vermont Academy, 48
Wolfe Hall, 48
Sharpe & Dohme, Inc., 64
Sigma Delta Epsilon, 158, 180, 202
Sigma Xi, 179, 202, 221
Smallpox eradication, 221
Smith Foundation for Medical Research, Douglas, 142
Society of American Bacteriologists, 44, 77, 90
(See also American Society for Microbiology), 124, 127, 130, 135, 206
Society of Illinois Bacteriologists, 202
Sodiedad de Laboratorio Clinico, 221
Sommerfield Distinguished Professor of Bacteriology, 209
Sowers Coins for Cancer, 66
Special Citation, DHEW Secretary's, 158
Sperry and Hutchinson Co., 231
Sprague Memorial Institute, Philadelphia, Pennsylvania, 37
State Institute for Serums and Vaccines, Teheran, 179
State Serum Institute, Copenhagen, 191
Sulfonamides, 144
Superior Service Award, DHEW, 153, 158

Transfusion reaction, 175
Trout Lake Station, 199
Trudeau Laboratory & Sanatorium, 36
Trudeau Medal, 64
Tubercle formation, 51
Tuberculin, 36, 57, 61–64
Tuberculosis eradication in cattle, 131, 197
Typhoid Mary, 24, 38
Typhus Fever Medal, 122

Uffizi Gallery, Florence, Italy, 99
Union of Soviet Socialist Republics (USSR) Gallery of Medical Honor, 210
United China Relief, 53
United States Department of Agriculture, 129, 131
Committee on Farm Animal Manure, 198
United States Department of Health Education and Welfare, 113, 154, 156
United States Department of Labor, 110, 111
Children's Bureau, 30
United States Geological Survey, 119, 120
United States Public Health Service, 30, 40
Bureau of Hygiene, 119, 120, 131, 142, 143, 152
United Public Health Service Hospital, Staten Island, 163
Trachoma Hospital, Rolla, Missouri, 120
Universities and Colleges
Albany Medical College, 100
Barnard College, 88
Bennington College, 226
Bethel College, 103
Bryn Mawr College, 52
Clark University, 114

Columbia University College of Physicians and
     Surgeons, 24, 63, 70, 71, 82, 89, 93, 96,
     100, 103
   Teachers College, 70, 109
Cornell University College
   of Agriculture, 72, 107, 128, 214
   of Medicine, 22, 82, 83, 103, 109
Delft University, 137
Douglass College of Rutgers University, 228
Federal City College (University of the District of
     Columbia), 138
George Washington University, 142
Georgetown University, 161, 163
Goucher College, 58, 59, 63
Greenville College, 214
Harvard University, 21, 93, 103, 106, 114, 226
Hendrix College, 172, 179
Hobart College, 100, 113
Howard University, 179
Iowa State College, 60, 136
Johns Hopkins University, 47–52, 55, 132, 215–
     218, 226
Karlova University, 198
Keuka College, 14
Lafayette College, 58
Marietta College of Ohio, 151
Massachusetts Institute of Technology, 227
McMurray University, 114
Mills College, 191
Mississippi University for Women, 95
Mount Holyoke College, 52
New Mexico State College, 162
New York University, 28, 52, 113
Oberlin College, 52, 114
Oglethorpe University, 52
Philadelphia College of Physicians and Surgeons,
     28
Princeton University, 232
Queens College, 72
Radcliffe College, 230
Reed College, 71
Rockefeller University, 69, 78, 82
Russell Sage College, 52, 113
Rutgers University, 228
Skidmore College, 114
Smith College, 48, 50, 55, 113
Stanford University, 137, 190
Syracuse University, 52, 214
University of Arkansas, 172
University of California
   Berkeley, 186, 190
   San Francisco, 186, 190, 192
   Santa Barbara, 51, 58, 186
University of Chicago, 51, 58, 61, 103, 105, 120,
     142, 143, 162, 173, 180, 206
University of Chungking, China, 147
University of Cincinnati, 151, 152
University of Colorado
   Boulder, 142
   School of Medicine, Denver, 54, 162
University of Ghent, 137
University of Glasgow, 179
University of Kansas, 103, 104, 111, 206–207,
     209
University of Massachusetts, 114, 162
University of Michigan, 114, 186, 206, 215, 218,
     220–222
University of Montana, 105, 215

University of Nebraska, 119
University of Oregon, 72, 189
University of Pennsylvania, 52, 62
University of Rochester, 142, 143
University of Strathclyde, Scotland, 179
University of Tennessee, 95
University of Virginia, 95
University of Washington, 104, 136
University of Wisconsin, 128, 138, 195–198, 200,
     226–227
Vassar College, 22, 81, 224
Wellesley College, 70, 141, 227
Wesleyan College, 141, 224
William Smith College, 100, 113
Wilson College, 52, 138
Women's Medical College of New York, 44
Women's Medical College of Pennsylvania, 59,
     61, 113, 138
   Yale University, 106, 107, 114, 227, 229
Upjohn Company, 175, 218

Vaccine, pertussis, benefit:risk ratio, 176, 179
Vaccine, plague, 191
Vaccine, poliomyelitis, 153, 154
Vectors, arthropod, 187, 191, 193
Veterans Administration, 83, 84
Virulence, typhoid, 177
Viruses
   Adenovirus, 151, 154
   Bacteriophage, 199, 200
   c-type virus, 166
   Encephalomyelitis virus, 190
   Epstein-Barr virus, 164
   Herpes virus, 164
   Influenza virus, 153
   Murine sarcoma virus, 165
   Oncogenic viruses, 155, 158, 161
   Poliovirus, 40, 153, 190
   Polyoma virus, 154, 155, 157, 161, 163, 167–169
   Rabies virus, 36
   SE-polyoma virus, 154, 163
   SV5, 166
   SV40, 155, 158
   Vaccinia virus, 37
   Vacuolating virus, 155
   Variola virus, 36, 37

Wales, 135
Walter Reed Army Institute for Medical Research,
     93
Warrenton, Virginia, 98
Weil felix Test, 121, 123
Weybridge Laboratory, England, 65
Willard Parker Hospital, New York City, 24
Wilson, Armine T, Oration, 78
Wolfe Memorial, 66
Woman of the Year, 113, 147
Women's education, 230, 231
Women's Equal Suffrage League, 30
Women's City Club, 30
World Health Organization, 64, 103, 111, 114, 175,
     176, 213, 219, 220
World War I, 40, 70, 131, 143, 190, 196
World War II, 64, 76, 110, 123, 175, 207–208, 224,
     226

Young Women's Christian Association, 228